EADERSHIP

SPIRITUAL LEADERSHIP

Wisdom for Work, Wisdom for Life

Erik van Praag

PARAVIEW
Special Editions

New York

Spiritual Leadership
Copyright © 2004 Erik van Praag
All rights reserved. No part of this book may be used or reproduced in any manner whatsoever without prior written permission except in the case of brief quotations embodied in critical articles or reviews. For information, address Paraview, P.O. Box 416, Old Chelsea Station, New York, NY 10113-0416, or visit our website at www.paraview.com.

From *The Tao of Pooh* by Benjamin Hoff, copyright © 1982 by Benjamin Hoff; text and illus. From *Winnie-the-Pooh* and *The House at Pooh Corner*, CR 1926, 1928 by E.P. Dutton, © 1953, 1956 by A. A. Milne. Used by permission of Dutton, a division of Penguin Group (USA) Inc.

Reprinted with the permission of Scribner, an imprint of Simon & Schuster Adult Publishing Group, from *Watership Down* by Richard Adams. Copyright © 1972 by Rex Collings Ltd.; copyright renewed © 2000 by Richard George Adams.

Spiritual Leadership was originally published as *Spiritueel Leiderschap* by Samson in 1999.

Cover design by smythtype
ISBN: 1-931044-88-0

Library of Congress Catalog Number: 2004102011

CONTENTS

Prologue

"The person who has the courage to know himself is the Warrior of the Heart."—Danaan Parry

THERE IS A HARROWING LACK OF LEADERSHIP IN THE world. Is this the way you see it, too?

Let's start with politics. What is your outlook on political affairs? Does the news inspire you? Do politicians generate hope for the future? Are your political choices and activities—both inside and outside the voting booth—clear and empowering? And, finally, do you feel that political action actually makes a difference? In all honesty, I have to say that I've answered no to all of these questions. As far as I'm concerned, there is very little leadership in politics.

I also perceive a lack of leadership in the business sector, too. Management is becoming sharper, planning and information systems are becoming more sophisticated, and technology is more intelligent. But do business leaders inspire us to solve pressing issues such as the endangered environment or the increasing rift between rich and poor? Is there vision in the current business sector besides the striving toward profit maximization? Are mission statements actively and passionately conveyed? Are they inspired by the personal convictions of management and staff? Is the function of business in society and the larger world actually taken into account? Do managers dare to let go of control and in doing so create room for creativity and initiative? Is a balance made between what the business costs—not only in monetary terms, but also in terms of pollution, energy consumption, manpower, stress—and what it yields: not only profit, but a better quality of life?

The answer to some of the above questions may be affirmative here and there, but as a rule I would say no, our business managers don't fulfill these functions.

Let's take a look at the non-profit sector, our art and culture, or the health care sector, or education. How many school principals, teachers, doctors, or theater directors do their work with inspiration and pleasure, and in this way inspire others? Twenty percent? Fifty percent?

This is no different on the world stage. Take the European Union, for example. I find the amount of discussion and negotiation distressing. Everything gets bogged down in limited personal interests, and there is scarcely a counterbalance in the form of vision or conviction. Although the great idea of the European Monetary Union exists, to me this seems to be more like an obsession than a vision. And if there is a vision at all, the bearer of this vision usually lacks the charisma or the authority to make this vision materialize. For that matter it is as if the vision of the authorities decreases proportionately in relation to the duration of their term of office.

Are my comments a veiled cry for a "strong man"? Not as far as I'm concerned. It is a cry for leadership. My perception of leadership cannot be compared to that of a strong man. In the first place, I don't ask for one leader at the pinnacle of society or the community. I request leadership—a quality of being which can be present in anyone, no matter what his or her status—because I find it lacking throughout society as a whole.

In addition, I don't request the sort of strength that is personified by a strong man, whatever that may be. I do not request the strength of an authoritarian or patriarch, someone who makes decisions for others. I request spiritual leadership.

The following are the most significant aspects of what I call *spiritual leadership*.

• Spiritual leadership is based on consciousness of unity. It is a realization of a connection between myself and another person, myself and the world. Of course, I can easily distinguish myself from another person, and myself and the world. However, in consciousness of unity, I am aware that there is a simultaneous inextricable connection: What I do with myself I do with my surroundings, and what I do with others I also do with myself. Consciousness of unity is also the awareness that the other person may be different from myself but, then again, not really. This has significant consequences for the way in which I communicate.

• Spiritual leadership is based on vision. I perceive vision here as what I wish to achieve in the world. This is not the same as purpose or life purpose. Rather, it's an image of what I want to create, possibly together with others, which is fed through my desires, my goal in life, my talents, and other factors. It comes from my whole self—from the mind, body, and soul—and is not just an intellectual aim.

• Spiritual leadership is based on honesty. By this I mean facing up to reality—both external reality and the reality within ourselves—in a direct manner. This isn't always easy. We have the tendency to perceive both the external and internal world in a more positive light—or at times even more negative—than it actually is. It takes courage to take an honest look at the world around us and to look inside ourselves without guilt, anger, disapproval, or judgment, but one must take a look at reality without all of those feelings and reactions or else it will become distorted.

There is often a discrepancy between vision and reality, which is experienced as a sort of tension. Robert Fritz calls this creative tension. A typical characteristic of a spiritual leader is his or her ability to allow this tension to exist and to know how to distinguish this from emotional tension (stress). I will deal with this in more detail in chapters 2 and 9.

Someone with consciousness of unity, vision, and honesty is charismatic. There are also other forms of charisma—for example, charisma based on an authoritarian attitude, good manners, or handsomeness. But spiritual charisma has a different effect. It invites the receiver of the charisma to develop the same qualities as the leader himself: consciousness of unity, vision, and honesty. This is why a spiritual leader doesn't create dependent followers. The reverse happens—he stimulates independence. Spiritual leadership cultivates spiritual leadership; it is contagious. Therefore, the call for spiritual leadership is something completely different to the call for a strong man (or a guru). There is a paradox here: a spiritual leader has significant influence, and thus can be very effective, and at the same time makes/leaves people free, as opposed to the strong man who pressures or binds them (to himself or an ideology).

Another consequence of spiritual leadership is the development of a spiritual community: a group of people who, from a consciousness of unity, work on the realization of a common vision. This is why the concept of community is inextricably bound to the concept of leadership I'll develop in this book. I will deal with this in more detail in chapter 7.

Therefore, spiritual leadership has nothing to do with gurus or sects or similar groups. It is a form of leadership which can occur anywhere, from the top to the bottom, in the business sector, government, education, the health care sector, the arts, and the church, with men and women, with young and old, and, yes, even in politics.

What would motivate you to become a leader? I ask this question explicitly of those who, in the formal sense of the word, are not currently working as managers. I am not referring to motives such as position, power, or status, because these desires motivate the creation of power, position, and status—not leadership. However, consider that everyone who wants something that concerns other people is (also) motivated to lead. He or she is in fact motivated toward achieving something that he or she wants to achieve *together with others.*

And what is it that we want to achieve? This is basically the same for most people—a happy life for ourselves and our loved ones. But what is happiness? We can make that very complex, but it is probably no more than a situation in which our basic needs are satisfied and in which we can make our talents available to the world. The latter requires a situation in which we can develop ourselves, in which we can grow.

Growth is a characteristic of life itself. There is no life without growth. If growth comes to a standstill, then this is the onset of the dying (off) process. When considering growth, I do not think only of quantitative growth; I consider it as being primarily a qualitative growth: maturing, developing talents, wisdom, gentleness, and so forth. The spiritual leader is motivated to create a world with others that is geared toward qualitative growth. He is also, just like everybody else, motivated to develop his own talents and to offer them to the world. One of those talents is his capacity to manage. Put another way: he loves life and wants to actively participate in it.

What is the purpose of this book? Let me first make clear what is *not* the purpose of this book. It does not provide short-term solutions to your current problems. It does not write prescriptions. It is not a cure-all for your personal or business problems. I have noticed that many managers in business and government, as well as politicians, are desperately searching for the one answer that will get rid of a specific problem once and for all. This requirement results in the delusion of the day. Management through objectives, quality groups, strategic planning, re-engineering, total quality management, the learning organization, visionary leadership, neurolinguistic programming, the emotional revolution—we have seen them all come and go. And although all of these methods, techniques, and approaches have some value, they lack one thing: the capacity to make your situation manageable to such an extent that you will no longer have any problems. In addition, the solutions from these techniques often create new problems that seem more extreme than the previous problems.

While I don't provide a quick fix for your problems, this book will help you find your own way as a leader, or as someone being led (externally or from within). It attempts offer you a new perspective of reality, one you actually want and one you can create with others— maybe not today or tomorrow, but during the course of your life. In this way it is a sort of handbook that you can reach for when you require support or inspiration. This book can assist you in finding your direction (again), even though the ultimate decision as to which path you take must come from within yourself. A good method of using this book may be to use it as an oracle: you can open it randomly, or at a page which you have found using a random process (for example, by drawing lots or with the aid of a table with "random" numbers). There, you will find exactly the message you need. Of course, you can just read the book from cover to cover.

But acute problems must also be solved. Sales must continue and the organization must survive. (Always? At what cost? Why?) Otherwise there is no longer a context in which to realize your ideals, or it will create so much trouble that the price may become too high. Even though this book provides useful tips for everyday problems, they do not constitute the core of the book. There are other outstanding books and courses which have been developed for this purpose. This book intends to make a contribution to long-term development, not only for your organization in particular, but for you personally and for the world as a whole. It may be a small contribution, but it is a contribution, because I would rather be a part, however small, of the solution to the problem than a part of the problem itself.

To help you bridge the gap with your own daily activities, a number of experienced leaders will share their spiritual and not-so-spiritual experiences in this book.

The intention of this book is to provide a contribution to the development of spiritual leadership in general, as I believe that this is what is needed in our world. We need a world in which political decisions are made effectively and with care, in which efficiency, compassion for work, and quality are the hallmarks of organizations. We need a world in which prosperity and happiness for everyone can be realized in harmony with the world which we are part of. I am convinced that spiritual leadership can make an essential contribution to this.

For the managers and politicians who are reading this book: the acceptance of the ideas in this book will not diminish your effectiveness in any way or compel you to earn less profits or fewer votes. Although this occasionally and temporarily may be the case, ultimately, the opposite will come true. Even though this book will not solve your practical problems immediately, it will not intensify them, either. It could not possibly lead to chaos in your life and work situation—provided, of course, that you are prepared to be and have the courage to be honest regarding yourself and your surroundings.

This book intends to put forward a number of insights from world literature and tradition that are within arm's reach for all of us, but which we very often tend to let slip by unnoticed. Furthermore, the book provides a number of practical tips and exercises that enable you to develop the sources in yourself, and with this execute your own capacity for spiritual leadership. It can also assist you in recognizing spiritual leadership when you see it (for example, with staff members) and to submit to it in a wholesome manner. In both cases this will lead to a more satisfying life for you and to the disappearance of the feeling of powerlessness. In the theory that unfolds in this book, there are no fundamental differences between leaders and those being led. You are now both, even though you may not be fully aware of this. There is always a choice to be made, an action to undertake, or an influence which can be exercised.

This book is divided into three sections: foundations, instructions, and education. In the first section, chapters 1 to 4, I explore the sources from literature and tradition that can provide us with the understanding and wisdom to become a spiritual leader, sources from which we can extract consciousness of unity, vision, and honesty. Chapter 1 is to be considered as an initial exploration of the whole field based upon a number of novels, in particular *Watership Down* by Richard Adams. Chapters 2 through 4 then lay the foundations for spiritual leadership. Each of these chapters provides one of the pillars upon which this book is based. Chapter 2, The Law, treats the law of manifestation, which defines how we create our own reality. One of the conclusions that can be drawn from this chapter is that creation is always co-creation, in particular in cooperation with the life flow itself. This brings us to chapter 3, The Way, in which the concept of life flow is dealt with in detail. I base this upon Taoism, the second pillar of this book. Here we will observe that the life flow always manifests itself in two forms of energy—yin and yang. Chapter 4—The Goddess— explores how the yin variant, the book's third pillar, has gone underground in our society and also explains how we can retrieve it.

The following section of this book, chapters 5 through 7, is intended to provide levers with which we can develop spiritual leadership within ourselves. The classification here is in accordance with the classic Buddhist classification of the three "refuges": the Buddha, the teachings *(dharma)* and the community *(sangha)*. Chapter 5—God or the Buddha—deals with spiritual development. In this chapter I show how the foundations of our spiritual development have been lost because we are alienated from yin and yang energy. I make a distinction between soul, mind, spirit, personality, God, and the Buddha and provide instructions as to how we could be able to find our way (again), if we wish, in God's (or the Essence's) maze, to get our spiritual beliefs back on track. Chapter 6—The Teachings—sums up a number of insights from the Jewish, Christian, and Buddhist scriptures and traditions from which we can directly profit in practice (1). Chapter 7, The Community, deals with the spiritual community—what it is, why we need it, and how can we create this in the workplace or in politics. In order to achieve this it is imperative that we communicate well, which is why this subject is also dealt with in this chapter. In particular, I explore how can we communicate in such a way that we will consciously hear and be heard.

The last section of the book, Education, is about learning: How do we develop spiritual leadership in ourselves and in others? Chapter 8, The Soul, provides a number of exercises with the aim of getting to know oneself better, which can be seen as an exercise in honesty. Chapter 9, The Vision, provides a number of exercises for the development and realization of an individual vision and the collective vision which results from this. Chapter 10, The School, deals with education: How can we learn spiritual leadership? Can we create leaders? A distinction is made between those who are already functioning as a manager, director, or politician and young people who are yet to begin their careers. I subsequently provide a comprehensive definition of how, in my opinion, a leadership school for both categories should be constructed.

Each chapter is introduced with a motto, a guideline for the spiritual leader. Together these guidelines form the "Ten Commandments" (they are actually more like wisdom, principles, or statements (2) which make up the essence of spiritual leadership. In the epilogue I will once again summarize my opinion about spiritual leadership based upon these ten statements. Subsequently I will return to the fundamental choices we are faced with in life: God or Mammon, spirituality or the world of matter. I will conclude by sharing my planetary vision with you.

As stated above, I've also included contributions from experienced leaders who link theory to practical experience.

If you wish to write a book such as this, then you discover relatively quickly that everything has already been said before. Each time

I thought that I had an original thought I discovered that someone else had already articulated it and, in most cases, considerably better than I had, sometimes thousands of years ago. The sense of this book is therefore not related to the originality of the separate elements.

In the case that it is clearly obvious where specific ideas originated from, then I will indicate the source concerned. However, there are many things in this book which I have picked up during my learning process, but I no longer remember exactly where. Therefore I would like to thank all my teachers, everyone who has helped me become the person I am today, through word or script, if I was aware or unaware of it, and via communication in this life or another, from this reality or another reality, or even maybe through my genes.

Naturally there are people who I would like to thank individually. I have been inspired and nourished and brought to my senses by many people, and it will no longer be of interest to you as a reader to read all of that and you will skip it anyway. But I would like to personally thank those who through their textual criticism have significantly contributed to the quality of this book: J.Th. Blok, G. Broekstra, Gerrit J. Doeksen, Maarten D. van Dijk, Rein Gaastra, J.W. Ganzevoort, Aadt Jonker, H. de Korver, Huib Matthes, Isaac Van Melle, M. Prop, Jan Paul van Soest, A.Twijnstra, and Gerda Voorbij. For their selfless time, energy, and attention I am particularly grateful. What's more, many of these people have been willing to make a contribution from their own practical experiences and have made themselves vulnerable. That touched me deeply. I would also like to mention my friend Aadt Jonker, my spiritual traveling companion, who through his loving attention and his stimulating questions can be considered more than anyone else as being the co-author of this book. I would therefore like to dedicate this book to him.

I would also like to thank ERA Bouw bv. for their material support.

I would like to conclude this prologue by thanking you. Not only through buying and/or reading this book and in this way enabling me to write and publish it, but you have also, on a deeper level, through your willingness to learn from me, or to become acquainted with what I have to say, created the prerequisite for my own learning process. This provides me with a deep feeling of satisfaction and joy. May you experience this yourself through reading this book.

An Appeal for Contemplation

I HAD TWO REACTIONS WHEN ERIK VAN PRAAG announced that he wanted to send me a manuscript about spiritual leadership. The first was one of curiosity regarding what his competent pen would provide. The second concerned how I would respond to his request to provide an opinion on his writing.

Regarding my first reaction: my curiosity was more than satisfied. With this book, van Praag has utilized much of his extensive knowledge and experience. You, as the reader, must be careful that you do not become overwhelmed or overloaded by this. An almost effortless transition from literature, which analyzes leadership processes in apparently childlike fantasy stories, to opinions about actual elements of, for example, Christianity and Buddhism, made reading this book a personal exercise in flexibility and compelled my memory to function at a high level.

Concerning my second reaction: through van Praag's request that I provide a contribution from my own personal experience as an executive, I got more involved in this book. I did not wish to speak from my own isolated experience. Therefore I required permission from those whom I worked with very closely. This, however, would have resulted in abandoning my own spontaneity. But van Praag's request, and the thoughts stimulated by it, caused me to contemplate his ideas more closely, which I hereby offer.

The question that most concerned me was how a book that primarily deals with humanities and bears the title *Spiritual Leadership* could touch on business and organizations in a culture made up of bits and bytes and a no-nonsense attitude. Will enough attention be given to expressions that at best can fill up a Sunday morning but definitely do not belong in business communication?

My initial cynicism turned into enthusiasm. I think that this is the right time and the right place for something like this book, which is not exactly commonplace.

Like van Praag, I believe that we are experiencing a period in which, through a number of developments, that the ecological viewpoint is replacing motivation based on ego needs. I offer but a few points:

• Technology enables us to obtain a large amount of information from all over the world, without the assistance of others. Prior to this, and not so long ago, significant input by and study from staff was required.

• The same technology allows us to inexpensively and very quickly explore the world physically and subsequently develop it all by ourselves.

• The old hierarchies (within families, schools, church, business, and organizations) have made way for a greater emphasis on individual freedom, advanced participation, and cultural decay. Through this a binding agent has been lost and we are being increasingly left to our own devices.

• Permanent employment and the associated feelings of solidarity and loyalty are being forced to make way for different arrangements, such as flexible work time, job-share programs, staff detachment, and part-time work.

• Global thinking in terms of production, distribution, and consumption break down the national and regional structures, resulting in a decay of cooperation and team spirit.

• During this period socialism lost its basis. With good reason, attempts are being made to resurrect its elements of ethics and protection. However, this isn't an easy undertaking in today's society.

Within this framework and in these times of unrest I place van Praag's appeal for contemplation of the elements of spiritual leadership. For me personally the following is important:

• Delve more deeply into the question concerning whether a spiritual leader is a master of manifestation. In other words: how can he create the situations he wishes to achieve without pressuring his fellow man?

• Appreciate the fact that in our beta world the male energy has pushed the female energy into the background. This is an appeal to both men and women, starting with listening to each other better.

• Develop the spiritual (working) community by using open communication. If the leader lets himself be led through this then he makes himself autonomous and liberated, as well as liberating others.

All of this requires that we speak openly, listen openly, and have courage and honesty. I believe that with this we can contribute to possible solutions to a number of local and global problems. This book has put me on track to try, together with others, to reach a vision as Erik van Praag has defined in this book.

G.J. Doeksen, former vice chairman
RvB Internatio-Müller

Part 1
Foundations

CHAPTER 1

Watership Down

MOTTO:
THE SPIRITUAL LEADER FOLLOWS WHAT HIS HEART AND
HIS HAND DIRECT HIM TO DO.

"Where God has sown you, there you must manage to flourish."
—French proverb

This chapter is an exploration of the concept of spiritual leadership based upon a number of novels, in particular *Watership Down* by Richard Adams. Some of the people who read the manuscript found this chapter to be exceptionally amusing and instructive, others found it to be too elaborate. I left it the way it was, particularly for those who are not familiar with the novels concerned, and can therefore make their judgement based on the quotations. If this chapter doesn't appeal to you, then you may also skip it. The material illustrated here is also dealt with later in another manner.

ARE YOU FAMILIAR WITH THE NOVEL *WATERSHIP DOWN* by Richard Adams? If not, then I wholeheartedly recommend that you take the time to read it, especially if you're interested in leadership. It's relaxing, exciting, poignant, spiritual, and amusing. As far as I'm concerned, *Watership Down* should be required reading for every manager or anyone who intends to become a manager. At first sight *Watership Down* appears to be about rabbits, but it is, of course, an allegory about humans.

Watership Down begins with the description of life in a colony (a society, community, or organization). This is a strictly regulated community with a chief rabbit at the forefront and encircled by an assemblage or council (which is known in rabbit language as an "owsla"). This owsla is a highly status-based and authoritarian hierarchy based upon physical and mental achievements. It is akin to an enlightened dictatorship or a modern company.

The main character is Hazel (all rabbit names are derived from the plant kingdom), a young buck that as yet has no status (an "outskirter"). But based on his roots and achievements he may go far. He has a little brother, Fiver (the fifth from the nest), an unsightly rabbit who consequently has no status whatsoever. However, Fiver does have the gift of second sight and one day he has a vision of scenes of carnage and danger, from which he foresees the downfall of the colony. Based upon this vision, Hazel decides to ask for an audience with the Chief Rabbit, via an acquaintance of his, Bigwig, a member of the owsla. I've included this passage below, because it is so illustrative of the leadership in our world—or what must precede it.

"Hazel?" said Bigwig, sniffing at him in the deep twilight among the tree roots. "It is Hazel, isn't it? What are you doing here? And at this time of day?" He ignored Fiver, who was waiting farther down the run.

"We came to see the Chief Rabbit," said Hazel. "It's important, Bigwig. Can you help us?"

"We?" said Bigwig. "Is *he* going to see him, too?"

"Yes, he must. Do trust me, Bigwig. I don't usually come and talk like this, do I? When did I ever ask to see the Chief Rabbit before?"

"Well, I'll do it for you, Hazel, although I'll probably get my head bitten off. I'll tell him I know you're a sensible fellow. He ought to know you himself, of course, but he's getting old. Wait here, will you?"

Bigwig went a little way down the run and stopped at the entrance to a large burrow. After speaking a few words that Hazel could not catch, he was evidently called inside. The two rabbits waited in silence, broken only by the continuous nervous fidgeting of Fiver.

The Chief Rabbit's name and style was Threarah, meaning "Lord Rowan Tree." For some reason he was always referred to as "*The* Threarah"—perhaps because there happened to be only one threar, or rowan, near the warren, from which he took his name. He had won his position not only by strength in his prime, but also by level-headedness and a certain self-contained detachment, quite unlike the impulsive behavior of most rabbits. It was well known that he never let himself get excited by rumor or danger. He had coolly—some even said coldly—stood firm during the terrible onslaught of the myxomatosis, ruthlessly driving out every rabbit who seemed to be sickening. He had resisted all ideas of mass emigration and enforced complete isolation on the warren, thereby almost certainly saving it from extinction. It was he, too, who had once dealt with a particularly troublesome stoat by leading it down among the pheasant coops and so (at the risk of his own life) on to a keeper's gun. He was now, as Bigwig said, getting old, but his wits were still clear enough. When Hazel and Fiver were brought in, he greeted them politely. Owsla like Toadflax might threaten and bully. The Threarah had no need.

"Ah, Walnut. It is Walnut, isn't it?"

"Hazel," said Hazel.

"Hazel, of course. How very nice of you to come and see me. I knew your mother well. And your friend—"

"My brother."

"Your brother," said the Threarah, with the slightest hint of "Don't correct me any more, will you?" in his voice. "Do make yourselves comfortable. Have some lettuce?"

The Chief Rabbit's lettuce was stolen by the Owsla from a garden half a mile away across the fields. Outskirters seldom or never saw lettuce. Hazel took a small leaf and nibbled politely. Fiver refused, and sat blinking and twitching miserably.

"Now, how are things with you?" said the Chief Rabbit. "Do tell me how I can help you."

"Well, sir," said Hazel rather hesitantly, "it's because of my brother—Fiver here. He can often tell when there's anything bad about, and I've found him right again and again. He knew the flood was coming last autumn and sometimes he can tell where a wire's been set. And now he says he can sense a bad danger coming upon the warren."

"A bad danger. Yes, I see. How very upsetting," said the Chief Rabbit, looking anything but upset. "Now, what sort of danger, I wonder?" He looked at Fiver.

"I don't know," said Fiver. "B-but it's bad. It's so b-bad that—it's very bad," he concluded miserably.

The Threarah waited politely for a few moments and then he said, "Well, now, and what ought we to do about it, I wonder?"

"Go away," said Fiver instantly. "Go away. All of us. Now. Threarah, sir, we must all go away."

The Threarah waited again. Then, in an extremely understanding voice, he said, "Well, I never did!

That's rather a tall order, isn't it? What do you think yourself?"

"Well, sir," said Hazel, "my brother doesn't really think about these feelings he gets. He just has the feelings, if you see what I mean. I'm sure you're the right person to decide what we ought to do."

"Well, that's very nice of you to say that. I hope I am. But now, my dear fellows, let's just think about this a moment, shall we? It's May, isn't it? Everyone's busy and most of the rabbits are enjoying themselves. No elil [enemies] for miles, or so they tell me. No illness, good weather. And you want me to tell the warren that young—er—young—er—your brother here has got a hunch and we must all go traipsing across country to goodness knows where and risk the consequences, eh? What do you think they'll say? All delighted, eh?"

"They'd take it from you," said Fiver suddenly.

"That's very nice of you," said the Threarah again. "Well, perhaps they would, perhaps they would. But I should have to consider it very carefully indeed. A most serious step, of course. And then—"

"But there's no time, Threarah, sir," blurted out Fiver. "I can feel the danger like a wire around my neck—like a wire—Hazel, help!" He squealed and rolled over in the sand, kicking frantically, as a rabbit does in a snare. Hazel held him down with both forepaws and he grew quieter.

"I'm awfully sorry, Chief Rabbit," said Hazel. "He gets like this sometimes. He'll be alright in a minute."

"What a shame! What a shame! Poor fellow, perhaps he ought to go home and rest. Yes, you'd better take him along now. Well, it's really been extremely good of you to come and see me, Walnut. I appreciate it very much indeed. And I shall think over all you've said most carefully, you can be quite sure of that. Bigwig, just wait a moment, will you?"

"As Hazel and Fiver made their way dejectedly down the run outside the Threarah's burrow, they could just hear, from inside, the Chief Rabbit's voice assuming a rather sharper note, interspersed with an occasional "Yes, sir," "No, sir."

Bigwig, as he had predicted, was getting his head bitten off (p. 24-27).

A brilliant passage, and a splendid description of the type of leaders with whom we are all familiar: competent, intelligent, polite, decent, sympathetic, and certainly not lacking in significant merit. However, they do not have:

- Vision
- Awareness of unity
- The sort of honesty and courage the situation requires

Therefore, the Threarah can listen to Fiver, but not really hear and understand him. He is too wrapped up in his traditional ways of thinking and acting. The next time this extraordinarily relevant information won't reach him. (There is of course no next time, because, as you will understand, the colony falls.) Do you remember the Challenger space shuttle disaster? Or the Herald of Free Enterprise ferry? Or the nuclear power stations in Harrisburg and Chernobyl? Or the explosions at Muiden Chemie? All are partly due to this sort of leadership: leadership that cannot see further than the end of its own nose (short-term leadership) and isn't open to information—even ignores or withholds information. However, it has to be said that the choice is also extremely difficult for the Threarah. If he follows Fiver's advice, it will almost certainly result in trouble and there will be losses. Which leader feels up to this? Only the leader who can act based upon a personal inner certainty and intuition. This is therefore a leader who complies with the three criteria found lacking in the Threarah. Such a leader can also personally experience such a premonition, or sense which information is authentic.

In the story of *Watership Down* there are various leaders of this type, and Hazel and Bigwig are two of them. Prior to the disaster, they leave with a group of rabbits. They can be compared to the leaders who dare to make unpleasant decisions when required, such as politicians who advocate severe tax increases or the manager who refuses to make a profit at the cost of further damage to the environment and is prepared to pay the price for this.

Other conclusions can be drawn from this passage, such as the observation that leadership is not bound to position. All four characters fulfill leadership functions by applying influence. Further on it will become apparent that Hazel, Bigwig, and Fiver fulfill their own roles, which is crucial for the undertaking they are about to begin. In this case, leadership also comes from below.

Yet another conclusion is that effective leadership—leadership that achieves the required short- and long-term results with a minimum of damage or undesirable side effects—must be attuned with what is happening in the world. However, to discover what is happening in the world, we must be open to warning signs. Sometimes these signs come from external sources (this is the case for Hazel, Bigwig, and Threarah, but also for Fiver, who receives his vision following the sighting of an announcement), sometimes from within (this is the case for Fiver, but also for Hazel, Bigwig, and Threarah, who, in a way, vibrated along with Fiver).

Spiritual, effective leadership requires attunement. A prerequisite for attunement is that we dare to let go of old concepts and opinions, as only then can we be open to the signs that are being projected toward us. Old concepts and opinions act as filters and ensure that we fail to perceive these signs. Letting go, attunement, and cooperation are required for the path toward spiritual leadership. I will return to these processes at various points in the book.

A final comment in connection to this passage is that effective leadership is integral leadership. Rational and irrational factors and intellectual and emotional considerations also play roles. Intuition and extra sensory perception are likewise just as much sources of information as analysis and sensory perceptions.

If we were only to take into account what we can rationally and intellectually understand, then we would exclude a significant source of information and energy and in turn become unable to obtain the result that we actually desire.

Let's return to the story of *Watership Down*. A group from the colony decides, based upon Fiver's vision, to leave the colony and embark on an arduous journey to—indeed, to where? Fiver has a feeling about this too. An exciting, interesting story develops in which the rabbits journey to Watership Down, the place where they will ultimately establish themselves. During the journey, a leadership structure develops progressively. Each rabbit takes on a leadership role, each of his or her own personal nature and talents. Bigwig establishes his authority with the aid of his physical power. However, he eventually joins forces with Hazel and Fiver. He is a natural second man, a loyal aide. Hazel is the leader of the leaders: he is what may be called a "focalizer." I have taken this term from the Findhorn community, a living and working community in Scotland. This function can be defined as the focusing of energy: attuning desires, talents, and demands that are defined by the situation. Hazel also relies on inner wisdom and intuition. Blackberry is the most intelligent of the group: he thinks up creative solutions for complex issues and in this way influences the others. And, finally, Fiver is the guide who has the most feeling for the hidden destination of the undertaking.

Later on more functions develop. After all, each member of the group fulfills an essential role within the group as a whole. Even the weakest, Pipkin, fulfills a central role on a number of occasions, because he motivates Blackberry and Hazel to carry out feats which not only at that moment but also later in the story are of significant importance.

I would like to illustrate these processes by citing a few more passages from the story. They have to cross a river at one point, even though the weakest rabbits are too tired to swim across the river.

Hazel initially wants to rest and wait until ni-Frith (rabbit language for midday).

Bigwig returns after a reconnaissance.

"Well, Hazel, if I were you I shouldn't wait until ni-Frith. I should go now. In fact, I think you'll have to."

"Why?" asked Hazel.

"There's a large dog loose in the wood."

Hazel started. "What?" he said. "How do you know?"

[Bigwig explains how he saw this and then says] "Come on, let's get over quickly."

Hazel felt at a loss. In front of him stood Bigwig, sodden wet, undaunted, single-minded—the very picture of decision. At his shoulder was Fiver, silent and twitching. He saw Blackberry watching him intently, waiting for his lead and disregarding Bigwig's. Then he looked at Pipkin, huddled into a fold of sand, more panic-stricken and helpless than any rabbit he had ever seen. At this moment, up in the wood, there broke out an excited yelping and a jay began to scold.

Hazel spoke through a kind of light-headed trance. "Well, you'd better get on, then," he said, "and anyone else who wants to. Personally, I'm going to wait until Fiver and Pipkin are ready to tackle it."

"You silly blockhead!" cried Bigwig. "We'll all be finished! We'll—"

"Don't stamp about," said Hazel. "You may be heard. What do you suggest, then?"

"Suggest? There's no suggesting to be done. Those who can swim, swim. The others will have to stay here and hope for the best. The dog may not come."

"I'm afraid that won't do for me. I got Pipkin into this and I'm going to get him out."

"Well, you didn't get Fiver into it, did you? He got you into it."

Hazel could not help noticing, with reluctant admiration, that although Bigwig had lost his temper, he was apparently in no hurry on his own account and seemed less frightened than any of them.

[Then Blackberry, who has wandered off on his own to find the solution, finds a piece of wood which can be used as a float for Fiver and Pipkin. He explains how this can be done.]

Hazel had no idea what he meant. Blackberry's flood of apparent nonsense only seemed to draw tighter the mesh of danger and bewilderment. As though Bigwig's angry impatience, Pipkin's terror and the approaching dog were not enough to contend with, the cleverest rabbit among them had evidently gone out of his mind. He felt close to despair.

"Frithrah [the rabbit god], yes, I see!" said an excited voice at his ear. It was Fiver. "Quick, Hazel, don't wait! Come on, and bring Pipkin!"

[Hazel has a total blackout and doesn't react. Under guidance from Bigwig and Blackberry, Pipkin and Fiver were heaved onto the plank.]

"Frith and Inlé," said Dandelion. "They're sitting in the water! Why don't they sink?"

"They're sitting on the wood and the wood floats, can't you see?" said Blackberry. "Now we swim over ourselves. Can we start, Hazel?"

During the last few minutes Hazel had been as near to losing his head as he was ever to come. He had been at his wits' end, with no reply to Bigwig's scornful impatience except his readiness to risk his own life in company with Fiver and Pipkin. He still could not understand what had happened, but at least he realized that Blackberry wanted him to show authority. His head cleared.

"Swim," he said. "Everybody swim" (p. 49-52).

Although Hazel completely loses his grip on what's happening, he remains central. This is partly attributed to his leadership up until that point and also because Bigwig, Fiver, and Blackberry continue to see him as their leader. His solidarity with the weaker rabbits is of no lesser significance. However, his authority has not yet been definitely established. After a night of apparently aimless marching onwards across an extremely unpleasant piece of land, as the rabbits are nearing the point of exhaustion, a mutiny takes place. A group of three rabbits decides to return to the colony because they believe Fiver is mistaken. When Hazel is just about to explain that that is no longer possible, Fiver and Bigwig come closer.

"'Hazel,' said Fiver, "could you come up on the bank with me for a few moments? It's important."

"And while you're there," said Bigwig, scowling round at the others from under the great sheaf of fur on his head, "I'll just have a few words with these three. Why don't you get washed, Hawkbit? You look like the end of a rat's tail left in a trap. And as for you Speedwell—"

Hazel did not wait to hear what Speedwell looked like. [He followed Fiver up to the overhang and there Fiver showed him where they were headed: the downs along the southern skyline.]

"I don't think we could get the others to go as far as that, Fiver," he said. "They're frightened and tired as it is, you know. What we need is to find a safe place soon, and I'd rather succeed in doing what we can than fail to do what we can't."

[Of course they are both right—but they are talking about different time spans. When they are back down Hazel asks:] "Hello, what's happened? Where are the others?"

"Over there," answered Blackberry. "There's been a dreadful row. Bigwig told Hawkbit and Speedwell that he'd scratch them to pieces if they didn't obey him. And when Hawkbit said he wanted to know who was Chief

Rabbit, Bigwig bit him. It seems a nasty business. Who *is* Chief Rabbit anyway—you or Bigwig?"

"I don't know," answered Hazel, "but Bigwig's certainly the strongest. There was no need to go biting Hawkbit: he couldn't have gone back if he'd tried. He and his friends would have seen that if they'd been allowed to talk for a bit. Now Bigwig's put their backs up, and they'll think they've got to go on because he makes them. I want them to go on because they can see it's the only thing to do. There are too few of us for giving orders and biting people. Frith in a fog! Isn't there enough trouble and danger already?" (p. 65, 66, 68).

They proceed to carry on, seemingly aimlessly through the night across this wretched ground. They are approaching exhaustion and even Hazel loses all sense of aim and direction. He is on full automatic pilot.

All was confusion, ignorance, clambering and exhaustion. Throughout the bad dream of the night's journey, Pipkin seemed to be always close beside him. Though each of the others vanished and reappeared like fragments floating round a pool, Pipkin never left him; and his need for encouragement became at last Hazel's only support against his own weariness (p. 69).

However, at the break of dawn they finally arrive at a green meadow, which provides food and an excellent shelter.

"Oh, Hazel," said Blackberry, coming up to him round a puddle in the gravel. "I was so tired and confused, I actually began to wonder whether you knew where you were going. I could hear you in the heather, saying 'Not far now' and it was annoying me. I thought you were making it up. I should have known better. Frithrah, you're what I call a Chief Rabbit!"

"Well done, Hazel!" said Buckthorn. "Well done!" [...]

"Splendid, Hazel," [Bigwig] said. "Everyone's here.

Let's get them into that field" (p. 70-71).

And in this way Hazel establishes his authority. Luck? I would not know. In the context of *Watership Down* it seems more that Hazel does what his hand and his heart instruct him to do, in which his own limited self-interests are made subordinate to the greater interests of the group, which is also his own greater interest. The passage also teaches us that if you are not out for your own interest, but follow your heart instead, life will take care of you in times of personal failure. I will return to this in chapters 2 and 3.

The passage in which Bigwig re-establishes authority is also interesting. Maybe Hazel was right to think that the conflict could be resolved by talking. However, sometimes there's no time for talk. As Ecclesiastes continually states: there comes a time for everything. There is a time for discussion and a time for authority. There is a time for talking and a time for action. (I will come back to this in chapter 3.) At any rate it cannot be said that Hazel's leadership is more spiritual than Bigwig's. That hinges on the intention each person bases his leadership on. If this occurs through awareness of unity, vision, honesty, and courage, Bigwig's leadership can be considered as being just as spiritual as Hazel's or Fiver's. Later in *Watership Down*, Bigwig undergoes a complete transformation in this sense. By brushing aside Fiver's vision, he endangers his own life, at which point he learns his lesson and is in his leadership as spiritual as the next person.

Maybe it's now clear why I am so enthusiastic about *Watership Down*. I cannot think of a better description of both effective and ineffective leadership. The passages I just discussed are only a partial illustration of this, so I'd like to offer more highlights from this book.

Watership Down presents itself as a thriller or an adventure, but also as a philosophical work. The majority of people who have read it are extremely fascinated by it and read it in one go. However, there are also people—very few—who were unable to finish it. If you have not yet read it, and if you are considering doing so based upon what I what I have just illustrated, then maybe you should do just that before reading this—because I'm about to reveal part of the plot.

The rabbits come into contact with two other colonies. They are both models of societies or colonies that are familiar to us all and their descriptions are extremely educational. The latter colony is a dictator-ship, of which General Woundwort is the leader. In the book there is a description of General Woundwort's youth, which enables us to understand what leads people to authoritarian, dictatorial, or cruel behavior. This has helped me understand the causes of unpleasant aspects of myself and not to approve or disapprove of them but to trans-form them into more constructive behavior. Here's the relevant passage:

General Woundwort was a singular rabbit. Some three years ago, he had been born—the strongest of a litter of five—in a burrow outside a cottage garden near Cole Henley. His father, a happy-go-lucky and reckless buck, had thought nothing of living close to human beings except that he would be able to forage in their garden in the early morning. He had dearly paid for his rashness. After two or three weeks of spoiled lettuces and nibbled cabbage plants, the cottager had lain in wait and shot him as he came through the potato patch at dawn. The same morning the man set to work to dig out the doe and her growing litter. Woundwort's mother escaped, racing across the kale field towards the downs, her kit-tens doing their best to follow her. None but Woundwort succeeded. His mother, bleeding form a shotgun pellet, made her way along the hedges in broad daylight, with Woundwort limping beside her.

It was not long before a weasel picked up the scent of the blood and followed it. The little rabbit cowered in the grass while his mother was killed before his eyes. He made no attempt to run, but the weasel, its hunger satis-fied, left him alone and made off through the bushes. Several hours later a kind old schoolmaster from Overton, walking through the fields, came upon Woundwort nuz-zling the cold, still body and crying. He carried him home to his own kitchen and saved his life, feeding him with milk from a nasal dropper until he was old enough to eat bran and greenstuff. But Woundwort grew up very wild and, like Cowper's hare, would bite when he could. In a month he was big and strong and had become savage. He nearly killed the schoolmaster's cat, which had found him at liberty in the kitchen and tried to torment him. One night, a week later, he tore the wire from the front of his hutch and escaped to the open country.

Most rabbits in this situation, lacking almost all experience of wild life, would have fallen victim at once to the elil: but not Woundwort. After a few days' wandering, he came upon a small warren and, snarling and clawing, forced them to accept him. Soon he had become Chief Rabbit, having killed both the previous Chief and a rival named Fiorin. In combat he was terrifying, fighting entirely to kill, indifferent to any wounds he received himself and closing with his adversaries until his weight overbore and exhausted them. *Those who had no heart to oppose him were not long in feeling that here was a leader indeed* [italics inserted] (p. 313-314).

The story continues by describing how Woundwort—who's very cleverly named—projects his craving for power—the old repressed fear lie is at the bottom of this—to the whole colony. The entire colony is militarized and a police state is created. This has two functions: controlling Woundwort's authority over the colony, but also controlling the power of the colony over its surroundings. In this way the colony can even outsmart humans (and this is what started it all). The price to pay is actually that you can only achieve your objectives with battle and thus you win or lose. It's double or nothing. Later on in the book, this manner of thinking is confronted by Hazel and his friends' manner of thinking, the win-win model. Woundwort then besieges the Watership Down colony and can be found close to the perimeter of the colony in discussion with a few of his officers.

At that moment a rabbit came out of the grass and sat up in the middle of the track. He paused for a few moments and then moved toward them. He was limping and had a strained, resolute look.

"You're General Woundwort, aren't you?" said the rabbit. "I've come to talk to you."

"Did Thlayli send you?" asked Woundwort. [Thlayli is the alias of Bigwig, who General Woundwort has already met, and who misled the General.]

"I'm a friend of Thlayli," replied the rabbit. "I've come to ask you why you're here and what it is you want." [Hazel, who was wounded in another adventure, is speaking. It doesn't occur to Woundwort that a crippled rabbit smaller than Bigwig could be the leader. Note that Hazel doesn't spoil this illusion.]

"Were you on the riverbank in the rain?" said Woundwort. [This was where Hazel's colony miraculously escaped a destructive attack from Woundwort and his troops.]

"Yes, I was."

"What was left unfinished there will be finished now," said Woundwort. "We are going to destroy you."

"You won't find it easy," replied the other. "You'll take fewer rabbits home than you brought. We should both do better to come to terms."

"Very well," said Woundwort. "These are the terms. You will give back all the does who ran away from Efrafa [Woundwort's colony] and you will hand over the deserters Thlayli and Blackavar to my Owsla."

"No, we can't agree to that. I've come to suggest something altogether different and better for us both. A rabbit has two ears; a rabbit has two eyes, two nostrils. Our two warrens ought to be like that. They ought to be together—not fighting. We ought to make other warrens between us—start one between here and Efrafa, with rabbits from both sides. You wouldn't lose by that, you'd gain. We both would. A lot of your rabbits are unhappy now and it's all you can do to control them, but with this plan you'd soon see a difference. Rabbits have enough enemies as it is. They ought not to make more among themselves. A mating between free, independent rabbits—what do you say?"

At that moment, in the sunset on Watership Down, there was offered to General Woundwort the opportunity to show whether he was really the leader of vision and genius which he believed himself to be, or whether he was no more than a tyrant with the courage and cunning of a pirate. For one beat of his pulse the lame rabbit's idea shone clearly before him. He grasped it and realized what it meant. The next, he had pushed it away from him. The sun dipped into the cloud bank and now he could clearly see the track along the ridge, leading to the beech hanger and the bloodshed for which he had prepared with so much energy and care.

"I haven't time to sit here talking nonsense," said Woundwort. "You're in no position to bargain with us. There's nothing more to be said. Thistle, go back and tell Captain Vervain I want everyone up here at once."

"And this rabbit, sir," asked Campion. "Shall I kill him?"

"No," replied Woundwort. "Since they've sent him to ask our terms, he'd better take them back.—Go and tell Thlayli that if the does aren't waiting outside your warren, with him and Blackavar, by the time I get down there, I'll tear the throat out of every buck in the place by ni-Frith tomorrow."

The lame rabbit seemed about to reply, but Woundwort had already turned away and was explaining to Campion what he was to do. Neither of them bothered to watch the lame rabbit as he limped back by the way he had come (p. 427-428).

Once more a brilliant—and for me a touching—passage. It is obvious that there are two conflicting styles of leadership here. And, just as in the beginning with Threarah, Woundwort is faced with a choice. And just as with Threarah, his acquired manner of thinking gets in the way of his making the correct choice—correct, although not in the moral sense of correct, but correct in the sense of effective. Woundwort's way has the chance of succeeding (at least from his point of view) but there's also the chance it'll fail. Moreover, if he wins, it'll involve the loss of his own rabbits and the loss of the other party. Those same outcomes are then based on the destruction of (a part of) the world around you. From a long-term perspective this isn't a good strategy because you either invoke opposing forces, which in the long run will turn against you, or sooner or later you'll incorrectly assess the risks, and then you will be the loser. I will deal with this in more depth in chapter 7.

Another striking element about this passage is that Hazel does not consider his opponent as being an opponent in any way. He distances himself from making a moral judgment. He doesn't become angry and he doesn't condemn. He only displays what he thinks to be the most beneficial conduct for both parties. He treats others with respect. This type of communication is known as open or collaborative communication, as opposed to defensive communication. I will return to this subject later (also in chapter 7).

Watership Down also illustrates something else. All of us, leaders and those being led, follow the course that has been laid out for us. Laid by whom is also an interesting question, by us or by a divine being, or by fate or life itself. Much of the first part of this book is dedicated to the answer to this question. But in any case, the course we follow is not haphazard and random. We follow a course geared toward a specific destination. In *Watership Down* this destination is, on the one hand, physical (reaching the promised land, Watership Down, and making it habitable), but on the other hand also spiritual—the creation of a society based upon love and respect. In this way it is an exodus story like the exodus of the Jews from Egypt that's detailed in the Bible. All of the actions on that route are significant. In *Watership Down*, there are a few examples of this theme. Assisting a mouse results in the mouse later warning the group about the arrival of the besiegers, resulting in the besiegers losing the benefit of surprise. A similar act of generosity toward a gull also provides them with a partner in adversity. The river-crossing incident and a dog running free in the woods trailing a rope teaches them about using a boat later in the book. Through the combination of these occurrences they also learn how to chew through a guard dog's rope and how to use this dog to their advantage. Mistakes and crises also appear to have their own value, either because the rabbits learn something essential from their mistakes, or because they acquire something that later comes in handy.

Of course *Watership Down* isn't the only book that can provide a valuable contribution to our understanding of leadership. I have found novels to be more beneficial in this context than professional or technical literature. I sincerely hope that this doesn't prompt you to immediately toss aside this book. What I do hope is that this book will inspire you to find new meaning in novels, films, and theatrical performances. Ultimately, the intention is that you can relate them to your personal experiences and wisdom. I cannot teach you something that you don't already know. I cannot explain to you what sorrow is if you have never experienced it. The same goes for the concepts in this book.

I would like to conclude this chapter by naming a number of other novels that have influenced my vision of leadership. *Jonathan Livingston Seagull* by Richard Bach is the wonderful story about a seagull that is fascinated by, and lives for, perfecting the noble art of flying. This book has taught me that we have been put upon this earth to make ourselves and the world a place of perfection and that this results in leadership. It has also taught me that the meaning of life, in some sense, can be found in developing talents and in using them in any undertaking— an extremely significant perspective for leadership.

Richard Bach's *Illusions* taught me that we create our own reality (see chapter 2), often expressed by this sentiment: "and as he believed, so was it for him." *Illusions* is about a messiah, Donald Shimoda, living in these times, "born in the Holy Land of Indiana, raised in the mystical hills east of Fort Wayne," a playful reference to the story of the birth of Jesus and our tendency to retrospectively declare locations as being sacred. This messiah is a car mechanic, but he has another purpose. He talks so much in the workplace and draws such a wide audience that he doesn't repair many cars. He is subsequently dismissed and then decides to become a full-time messiah. This goes well for a while: he performs numerous miracles and people hang onto his every word, until he begins to feel uneasy. He then realizes that his followers aren't taking responsibility of their own lives, but are leaning on him instead. All is well if his shadow falls on them or if they can touch the seam of his cloth. This burdens him so much that he decides to climb to the top of a mountain—as Messiahs tend to do—and prays to the "Infinite Radiant Is" by saying, "not my will but thine will be done. However if it could be your will that this cup passes me by, then that would be just as welcome." He receives the reply, "My will is your will—I want you to do what you want to do." Upon hearing this he gives thanks, goes back down the mountain, and says to the crowd, "I'm resigning." This surprises them.

He subsequently makes a living by flying across the Midwest and selling tours for $3 per flight. This is how he meets the writer of the book, Richard Bach, who is not just any Tom, Dick or Harry, because he has already written *Jonathan Livingston Seagull*. They talk, especially after work in the evenings by the campfire, and pearls of wisdom drop from Donald's lips. One day Richard Bach says to him, "Donald, how do you get to know all these things?" Donald replies, "When you do your Messiah's course you get a book and everything is in the book." Richard says doubtfully, "A book?" "Yes," replies Donald. "I've got a copy here somewhere, it's in the cockpit." And he gives the bewildered Richard the *Messiah's Handbook: Reminders for the Advanced Soul.* From this moment on the story is peppered with quotations from the book, a new source of wisdom.

This amusing story was and still is a personal source of inspiration and insight. Interesting conclusions can be drawn from the above synopsis, such as how leadership doesn't make one dependent, and that spirituality is not something solemn, but an everyday occurrence and one that can be witty, too. In addition, it also explains that it's spiritual to follow one's own heart. Care for another can only be based upon care for yourself.

Hollands Glorie and *De Kapitein* by Jan de Hartog have taught me about the significance of dedication and our destination. (The proverb at the beginning of this chapter was taken from the latter book.) I believe that we all have a personal assignment in life, which we can consider as being our destination. It is what we are to learn, to do, and to give in this life. This is what I refer to above as the course that is laid out for us. We have been given talents for this purpose and it is also our task to discover and develop these talents and make them available to the world. Only then can we make a contribution to perfecting the world and fulfilling ourselves. Spiritual leadership can be seen as assisting others with this purpose.

Other books that have inspired me include *The Lord of the Rings* by J.R.R. Tolkien and *The Chosen* by Chaim Potok—and many more. Novels, of course, do not prove particular insights. I believe that the most significant insights in life cannot be readily proved, but they correspond with our deepest wisdom and experiences. Novels and also films, theatrical productions, and poems can be exceptionally useful. Moreover, it is certainly not true that only art and literature can contribute to these insights. In the following chapters I will be dealing with other sources, such as professional literature, wisdom from a number of spiritual traditions, and last but not least, reality itself. Art and literature in my life are like the sauce and the spices included in a meal: they give it a refined taste.

CHAPTER 2

The Law

MOTTO: THE SPIRITUAL LEADER IS A MASTER OF MANIFESTATION.

"The World is your exercise book. The pages on which you do your sums. It is not reality, although you can express your reality there if you wish. You are also free to write nonsense, or lies, or to tear the pages."—Richard Bach, *Illusions*

"Some say life is like a little feather, that's fluttering in the wind. Others say: we have a destiny that we have to find and to follow. Maybe both is true."—Forrest Gump

IMAGINE YOU WANT TO CREATE A LAWN. WHERE DO YOU begin? Most people will describe an action: buying grass seed or turf, turning over the soil, removing weeds, or leveling the ground. However, the reality is that, initially, you imagine the lawn. In your mind's eye you "see" the lawn: its color and form, its location within the surrounding garden, and so on. Once you have imagined it you can get on with creating it.

Actually, it isn't true that you actually grow the grass in the most literal sense. Nature, or the grass itself, actually does the growing. You create the conditions in which nature can take its course. You do, however, have an influence on the quality of the result. If you carry out your actions with care and attention, then the result will generally be better than if you fail to do so. If you apply the correct fertilizer to the soil, water it when it's dry, and mow it at the correct time, not too often and not too infrequently, then you can expect a good result. In order to do this you must submit to the rhythm of nature. For example the grass will not grow more quickly when you tug at the blades or if you apply more fertilizer or water than is necessary. On the contrary, all of these actions will be detrimental to the result, or have long-term damaging effects. There is a time and place for everything and you cannot make the river flow more rapidly by pushing it.

Let's take our mind game one step further. Your neighbor, who has exactly the same house as yours, wants to lay down exactly the same lawn, too. He works in synchrony with you, and carries out exactly the same actions. The conditions in his garden are identical to yours. However, as you already know, the grass is always greener on the other side, and in this case this is actually so. He has fewer weeds, the grass is more uniform, and, to make matters worse, you end up with a grass ailment—brown patches. What's going on?

Upon closer inspection it becomes apparent that there is a difference. The neighbor had been talking to his grass; you consider this ludicrous. He developed a relationship with his grass, just as some people do with their plants (he could have indeed done this without talking). His intention is therefore different. Maybe you are more geared toward the result and wanted to outdo your neighbor in achieving the best lawn. For you the lawn is the means and for him it is the aim. Or to put it better: he sees the lawn as if it were his child. To him, creation (laying the lawn) is an act of unadulterated love, even though he may never refer to it as that and would be completely bemused if someone should say so. To put it yet another way: he is at one with his lawn and he also experiences it this way. This is what we call *awareness of unity.*

This scenario stirs up a number of interesting questions. Is it true that the underlying intention of actions determines the result, even if on the surface the actions appear to be identical? A more general question is: To what extent do we determine the reality surrounding us? In other words: To what extent is the reality surrounding us the result of our own process of creation? These questions are significant if we wish to gain an understanding into what the effectiveness of our actions, and thus of leadership, determine. I will now deal with both of these questions comprehensively.

DO WE CREATE OUR OWN REALITY?

The Effect of Our Intention

Let's look at the first question: Does the underlying intention of the action determine the result? Some people have difficulty believing this. Nevertheless, there are many indications that this is true. For example, we know that some people have green thumbs, while plants fail to thrive in the care of others who do everything by the book. Some teachers create a pleasant working atmosphere in the classroom, whereas others who apparently do exactly the same things cannot seem to achieve this. Like all living creatures, people are able to tune in to the underlying intention of actions. In bio-energetics, body work in which manual techniques are applied, it is a well-known fact that if your intention towards the client is pure—loving, healing—you can proceed vigorously, without any danger of hurting the client. If, however, the body worker's intention is not pure—for example, thinking "I'll break your resistance"—then even an apparently harmless action can result in bruising, contusions, or psychological damage. Even matter appears to adapt to the human psyche, as is apparent from both subatomic physics and from scientific parapsychology (see for example *Experiments with God* by the physicist Cornelis Rietdijk). I am going to explain below how our intention influences our actions, but first I must deal with the second question.

Three Reality Concepts

To what extent is the reality surrounding us the result of our own process of creation? The traditional opinions regarding this matter are extremely divided. Roughly speaking, there are three concepts. The first is that everything is predetermined. This is a concept that can be found among the ancient Greeks, for example, and is expressed in particular in the classical Greek tragedies. According to this opinion, everything will occur as the gods have determined. No matter what, fate will prevail. A fine example of this is the classic story of Oedipus. It was prophesied at his birth that Oedipus would murder his father and sleep with his mother. In order to prevent this from happening, he was sent away to another country. However, the outcome of this, of course, is that due to a twist of fate he encounters his parents at a later time and does not recognize them, at which point he comes to blows with his father, killing him, and sleeps with his mother.

A modern—although not really modern—version of this reality concept is the Protestant doctrine of predestination, which states that it is predetermined whom the chosen ones are, who will be graced with celestial salvation. This concept has always appealed to the imagination of many people (P.N. van Eijck's poem "De Tuinman en de Dood," which can be translated as "The Gardener and Death," is a good example). But at the same time, this idea causes impotence, resulting in resignation and apathy.

DE TUINMAN EN DE DOOD (THE GARDENER AND DEATH)

A PERSIAN NOBLEMAN:
This morning my gardener made haste, pale from fright,
Into my home: "Sir, Sir, one moment!,
There in the rose garden, I was pruning cutting after cutting,
Then I looked behind me. There stood Death.
I was shocked, and hurried along the other side,
But still happened to see the threat of his hand.
Sir, your horse, and let me dash off,
Before nightfall I will be in Ispahaan!"-
This afternoon (he was already long gone)
I met up with Death in the Cedar Park.
"why?" I asked, as he waits silently,
Did you threaten my servant this morning?
Smiling he replied: It was no threat,
From which your gardener fled. I was surprised,
When I saw him this morning here peacefully working
The man I must collect tonight in Ispahaan.

The second concept of reality is that we are directly or indirectly completely responsible for the occurrences in our lives—everything is the result of our actions or decisions. This concept can also be found in Christian circles (and is as ancient as the book of Job in the Bible, where it is expressed by Job's friends) and can be stated as follows: the course of your life is determined by whether you have sinned or not. Happiness and prosperity are the result of God's discretion, while illness and troubles are the consequence of our sinful behavior or thoughts. A variant of this idea can be found in the Eastern concept of karma: that in this life we must deal with or work out what we have left undone in our previous lives. This often has a negative tone, for example if we believe that in a previous life we were not loving and caring enough and this is why we are now exposed to unfairness and cold-heartedness.

Another variant of this is the magical thinking which can be seen in children and with certain primitive populations and their magicians: the fantasy that we can totally mold life to our own desires (otherwise known as an *omnipotent fantasy*). Conversely, it can be said that everything that occurs in our lives has been caused by ourselves or by someone else, and if it is someone else then we must have directly or indirectly incited this. This reasoning was observed with many Surinamese people regarding the airplane catastrophe in the Bijlmer area of Amsterdam in the 1990s. When the airplane crashed into the high rise, resulting in the death of many Surinamese people, it was said that catastrophe was pursuing the Surinamese people, as politicians and Surinamese citizens didn't take responsibility for the poor conditions within Suriname. This accident was also linked to a prior airplane crash in which virtually the whole Surinamese national football team was killed. Magical thinking is also popular in other circles, in particular in New Age ones, and provides the pleasant feeling that we can understand everything and therefore can gain control over everything. If this doesn't bear out in reality, then disappointment and cynicism can set in.

The third concept of reality is that everything in the universe occurs completely randomly. While there is a cause of each action, no systems or definitions can be identified. For example, a long time ago the Big Bang created a chain of events that can be thought of as an entirely random series of matter displacement. This idea has typically caught on in the modern industrial world. It is a mechanistic conception of the universe with no room for consciousness or for God, just material matters. The advantage of this idea is that you can attempt to explain the world in the physical science sense, but you will never be able to understand it—as there is in fact nothing to understand. Therefore you don't have to feel unhappy if you do not understand something; for example, the origin of evil. The downside is, of course, that all criteria for good and evil are lacking, other than the strict individual plane of personal choice. This is in time very unsatisfactory and causes despondency.

The common link between the first and the third concepts is that it makes us powerless. In both cases we are not in the position to—both at the personal and at the collective levels—create the reality we desire. The advantage of this of course is that we are not responsible, either, and in a way that is easy. Conversely, the second concept makes us excessively responsible. Every occurrence in life is seen as a punishment or a reward. This is a concept that amplifies feelings of guilt and fear, because it depicts the existence of a judgmental God or entity whose demands are almost impossible to fulfill. Therefore, we always fail, and the paradox of this concept is that we become fully responsible and at the same time are completely powerless. Responsibility in this manner is seen as sin and our life becomes one of guilt and penance.

A FOURTH MODEL

Are we powerless? Or do free will and free choice exist? Let's return to the example of the lawn. If its underlying presumption is true, that intention does in fact determine outcomes, then we can in fact create our own reality. However, we do this in co-creation with the world around us.

We cannot create the lawn without submitting to the powers of nature. Likewise, we are unable to create a pleasant atmosphere in our department or organization without submitting to the power in the people around us.

If our intention is pure, if we are honest with ourselves and others concerning what we actually desire and don't deceive ourselves or others, then we can achieve everything we desire, provided that we do this in harmony with the powers within ourselves and around us. This does not mean that we should always let ourselves be carried along by these powers with no will of our own. However, it does mean that we must acknowledge these powers and utilize them for our aim, like a true Aikido master does. We are as sailors on a lake: the wind and the waves determine what we can do. However, we can determine where we want to come ashore if we yield to the winds and the waves and do not fight them. We can use them by sailing against the wind, or if necessary, by tacking. We can strike sails at the onset of a storm.

Thus we cannot determine how and when we will reach land, but generally that we will reach land, if we are skillful and sensitive. The wind and the waves always side with the superior seaman. I will deal with this comprehensively at a later point.

(The objection could be made that we are not in control of surviving the storm, or being overcome by hunger or dehydration as a result of long-term drift at sea, but if you think about it you will realize that even these occurrences are partly the consequence of decisions that were taken prior to the event. I will return to this type of question later on.)

The above can be brought together in one law, a law of manifestation which has long been occult and veiled and was only known to sorcerers, shamans, and sects, but which is now becoming increasingly widely accepted. This law of manifestation is formulated as follows: we create in our own reality what we give energy to in our mind.

Manifestation

Let us take a closer look at this theory. First, let's look at the word manifestation. We understand this as becoming visible, public. This means that the thing that becomes visible already exists—it just isn't yet visible. In this way, a music composition already exists in the composer's mind, or, prior to this, in any form in the universe, before it becomes visible in the form of music sheets. A subsequent form of manifestation occurs when the composition is actually played. Therefore, manifestation is in fact not much more than a conversion from one energy state or state of being to another. In the case in question it is the conversion of spiritual and mental energy into material energy and subsequently from one form of material energy into another. If this also results in emotions being felt—the experience of beauty, sentiments—then a conversion into emotional energy also occurs.

Whether forms or entities can originate from nothing is an interesting (philosophical) question. We are incapable of imagining this. However, this question is not of significant importance to practice anyway. For practice, it is more convenient to make the presumption that manifestation is nothing more than the conversion of something from one energy state to another. Here are a few more examples:

- A designer mentally designs a piece of furniture. He makes a sketch. A carpenter makes a prototype. The engineer designs an industrial production process. The item of furniture is manufactured. Mental energy is therefore converted into material energy.
- A manager has a mental picture of how he wishes to have his department operate. By conveying this mental picture through his actions, the department begins to change. People begin to enjoy their work more. Mental energy is converted into emotional energy.
- A log is burned in an open hearth. One form of material energy is converted into another: structure and order into warmth and light.

• Bread can be made from wheat. Two forms of physical energy (the wheat grain and warmth) are converted into another form, which in turn is once more converted into emotional and mental energies (food as a prerequisite of life).

As is evident from these examples and the lawn example, every process of manifestation begins with a process of awareness. This awareness is therefore the origin of the material and not, as stated in the third reality concept above, the other way around.

Creation

The second word I would like to look at is creation. Creation is in fact nothing more than manifestation: making the conversion from one state of being to another. Therefore, it is not creating something that does not yet exist. When we think of creation we visualize the origin of doing something or making something. However, we know that this is only a part of the creation process.

The process of creation actually occurs at four levels:

1. The physical level: creation through work, deeds, and actions
2. The emotional level: creation through will
3. The mental level: creation through thinking, visualizing, and imagining
4. The spiritual level: creation originates from belief

All four levels play a role in most (but not all) acts of creation. First there is a vision, concept, or idea of what is to be created. Then there must be the will to actually realize this (although in some cases the will precedes the specific vision). This is followed by action. The whole process is supported by the belief that what is being created will actually come into being. It is important that we realize that the action arises from the other sectors of the process of creation. In some cases, when belief is lacking, or the image is unclear, or the will is weak, we attempt to force the process of creation by means of extra activity. Effectiveness and efficiency in such a situation are actually slight, often due to the occurrence of many undesired side effects. (Think once more of the sailor on the lake who challenges the wind.)

Faith is crucial to an effective and efficient process of creation. Faith is in fact made up of two elements: faith in yourself and the faith that life will provide you with what you require. You could say that life provides the power and energy we require for the realization of our own process of creation. But this also means that in order to create we must be in touch with this power and energy; we must become familiar with them and submit to them, as shown by our examples. This is an important aspect of what we previously called the awareness of unity. You could also put it another way: our own process of creation must be in harmony with the processes of creation around us, the universal process of creation. We are created in God's image and likeness—this a wonderful metaphor—we are created by God as a creator together with God, or, in more worldly terms, we are both a part of and a contributor to the ever ongoing process of creation. Therefore, we are required to attune ourselves. We humans may well have the power and the right to go against the flow, but this takes a lot of time and energy and often results in disasters or crises in the form of failures, depression, breakdowns, dysfunctional relationships, or illnesses. (This does not necessarily mean that these occurrences are always the result of going against the flow.) Going with the flow is by far the preferable option (this is something completely different to letting yourself be carried on the wind or aimlessly following fashion).

In practice, the significance of belief and attunement are quite often forgotten. This results in a number of misconceptions that cause the process of creation to deviate from what was anticipated or expected. This once more undermines the faith in personal creative capacity. A few examples of such misconceptions include:

1. If the law of manifestation is true, then we are in complete control of our lives. With this it is often forgotten that we are co-creators and that we can only function through submission to the powers surrounding us (with which we initially have to become familiar).

2. We consider what we manifest as an isolated entity, and forget that it is an inextricable part of the world of which we are also part. In practice, this leads to insensitivity toward the unforeseen consequences of our process of creation. (Consider, for example, a compa-

ny that produces a specific product without taking into account the environmental consequences.)

3. The law of manifestation appears to be an example of the law of cause and effect; there is an unambiguous one-to-one relationship between cause and effect. Under the same conditions, every occurrence will continually result in the same effect. If we could learn to completely control our energy process, then we could also completely control our own process of creation. However, this does not take into account the circumstances we dealt with in the first point. In addition, it isn't certain that the law of cause and effect always follows the previously formulated form. In any case, this isn't so at the level of subatomic physics. Since Heisenberg, who formulated the so-called uncertainty relationship, we know that the relationship between cause and effect is a statistical relationship at that level. Specific causes increase the probability of specific effects. However, this is not certain. There is room for coincidence. This may also be the case with manifestation. If we provide something with energy, the probability of its manifestation increases. However, there is no certainty. Free will is therefore nothing more than the opportunity to influence the probability and not the certainty that what we have chosen will actually take place.

4. We forget that manifestation is not much different than making something visible which already exists and thus we forget to attune to what already exists.

5. You can achieve what you want, if you really want it. This is the theory of positive thinking. It contains an element of truth. However, the processes of attuning and coincidence are underexposed. Another objection to this theory is that the element of time is mostly forgotten. When do you achieve what you wish to achieve? And, finally, this theory simplifies the energy-giving process (see below).

This manner of thinking results in viewing creation as a (small) technique. Manifestation then degenerates to manipulation or magic. Processes such as these can go well for a long time, but sooner or later one's lack of contact with the universal process of creation results in decreasing effectiveness (and thus faith) or a crisis.

In summary, the following is required for an effective process of creation:
- Belief in one's self
- Faith in life
- Attunement

What if you lack one of these qualities? Some spiritual exercises can aid you. They can be found in chapter 8.

Giving Energy To

The third expression in the law is the expression "giving energy to." This is a sort of collective name for the following psychological processes:
- Paying attention to
- Being afraid of
- Suppressing
- Fantasizing about
- Longing for
- Evading

It can be seen that both attraction processes and rejection processes have a manifesting effect. With regards to this, energy is completely neutral in its actions. We are just as capable of creating what we evade as well as what we desire. (The poem "The Gardener and Death" can also be interpreted in this manner. The gardener is, in contrast to the nobleman, afraid of Death and therefore attracts him.) This explains why we often create many unpleasant occurrences in our lives. Someone who wants to learn how to ski, and expends the majority of his energy on his fear of falling, will fall often and have difficulty learning to ski.

What are the matters to which we give energy? This can be all sorts of things: concepts, convictions, thought models, impressions, ideas, emotions, tendencies, desires, our intuition, our love, our fears, and much more. Giving energy is just like sowing seeds and we reap what we sow. In practice, we actually harvest a mixture of things, because our energy processes proceed in a quite chaotic way. The reality that we create is thus a wonderful projection of that which is taking place within ourselves.

In this context, I would like to turn our attention to the word "in" in this theory. It does not say that we create reality, but that we create "in" reality. To put it another way, we create our own personal subjective reality. In fact, it's surprising that we are often in agreement about shared situations, and isn't surprising that we are very often in disagreement regarding the reality in which we co-exist in unison. (An important principle of communication stems from this, which I will deal with in chapter 7.)

The law of manifestation does not state that we can only manifest if we consciously give energy to something. These processes very often occur subconsciously. In this way we can suppress images and feelings which we would rather not have—subconsciously give energy to—instead of expressing them and sharing them, and in doing so make them conscious and subject to choice. We then can no longer expend energy on them. (This is often stimulated by a superficial application of theories on positive thinking.) These images and emotions then manifest themselves in any shape in our reality.

Subconscious energy processes are, sometimes significantly, responsible for the results in our lives. For example, if we wish to trust people. If, subconsciously, we do not trust people—perhaps because we have been deceived in the past, which we may have "forgotten," as it was such a painful experience—then it may be the case that we continually meet up with people who violate our trust. In the end we can become suspicious and skeptical and eventually create a reality we do not seem to want, but to which we have subconsciously given a lot of energy. It is these negative feelings and thoughts we do not want, or do not allow ourselves to have, which are often suppressed and subconsciously play a significant role in the process of the creation of our lives.

Chapter 8 provides a number of techniques regarding this. The general idea is that being honest with yourself and observing yourself without judgment and disapproval provide the most insight into oneself. The subsequent step is then to give no more energy to these feelings and thoughts. Sometimes there is so much energy involved—the thoughts and feelings are so emotionally loaded—that this cannot take place easily or immediately. In cases like this, it is then necessary to first express these feelings and thoughts with the accompanying emotional charge to an impartial listener (this is often someone other than the partner). Sometimes this has to take place several times. However, at some point the moment arrives that the solution is to give no more energy to the thoughts and emotions concerned, to pay no attention to them. Every time these thoughts arise, acknowledge them and then proceed to the order of the day.

The technique of paying no attention to thoughts and feelings you no longer wish to have is no mean feat. In general it's impossible to pay no attention to something. When you have read this, attempt not to think about a pink panther. You will notice that this is not so simple. How does one in general not pay any attention to something? By paying attention to something else—for example, a thought or feeling that you want to have.

Using this approach, we can acquire a command of the process of giving energy and through this acquire a command over our own lives, mindful of the statements above about attunement. With this it must be taken into account that the law of manifestation does not state that we can immediately manifest what we give energy to. This may certainly take some amount of time. The time can be a few minutes or it could be years. That which we now focus on and provide energy to can only manifest at a later point in time.

Our current reality is therefore a manifestation of our process of attention throughout our lives, within our inner self, up until this current moment, and, according to some, even in the period preceding our lives.

Objections to the Law: Taking Responsibility

It is shown that the manifestation theory is a totally different approach to reality and our part in it than the previously mentioned approaches of reality. Is this law the Truth? Is this the way it is? Naturally, we do not have the answer. Such things cannot be scientifically proven. Everything that I claim in this book may very well be untrue, but that is beside the point. The point is that it may appeal to you or be beneficial in practice.

If you are experiencing difficulty in believing that the law works in the manner I have defined, then I recommend that you treat it as a working hypothesis, particularly if an unpleasant incident occurs. I did this when I was diagnosed with cancer in the fatty tissue in my groin. The cancer did not make me sick, but even so it was an extremely threatening experience. At first it seemed highly probable that the cancer could spread. If this had happened, then I wouldn't be able to tell you about it now. Even though I did not feel ill, it was nevertheless an existential crisis. I had to consider that I may die from it. One of my first thoughts was: "I didn't create this. Why is God's name would I do something like this to myself?" My second thought was, "Wait a minute, not so fast. Suppose that you did partly create it. But in the name of God, how and why?" I can assure you that if you pose these questions you will always receive an answer.

It has, for example, taught me to be truly loving toward myself and, as you know, you cannot love thy neighbor more than you love yourself. I wonder if I could have learned this without my illness and it is certainly one of the reasons why I did this to myself (if you want to know more, I would like to refer you to my book *Room for Happiness*).

Therefore, considering the law as a working hypothesis provides questions and answers. It is of course difficult to consider the law as a working hypothesis if you do not believe in it. The children who get cancer? Or natural disasters? Who is creating what in whose life?

Naturally, I do not have definitive answers to these questions. However, what I do know is that you will never receive answers to these types of questions if you pose them in the general sense. Answers can only be obtained if the questions are asked by the person concerned regarding the occurrences in his or her own life.

A friend of mine got cancer after she had finally, after many years, renounced her destructive behavior toward herself, her children, and her loved ones. She found this to be very demanding. However, eventually she died an extremely peaceful death, and her life left behind a trail of vibrancy. The son of another one of my friends became extremely psychotic during puberty and I can assure you that this was an enormous tragedy for those involved. It seemed to be extremely unfair after all the care given to him by his parents and also after all the work they had done on their personal growth.

In cases such as these, who creates whose reality? In my mind, the answer seems to be that everybody involved in this case is involved in a huge co-creative process in which each person has his or her own share. It is remarkable that if each of the persons involved actually consults his or her self—and asks, How and why have I contributed to this?—the answers always come.

It is also important that the guilt question be kept out of this sort of investigation, because just as manifestation doesn't mean having everything under control, co-responsibility—which is often realized subconsciously—can never mean guilt. Guilt is a state of cold-heartedness toward yourself—and often toward the other person who appears to be making you feel guilty—and no one has ever benefited from this. There is a real difference between guilt and co-responsibility; the latter means that you take responsibility for co-creating your own reality. And this is the beginning of the discovery of the answers.

Responsibility is often is entirely denied. We know that a large earthquake will probably occur in the next century in the Los Angeles area. The situation in Los Angeles can be compared to that of Kobe prior to the earthquake there. Even with this knowledge, however, millions of people live in LA. I'm not saying that this is not comprehensible. However, it will be hard not to say when it does happen that the people co-created their situation themselves. Something similar can be said about those who choose to build in and live in the areas of Zuid-Limburg which are under threat from water. Once again, the law does not state that you create reality—the earthquake and the floods—but that you create your own reality, which is in this case experiencing an earthquake or flood. People live on the slopes of volcanoes, in war-torn areas, or in areas with periodic floods often because they cannot perceive any other possibilities—which doesn't mean that such possibilities are not present—or because they do not want to give up what they have.

Mind you, taking 100 percent responsibility is also threatening for another reason. If you do this you cannot blame someone else for your troubles. Sometimes things can happen which are incomprehensible or are considered unjust. However, you can only blame yourself or God or Life, if you at any rate believe in an unloving God or a Life which does the dirty on you every now and again. (This is thus a very humanized Life.)

Taking 100 percent responsibility for your own life means unconstrained freedom. We are free to be honest or to lie, choose to go with or against the flow of life, or to live a futile or constructive life, to be loving or uncaring. Many people consider freedom to be threatening because no one makes decisions for you, not even Life, and not your sense of duty, either. You are all alone. This can create a feeling of strength and power, but also a feeling of being adrift in the universe.

In conclusion, we have ascertained that the question as to whether the law of manifestation is true is not such a significant question. The true question is: am I going to use it or not? This is also a choice. I may have made it plausible that choosing the law contributes to greater effectiveness. Faith, trust, and attunement are prerequisites for working with the law. However, making use of the law as a working hypothesis also makes a contribution to the development of these qualities. American literature refers to this process as "empowerment," becoming more powerful. I have given this another name: "personal mastery," being the master of your own life.

THE LAW OF CREATIVE TENSION

In recent years, a number of alternative laws have been formulated which can all be considered as being variants of the law of manifestation. I would like to deal with a number of these, as they provide deeper insight into the process of manifestation.

Robert Fritz has developed an interesting model for using the law of manifestation. It is a model of creative tension, or the path of least resistance (see figure 2.1).

The lower square is the impression we have of (our own) reality,

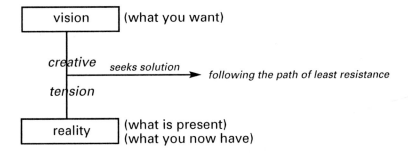

Figure 2.1 Robert Fritz' creative tension model.

including our inner reality—our thoughts, concepts, and so on. The top square is the vision we wish to achieve. The distance between these is known as creative tension. Just like every other tension, this tension searches for relief (a solution) which is along the path of least resistance. Just as a mountain stream flows along the path of least resistance, and just as electrons flow from the negative pole toward the positive pole along the path of least resistance, creative tension is also released in this manner. This can be formulated as a law that is an exceptional circumstance of the law of manifestation: the creative tension between vision and reality resolves itself along the path of least resistance.

A number of interesting conclusions can be drawn from this exceptionally illuminating model. The first is that in practice the tension can be reduced in two ways, because the vision moves toward the reality, or the reality moves toward the vision. In the first situation, the vision becomes diminished and degenerates to no more than what is feasible or even less than that. However, thinking about the feasibility of something is not part of the vision; this is a part of reality. In practice, a vision often becomes weakened or indistinct because often we do not want tension, possibly because this is confused with stress. However, stress is a completely different type of tension and involves suppressed emotions and desires.

Creative tension can be more readily compared to a challenge or excitement. If we do not wish to have this tension, then we pay dearly for it by not achieving what we actually want. This process also occurs collectively in business and in politics and it is one of the reasons why we observe such an alarming lack of vision and leadership.

Another reason why we often weaken the vision is that we are afraid of disappointment. Desiring what you actually want also includes being confronted with the large distance between vision and reality and living with the fear that your vision will never become reality. However, once more there is a price to pay for weakening our vision: slowing down the movement of reality in the direction of the vision. This feels like a standstill or stagnation and eventually results in dissatisfaction with your own life and with life as it is.

We often have difficulty with the concept that Rome was not built in a day. Let us take the example of the mountain stream. All the water that falls on the mountain or wells up from a spring eventually reaches the foot of the mountain. Sometimes this is rapid—rainwater, for example—but sometimes it takes longer, if the water has become snow. Sometimes it takes centuries, if the water is ice in a glacier. Sometimes there is a deviating route, such as when the water evaporates or is dispersed as mist. But this much is true: the water will eventually reach the ground. We can also view reality in this manner. We want what we want and if we uphold our vision and supply it with enough energy (obey the law of manifestation), then the reality will, no matter what, move toward the vision, even if it is very slowly. However, if we abandon the vision, then nothing will happen. Thus we must have the courage to want what we actually want. I find this a heartening thought when I think of the things I desire—world peace, for example.

It is important to realize that, in this context, there is no direct relationship between creative tension and satisfaction. Some people believe that the presence of creative tension results in dissatisfaction with what you have. It is more likely that the opposite occurs. Satisfaction and fulfillment occur through the experience that your reality is moving in the direction you desire. You then know that you are a part of the process of creation and have the feeling of living a constructive life—you feel your life is leading toward something. If, on the contrary, your reality does not move, because you desire nothing—or think you do not desire something, or because you think that you should be satisfied with what you have—then you are not actively taking part in the process of creation. Life then comes to a standstill, becomes pointless. There is no longer any growth, and thus through time no life, because living is growing.

Another way of reducing creative tension is to represent reality better than it actually is. Then the reality will not shift toward the vision, but our perception of reality will. In doing so, our reality may well change (law of manifestation), but not very satisfactorily, because deep down we know that we are leading ourselves up the garden path and this realization forms an opposing force. This is why Fritz implores that reality should be seen in the most objective way possible and to use this as a base for our vision. In other words, we fence in our vision against reality. This also incorporates a reality check and a safeguard against "freaking out" or not making our vision "realistic" or "feasible." If Martin Luther King or Gandhi had limited themselves to a vision which seemed to be feasible, then they would not have had the impact that they had. Of course, we don't all have to be a Martin Luther King or a Gandhi (after all, we do not all opt for death by murder). But being ourselves is just fine. I would like to plead for some grandeur in what we want. Otherwise we will never get to where we want to be in the world.

A second conclusion that can be derived from the model is that the tension energy chooses its own course. Many roads lead to Rome, many more than we could possibly know, let alone that we do know, which provide the path of least resistance. It can be derived from this in practice that it would be beneficial to focus our attention more toward the development of our vision and provide it with more energy, rather than occupy ourselves with the question of how we can achieve our vision. If we do this our actions will arise in a natural manner from our process of awareness and we won't force the realization of our vision through excessive activity, planning, and organization. A habit of natural, organic acting instead of rigid planning and structuring is not popular in our Western industrialized society and very difficult to sell in the business world and in politics. We are geared toward results and indoctrinated to making haste, doing, organizing, and managing. However, the greatest effectiveness lies in

If You Do Not Have Enough Time, Go and Sit Down for a While

After setting up a new chemical factory, things didn't work out as expected. This meant that the required production wasn't achieved, which resulted in enormous pressure both financially and time-wise, as the old plant had been condemned. Nervous technicians and operators ran from pillar to post robbing Peter to pay Paul, solving problems by creating other problems. The new plant was repeatedly shut down and the deadline for the plant being operational was continually reestablished. Overwork and nervous exhaustion were the order of the day. The company's entire focus was geared toward the problem, which, thanks to the law of manifestation, became increasingly larger.

How could this be dealt with differently?
In a situation like this, it would be useful to ask yourself: what was it again that I actually wanted to achieve? The focus then shifts from the problem to the vision, from reaction to creation. (It all depends on how you "c" it.) Reality then becomes a reference point instead of the main focus of attention. Moreover, the tunnel vision that allows us to only see one solution or path for each problem, which may not be the path of least resistance, disappears.

My view is: If you do not have enough time, go and sit down for a while. This is exactly what a group of technicians from the company in question did one day. They left the factory and went to a nearby restaurant and took the time to sit down for lunch and think about it. What was it again, our aim? What was it all about? A modern company with pleasant working relationships and a pleasant working atmosphere? A company that normally functions well and produces an excellent product? Once they had determined their aim, the way toward a solution became clear. Necessary actions came forth automatically from their vision. Not surprisingly, this route wasn't the same path they had originally chosen to follow.

This is not a complete success story, because the new route was only partially adhered to, and exceptionally difficult external circumstances brought the company into deeper trouble. The greater the pressure, the more difficult it becomes to not fall back into the old work methods which up until that point had been in a certain sense beneficial. The extent to which the new vision has been integrated into the (collective) thought, or is only a superficial manner of thinking and operating, becomes clear in such a situation. Can you sustain a new way of thinking and working under pressure? The company in question was eventually extremely successful in doing this.

submitting to the process, which in turn does the work itself. As I have already said, you cannot make the grass grow quicker by tugging the blades. The East Asian business world in general appears to have a better understanding of this than we Westerners do, which partially explains their success. This will be thoroughly dealt with in the following chapter (the principle of Woe, Wei, acting without doing). In chapter 9 we will meet the reader who still wishes to activate the process. Here I would like to illustrate this principle using a single example (see box; the history of this example can be found in chapter 9 under the heading We Make the World Lighter).

A third conclusion can be drawn from Fritz's model: the path of least resistance is determined by the underlying structure. An example given by Fritz is a river: water follows the course of the least resistance. However, the riverbed determines the route. This means that if we, in spite of the second conclusion, still want to focus on making the route through which we wish to achieve our vision more efficient, then we can only do this by changing the underlying structure—and not, as often happens in practice, by fighting against the underlying structure. The underlying structure is in fact nothing more than the powers within ourselves and around us.

We must first know these forces (through attunement) and it then becomes apparent that some forces are unchangeable—for example, the wind and the waves and the forces of nature are unchangeable, even though man in his arrogance believes that everything can be changed and controlled. There is, however, one important aspect of the underlying structure which can be changed, and that is our own system of concepts or our belief system, the coherent system of what we perceive as being good and true. If we achieve results in our lives that we do not desire, then it is recommended that we examine our underlying concept system and which part of it is no longer functional. It will become apparent that letting go of old concepts isn't so easy, which is why it was previously stated that letting go is the first stage of our personal growth process and the first step toward a greater personal effectiveness (as a leader).

OTHER LAWS

I would like to bring this chapter to a close by naming a few other laws of creativity and effectiveness that in my opinion are special cases of the law of manifestation. As they are special cases, they are only effective in specific circumstances.

The first I would like to deal with is the law of creativity: we create our own reality (as seen in the Jane Roberts/Seth books). This law is a simplified formulation of the law of manifestation. How we create our own reality is not stated. An advantage of this formula is that it becomes even more obvious than with the law of manifestation that our—not *the*—reality does not exist independently from our process of creation. Another obvious consequence of this law is that we realize that we are all creators, because we all live in one—namely our—reality. The law makes short work of statements such as "I'm not creative" or "I have no capacity for creativity."

Another law worth discussing is the law of belief: what you believe in becomes reality (Murphy). This is also referred to as the law of positive thinking. This law is often applied to healing processes (Louise Hay). Affirmations, visualizations, and (auto)suggestions are used to suggest a specific belief which then for you personally becomes reality. It has been shown above that the theory is valid, but that it is not only faith but also other capacities of the human spirit, such as desires, inclinations, and feelings, which determine reality. Moreover, the desired result can only be achieved when the forces of the internal and external surroundings (the underlying structure) have been attuned. In this context it's important that a distinction be made among faith, trust, and something in which you believe (belief). Your beliefs, as we have already seen, only become reality if they are attuned to its context and based on faith in yourself and trust in life itself. Autosuggestion can sometimes achieve this, but not always.

The following law provides a better understanding of this. It is the law of converse effort: if your wish and your fantasy are at odds with each other, then the outcome is in accordance with the fantasy. The law is aptly named, because in this case we will very often see the storm coming and put in extra effort to realize our aim anyway. According to the law of manifestation this has an adverse effect, because the exertion doesn't stem from desire but from fantasy, which in this case is very often negative (such as the fantasy that you fall when learning to ski, or fear new disruptions and problems at the chemical plant). Thus fantasy and not the wish receives extra energy, and therefore fantasy is more likely to become reality. This is actually a unique case of subconscious repression. This shows once again that what you believe in only becomes reality if it is supported by your faith in yourself, trust in life, and attunement.

IN CONCLUSION

I hope that it has become a little clearer how crucial a vision is to leadership. It is the only attribute a leader possesses in order to achieve what he wants to achieve without pressuring people or manipulating them; this is truly effective leadership. By developing his vision and subsequently energizing it, he obtains a certain charisma, and with this also influence, without making his staff dependent. In chapter 9 I will delve deeper into discovering and developing one's personal vision and also the process that leads from individual visions to collective visions. Methods for enhancing visions will also be dealt with, creating more energy and in this way advancing effectiveness as a leader. If a vision can move mountains, what is a collective vision capable of? We find that we can let the process of manifestation work for us through vision, in particular if we energize and focus on the vision and use reality as a set base point. Energizing reality in excess, in particular the undesirable part or the part we wish to change, is inadvisable, as this causes a preservative effect according to the law of manifestation.

The following example illustrates the power of vision and the law of converse effort. First, a transition occurs in the direction of vision. The process is then forced and the path of the least resistance is not taken. It is forgotten that "it takes as long as it takes" in the Transformation Game, a game I'll explore later in this book. You can also ask yourself whether a collective vision was actually present in this situation—it is obvious that this was not the case. These subjects will be dealt with further in chapter 9.

Unity Divided

It has become clear to me that things cannot continue in this manner. We are driving ourselves and the world crazy. The deeply felt feeling of unity within me is being torn; it is screaming in agony. It is banging on the walls with its white-knuckled fists. Stop this, stop, stop, stop! But no one hears it, everyone just carries on, what can you do? Fight, wrestle with it, make sure the world around me changes. Ensure that it is bearable. Yes, I'm tough, I can take a lot, I have energy so let me have a go at it. I will manage to give shape to that feeling of openness and harmony, love and vulnerability, from the deep-down knowledge of how this world is meant to be.

For a long time I've believed that information and automation are the way to prepare society for necessary change. Just as the complexity and specialization in organisms has to increase first in order to develop consciousness, this is how the world will fare as a whole. Teilhard de Chardin saw all of this in '48 and put it in his book, Le Phénomène humain. This book was my dream as a boy. I read it when I was 17 or 18 years old and de Chardin's body of thought was my guide. It influenced my decision to go into the field of automation so that I could offer a tool to society with which unity could be re-established.

I now realize that a development of awareness must follow this computerization surge, that this awareness holds the actual key to our changes. This isn't merely knowledge and expertise—what you would expect from a good engineer—it is about Being. It is no longer about others and the world around me—it is about starting with my own self and the world within me. The key to changing the world is in all of us. Turning this into reality is actually quite simple yet at the same time a very difficult task which requires a significant amount of effort. For myself, the breaking point occurred when I was around the age of 55, when I switched from a being a manager to having a more indirect advisory role. (I'd long known that this would happen at this time so that I could devote more of my attention to personal matters.)

I was inspired throughout my career to create tools for change and at the same time help to create a world in which sufficient awareness is present to make these tools applicable. How naïve and arrogant, yet at the same time so full of good intentions and idealism.

My career with Raet automation consultancy began in 1972. I was director along with another colleague; we were a loyal team. Raet grew from a small pioneering company in the 1970s to a medium-size enterprise with a clear-cut market and partnerships. It was a company with decency, with a good social climate, with friendship. But there was also distance, and feelings that were difficult to overcome from throughout the layers of the company.

Raet's growth accelerated in the 1980s through takeovers geared toward creating market volume in order to be able to offer total solutions. This meant choosing specific markets for problematic fields such as health care and welfare, municipal authorities and other local administrative organizations, and associations and fundraising organizations.

These choices were not solely based on profit potential and commercial opportunity, but also on the contribution that automation could offer individuals and society as a whole.

The accelerated growth up to a turnover of circa 600 million guilders in the Netherlands led to the inevitable delegation of power and authority. We made the transition from a small company to a big business. In order to maintain our identity, we formulated and tried to practice certain values. We questioned our identity ("Who are we?"), our mission ("What is our purpose?), our market and society, our human relations, our investor relations, and other pressing issues. These values were meant to realize the unity and the awareness I strove for, both externally and internally.

The ideal was propagated in conferences, such as one called Art Meets Science: How to Let Go and Keep Control?, and at personnel gatherings, including a trip to Malta with more than a thousand people. I also tried to live by this ideal, but I don't think that everyone recognized this.

The management of this process in the Netherlands was handed over to my potential successors, a total of three, one for marketing, one for technology, and one for finance and human resources. I remained chairman from a distance, and was operationally involved with the internationalization of the company, an expansion which had to take place simultaneously with consolidation in the Dutch organization.

But things didn't go as expected. It appeared that my views weren't supported, that power games were being played, and that the space was not being used to create and mature, but to make each other's lives hell.

My conclusion was that action was required. We had to slow down the international expansion in order to give the home base the opportunity to recover. We drew up a strategy in the summer of 1992 based on this plan, which was widely supported within the board of commissioners and the employees' council. Furthermore, I thought that the operational managers in the Netherlands should be replaced. However, the chairman of the board disagreed. He wanted me to get involved once more with the Dutch operations and, together with the existing directors, make necessary changes. I did not see the point in this, but I couldn't convince him otherwise.

Unfortunately this difference of opinion escalated into a conflict that resulted in my departure. It was hasty, but just at the right time to move on to a new phase and new challenges in the beginning of my 55th year. This sounds fine now, but I still feel disappointed because, after all, I hadn't achieved what I wanted to achieve.

Spiritual leadership is obviously more than the ideal alone . . .

Ir. Huib Matthes, organization advisor and former chairman of the board of Raet Automatisering, 1970-1992

CHAPTER 3

The Way

MOTTO: THE SPIRITUAL LEADER LOOKS AFTER HIS AFFAIRS WITH-
OUT ACTING. AND YET NOTHING REMAINS UNDONE.

"The Tao is hidden and nameless."—Tao Te Ching 3/41

*"Thou shalt not make unto thee any graven image, or any likeness
of any thing that is in heaven above, or that is in the earth beneath,
or that is in the water under the earth."*—Exodus 20:4

THIS CHAPTER DEALS WITH TAOISM AS A WAY OF LIFE OR
an attitude toward life. Not that I am a Taoist master, nor do I see
myself becoming one. But after I had completed writing one of my
previous books, *Management zonder Controle (Management Without
Control)*, I was given, by coincidence—is there such a thing?—the *Tao
Te Ching* (literally: the Classic Book of the Way and Integrity). I was
deeply struck by its beauty and wisdom and I recognized a philosophical similarity to what I was trying to convey in a stumbling
manner in my own book. I have read a lot more since then (including
the I Ching and books by Stikker, Master Mantak Chia, and Jolang
Chang). However, the one thing I do know is that you cannot learn
Taoism from a book. You can only learn it by practicing it, both as a
state of mind and on a practical level.

But, for me personally, just being occupied with it in my daily life
has been so beneficial that I am convinced that someone who wishes to develop into a spiritual leader—you—will find it to be extremely beneficial.

This is why I have—as a student with no master—allocated
myself the position of messenger to relate to you a little of this age-
old wisdom. Maybe I am capable of awakening your interest to such

an extent that you will go directly to the source. This is not difficult. Excellent translations of the old Chinese books are available in all bookstores and libraries, and practicing Taoist masters are everywhere. Plus, Taoism can be found where you expect it the least—in the Bible, for example, in Matthew 6:25-34 and 7:7-8, Ecclesiastes, and the example cited above. However, the book that appealed to me the most is *The Tao of Pooh* by Benjamin Hoff. He wrote:

> That was after some of us were discussing the Great Masters of Wisdom, and someone was saying how all of them come from the East, and I was saying that some of them didn't, but he was going on and on, just like this sentence, not paying any attention, when I decided to read a quotation of Wisdom from the West, to prove that there was more to the world than one half, and I read:
>
> > "When you wake up in the morning, Pooh," said Piglet at last, "what's the first thing you say to yourself?"
> > "What's for breakfast?" said Pooh. "What do you say, Piglet?"
> > "I say, I wonder what's going to happen exciting today?" said Piglet.
> > Pooh nodded thoughtfully.
> > "It's the same thing," he said.
>
> "What's that?" the Unbeliever asked.
> "Wisdom from the Western Taoist," I said.
> "It sounds like something from Winnie-the-Pooh," he said.
> "It is," I said.
> "That's not about Taoism," he said.
> "Oh, yes it is," I said.
> "No, it's not," he said.
> "What do you think it's about?" I said.

"It's about this dumpy little bear that wanders around asking silly questions, making up songs, and going through all kinds of adventures, without ever accumulating any amounts of intellectual knowledge or losing his simple-minded sort of happiness. That's what it's about," he said.

"Same thing," I said (p. ix-x).

And so he decided to explain Taoism based upon *Winnie-the-Pooh* and vice versa. The success of this is apparent from the mere fact that this passage from *The Tao of Pooh* is a fitting definition of Taoism. How that can ever lead to spiritual and efficient leadership remains to be seen. Let us start at the beginning, for, as the Taoist says, "A journey of a thousand miles begins with one step."

TAO

The concept of Tao lies at the very foundations of Taoism. One of the most significant sources of the concept is commonly known as the *Tao Te Ching*, which for a long time was attributed to Lao-tse (literally Ancient Master), who is said to have lived around 500 BC. Whether Lao-tse actually existed is, however, exceptionally doubtful. It is more probable that the *Tao Te Ching* is a codification of wisdom which was passed on verbally around 300 to 250 BC. There are various versions; the last one came into circulation after 1973 and is based on the Ma-wang-tui manuscripts, which were discovered in that year. I have mainly used this version in this book. The numbering of the chapters deviates from previous versions of the Tao. I will use the old reference numbers after the 1973 ones in my citations.

The concept of Tao probably existed before 500 BC. The Taoist manner of thinking can also be found in the *I Ching*, which dates back to the ancient Chinese wisdom of 3,000 years ago. Confucius, who lived circa 500 BC, was opposed to it; maybe he didn't fully understand it. And, finally, there is an obvious affinity between the Taoist manner of thinking and the *Bhagavad-Gita*, one of the most significant scriptures forming the basis of Hinduism and yoga, which probably appeared in northwestern India up to two centuries before the *Tao Te Ching*. The link between China and India only came into its full existence around 300 BC, when the climate became warmer and the mountain passes in central Asia became free of snow. This implies that the *Tao Te Ching* was therefore influenced by the Hindu and yoga traditions.

But what is Tao? It is normally translated as "the way," but that doesn't explain anything. The essence is that Tao cannot be grasped using words, because it must be seen as the source or the beginning of everything. The Word originates from the Tao itself (compare with John1:1: In the beginning was the Word, and the Word was with God, and the Word was God) and therefore cannot be articulated in words. The same notion can also be seen in the Old Testament, where God had no name other than J.H.W.H. (I am what I am). It can be seen again in the second of the Ten Commandments. A word is like an image, a symbol, and is therefore not the All-One itself. Every image or denotation can become an idol and this does not only injustice to the All-One, but also presents the danger that we lose our independence through our relationship with the All-One, as adepts are part and parcel of idols. The All-One is in fact too vast for words and exactly because of this we are not in danger of submitting ourselves to it.

I have just drawn a parallel between the Old Testament's concept of God and Tao, but there is a significant difference. The God of the Old Testament is clearly seen as a human entity with whom you enter into a personal relationship. Tao is not a human entity. It is a power, energy. There is a reason as to why one of the meanings of Tao is the Way. On occasion, I have personally translated it as the universal process of creation. Indeed, Tao is just as much the Creating as the Continuing as the Completing (*I Ching, The Great Treatise*, V and VI). The Alpha and the Omega. The eternal. "The Tao is always nameless" (*Tao Te Ching*, 76/32). We are part of Tao as well as a manifestation of Tao.

The fact that we cannot capture Tao in a name or word doesn't mean that we cannot make a few statements about it. I will indeed do so, although in fact we can only understand the Tao through a specific manner of living and working. "Truth seems contradictory" (*Tao Te Ching*, 43/78). Nevertheless, I hope that my words and quotations are enough of an incentive to you to try out this style of living and working.

I just stated that we are both a part of Tao as well as a manifestation of it. However, we are often unaware of this. We disconnect ourselves from our origins. In doing so we also lose our sustenance, which in turn results in a feeling of uncertainty and reduced efficiency. We then compensate for this with excessive actions and attempts to mold the world to our will. For example, we exploit the world, instead of adopting an attitude of respect for the world and allowing ourselves to be nourished by it. Humanity as a whole is afflicted by this and the global environmental issue can certainly be partially accounted for through this.

Harmony and balance are key words in Taoist thought. Harmony can only be achieved through not forsaking the Way. I interpret this to mean remaining in touch with our inner source, our intuition, love, and wisdom. If we forsake the Way then we do not reach what I defined as awareness of unity. But if we are in touch with our inner source, then we can also experience this same source in another person, in nature, and in the world. When that happens, we no longer exploit the world and we do not use our fellow human beings or manipulate them, but we work in co-operation with them. We then find ourselves in a harmonious relationship with our surroundings. We become capable of seeing the source in our enemies—even though we cannot relate well to their behavior. We can achieve awareness of unity.

Harmony is the father of efficiency. Harmony enables all the energy at our disposal to become available and therefore we squander no energy on opposing forces. We can now begin to appreciate the value of Taoism for effective spiritual leadership. Naturally, questions crop up: how do we achieve this harmony in this hectic world, where we are constantly tempted to react, where there are continual contradictions, where we believe that we have to fight for our status, where it is a struggle for life and the survival of the fittest?

For answers, I refer you to the previous chapter. If you really desire harmony, then you should include this in your vision. According to the law of manifestation you will then evoke the forces in the direction of that harmony. In this case, that is no different to the Tao itself. There is more information on how to deal—or not deal—with this in chapters 7 and 9.

TE

Balance is a characteristic of the Tao itself. As I have already said, Tao is the creator and the receiver, beginning and end, the light and the dark, the strong and the weak, the male and the female, fire and water, yang and yin. In Tao everything is still united. However, "one produces two, the two produce the three, and the three produce the ten thousand things"(*Tao Te Ching*, 5/42). In this statement, the process of creation is defined in a single poetic sentence. The original unity is still present in the created, but in the form of a polarity: yin and yang. In all that is created yin and yang are present, but sometimes yin is on the surface and yang is inside, and sometimes it is the other way around. What we humans must do is integrate these energy forms. Men ought to become familiar with the feminine in them and to integrate it (and of course the opposite applies to women). The word "integrate" contains the word "integrity," wholeness (from the Latin integer: whole). Te (pronounced as *doo* in ancient Chinese) is the second word in the title of the *Tao Te Ching* and means integrity.

Our society as a whole is definitely out of balance. This doesn't only apply to the Western or northern civilization alone; it is a global problem. To see this, it is useful to make a list of some yang concepts with their corresponding yin polarities.

Yang	**Yin**
Penetration	Receiving
Speaking, asserting	Listening
Analysis, reasoning	Synthesis
Aggression	Tenderness
Free will	Intuition
Will power	Willingness
Arranging, organizing, controlling	Caring for
Ego oriented	Eco oriented
Initiative, power	Surrender
Hard	Soft
Perseverance	Patience
Consistent	Flexible
Aim oriented	Relationship oriented
Light	Dark
Peaks	Valleys

There is nothing wrong with the concepts and processes in the yang column, except when they lack connection with the concepts in the yin column. The same applies to the reverse. Further consideration shows that the yang side has a much greater emphasis in our world. Through this we create a scene of battle, a situation of victory or defeat, instead of a situation of harmony and balance. We subsequently view reality as being a battle for survival. This in turn enhances in us the (often subconscious) fear of losing: losing our job, our position, our safety, and, ultimately, our very own life. This is a gigantic waste of energy on a global scale. This can also be perceived in the (rest of) nature. However, in that case, this process is balanced by extraordinary processes of cooperation and symbiosis—except that we humans just happen to have been given the ability to diverge from the rest of nature. We are currently doing this, but not in a beneficial manner. We are busy creating a world of conflict—with each other, with the Earth itself—instead of a world of cooperation.

At an individual level, the price we pay for becoming unbalanced is the loss of our integrity. I use this term in both senses: as wholeness and as being true to oneself. We lose wholeness by one-sidedly not using parts of ourselves temporarily, and in doing so we also lose a part of ourselves. This is obvious for men. By living one-sidedly from the yang energy, they neglect or suppress their feminine side, the tender inner side. It is more complicated for women, because society is a male society. Because of this, some women in addition to their masculine side also suppress a part of their feminine side, career women in particular. One of the greatest tragedies of feminism is that it has not actually helped women to rediscover their own identity and integrity. It was too one-sidedly oriented toward the position of the woman in society—important, but nevertheless a yang process. Through forsaking or suppressing parts of our nature we are not true to ourselves. We miss our destination, which is to develop ourselves fully. This results in a feeling of dissatisfaction (often subconscious) and we focus on external aspects: money, possessions, position, being proved right, being successful, etc. Through this we enhance the yang side in ourselves, and in this manner contribute to the yang nature of our world. What is even worse is that we adopt a defensive attitude—we want to hold on to what we have—and we also adopt a guarded attitude, a lack of trust. We start focusing on our conditions (political, social, managerial) and our energy is completely consumed by reacting to those situations instead of being used for creating the thing we actually want. We have the tendency to make other people our stooges. We start thinking and playing games diplomatically and politically. In short, we have totally lost our integrity, besides wasting our energy. "Therefore, a man of integrity pays attention to his debts, a man without integrity pays attention to his claims" (*Tao Te Ching*, 44/79). This of course does not only refer to money. We are all occupied with what we are worth and we make ourselves dependent on our surroundings. We no longer feel that we are the masters of our own lives, which of course intensifies all of the processes stated, creating a vicious cycle.

Maybe you consider this description to be slightly extreme. I hope you are right. However, I see that many people are completely out of balance. I do not have to look very far. I myself was raised one-sided—even though I do not come from a particularly competitive family—and I continually sense the inclination to neglect my yin own side. I do not find it at all easy to let go of my attempt to have control over my surroundings, or to display my gentle powers to the world. Gentleness is perceived by most people, including myself, as being weak or feeble. It took a great amount of effort to make myself aware of these processes, and I see all around me that there are many others who often subconsciously wrestle with the same things.

The yin energy is often called the weak, the feeble, or the dark power. All of these concepts have unfavorable meanings in our world. However, there is no soft without hard, no feeble without strong, and no darkness without light. The dark is like a shadow (the Taoist would say: the northern side of the mountain), and it is the suppression of the shadow in ourselves that causes our light to be depleted and destroys the Earth (see chapter 8). Yang without yin is like the desert. Yin power is like water. "In the world there is nothing more submissive and weak than water. Yet for attacking that which is hard and strong nothing can surpass it. This is because there is nothing that can take its place." Water can grind stones and extinguish fire. The yang power is bright, light, consuming, with rapid effects. But, according to this poem by Henriëtte Roland Holst:

> The gentle forces will surely win
> in the end—a gentle inner voice declares this to me;
> if it were to fall silent, all light would be banished,
> all warmth would be frozen within.
>
> The forces which still fetter love
> will be conquered as it steadily moves on, hence
> the encompassing joy may commence
> which we, if we listen attentively with our hearts,
>
> in all tenderness may hear as the sound of the sea in a small
> shell.
> Love is the essence of planets and man and beast alike.
> Nothing can interfere with the ascension into love.
> This much is for certain: up to perfect Love everything
> rises.

As I have already said, our task is to arrive at wholeness, to integrate the yin and the yang energies, the masculine and feminine sides in ourselves. The psychologist Carl Jung also indicated this when speaking of the veiled feminine side in men as being the anima—the female soul—and the masculine side of women as the animus. *The Legend of the Grail* (in the Chretien de Troyes version) also provides a wonderful symbolic definition of the course of this process for men (see for example Johnson, as well as the next chapter); the Greek myth of Psyche for women (written by Apuleios; see Johnson once more). The theme recurs in other myths and fairy tales. The wonderful thing about these stories is that by integrating the feminine and masculine in ourselves we arrive at our divine nature and achieve the Tao, allowing us to be harmonious in life. According to the *Tao Te Ching* (72/28):

Know the masculine,
but preserve the feminine:
and be a ravine for everyone under the sky.
If you are a ravine for everyone under the sky.
eternal wisdom will never leave you.
And if eternal wisdom will never leave you,
you will become as a little child again.

Know you are innocent,
Stay steadfast when you are insulted,
and be a valley for everyone under the sky.
If you are a valley for everyone under the sky,
Eternal integrity will be sufficient,
If eternal integrity is sufficient,
You will return to the simplicity of the uncarved block

Know what is white,
yet preserve the black:
be an example for everyone under the sky.
If you are an example for everyone under the sky,
eternal integrity will not err,
and if eternal integrity doesn't err
you will return to infinity.
If the uncarved block is sawn to pieces
utensils are made from it.
If the sage is made subservient
he is appointed as the master of civil servants.

For, he who carves rightly, doesn't chop.

To conclude our dealings with the Te, let us examine this excerpt closely. The terms "ravine" and "valley" are used to symbolize the feminine (mountain or top is the masculine: other translations use dales, channels, or stream). We can see here that even 2,300 years ago the Taoist was aware of the fact that we had to direct ourselves more toward the yin side. After all, it doesn't ask us to be both a mountain and a valley, but to be the valley. Then the balance will occur of its own accord, then we become as innocent as a baby: "One who remains rich in virtuous power is like a newborn baby"(18/55). This reminds me of the Fool card from the Tarot, which also symbolizes the beginning and the end of human spiritual development. We came from the child and we will return to the child—this is at the same time the unity with the All-One.

The uncarved (untreated) block ($P'oo$) in Taoism symbolizes the same simplicity personified by Winnie the Pooh, whose name is a fine coincidence. If we return once more to this simplicity we also return to the Way and with this to infinity (literally: with no boundaries). That is a pivotal Taoist doctrine. We can in fact become immortal. The Taoist believes that we are in fact immortal. However, we can become lost and lose our way (by being unconnected to Tao). That is the Taoist equivalent of Hell (roaming, destitute spirits). Our true destination is our return to the Way. This can be achieved in this life, or at least we can come close to it. In this matter Taoism is more optimistic than Buddhism (see chapter 6), which indeed states that enlightenment is possible in this life but at the same time makes the assumption that we must endure many lifetimes of suffering before we become enlightened. This makes Taoism an exceptionally practical philosophy, whether you believe in immortality or not. Infinity can be achieved through a Taoist attitude and way of life, but also through physical exercises and meditation. When it comes down to it, Tao is similar to yoga, an idea I'll return to this later in this chapter. Now I would like to deal with the Taoist way of life in practice.

WU WEI

> "By the time it came to the edge of the Forest the stream had grown up, so that it was almost a river, and, being grown-up, it did not run and jump and sparkle along as it used to do when it was younger, but moved more slowly. For it knew now where it was going, and it said to itself, 'There is no hurry.

We shall get there some day.'"
—A.A. Milne, *The House at Pooh Corner*

Wu wei means no actions. *The Tao Te Ching* says the following about this: "Therefore the sage" (in the *Tao Te Ching* the sage is the sage leader) "abides in the condition of wu-wei" or unattached action (46/2). "Do without doing, get involved without manipulating" (26/63). "Through not doing, nothing is left undone"(1148). This seems rather enigmatic, all the more so because the *Tao Te Ching* was written for civil servants and administrators, for those who we could call managers. Could wu wei possibly be a plea for far-reaching delegation? Maybe so, but it is certainly more than this because the principle of not acting is also valid for the civil servants further down the ranks. (However, it is definitely not a call for laziness or sleepiness!) We have to look further. As the Tao Te Ching is influenced at this point by the *Bhagavad-Gita*, it makes sense to consult it as well.

There is no work that affects Me [Krishna]; nor do I aspire for the fruits of action. One who understands this truth about Me also does not become entangled in the fruitive reactions of work (IV:14).

One who sees inaction in action, and action in inaction, is intelligent among men, and he is in the transcendental [spiritual or religious] position, although engaged in all sorts of activities.

One is understood to be in full knowledge whose every act is devoid of desire for sense gratification. He is said by sages to be a worker whose fruitive action is burned up by the fire of perfect knowledge.

Abandoning all attachment to the results of his activities, ever satisfied and independent, he performs no fruitive action, although engaged in all kinds of undertakings.

Such a man of understanding acts with mind and intelligence perfectly controlled, gives up all sense of proprietorship over his possessions and acts only for the bare necessities of life. Thus working, he is not affected by sinful reactions (IV: 18-21).

An important added bonus of only acting in order to provide oneself with the necessary daily needs is that competition is avoided. "It is exactly because she does not contend, that nobody can contend with her" (*Tao Te Ching*, 67/22). Such peace! Such liberation! Imagine that you no longer have to be better than someone else, no longer have to defend what you have. That your company no longer has to be fully occupied with capturing the market share from its competitors, but just has to expend its energy on creating a good product at a good price—good in the sense that it contributes to the welfare of the world as a whole (including the company itself).

It is apparent from the above passage from the *Bhagavad-Gita* that it, in fact, is not dealing with not acting, but dealing with non-attachment to action and the results of the action (such as possessions). There is a striking parallel between this and the Gospel (Matthew 6:24-34), which I will deal with later in chapter 6. It seems as though the attachment to the results of one's actions blocks one's spiritual way, and inversely that the spiritual way is a way of detachment. I believe that this doesn't necessarily mean that wanting all sorts of things in life is detrimental. However, your spiritual development and your satisfaction depend on the quality of the wanting. When it comes to desire, your welfare depends on the fulfillment of that which is desired. If on the other hand we are dealing with a longing for what you find to be essential and valuable (for example, beauty) then you are not so much dependent on the result (which for that matter is immeasurable), but you encounter complete satisfaction through following the path of least resistance (see also chapters 2 and 9; though it is obvious that there is only room for longings such as these, if the most basic living requirements are fulfilled: cf. Maslow). The *Tao Te Ching* would say: "The sage produces without possessing, acts without expectations, and accomplishes without abiding her accomplishments"(46/2). And the *Bhagavad-Gita* states:

"A person who is not disturbed by the incessant flow of desires—that enter like rivers into the ocean which is ever being filled but is always still—can alone achieve peace, and not the man who strives to satisfy such desires."

Someone who, in this sense, is truly independent exudes extremely strong charisma, peace, and influence. This is why this is a significant perspective for leadership.

Thus if we act in a natural and spontaneous manner then we will automatically end up in a sea of tranquility and peace. This seems rather inconsistent with our modern-day hectic existence.

> Rabbit hurried on by the edge of the Hundred Acre Wood, feeling more important every minute, and soon he came to the tree where Christopher Robin lived. He knocked at the door, and he called out once or twice, and then he walked back a little way and put his paws up to keep the sun out, and called to the top of the tree, and then he turned all around and shouted "Hallo!" and "I say!" "It's Rabbit!"—but nothing happened. Then he stopped and listened, and everything stopped and listened with him, and the Forest was very lone and still peaceful in the sunshine, until suddenly a hundred miles above him a lark began to sing.
>
> "Bother!" said Rabbit. "He's gone out."
>
> He went back to the green front door, just to make sure, and he was turning away, feeling that his morning had got all spoilt, when he saw a piece of paper on the ground. And there was a pin in it, as if it had fallen off the door.
>
> "Ha!" said Rabbit, feeling quite happy again. "Another notice!"
>
> This is what it said:
> GON OUT
> BACKSON
> BISY
> BACKSON.
> C.R.

Rabbit didn't know what a Backson was—in spite of the fact that he is one—so he went to ask Owl. Owl didn't know, either. But we think we know, and we think a lot of other people do, too. Chuang-tse described one more accurately:

There was a man who disliked seeing his footprints and his shadow. He decided to escape from them, and began to run. But as he ran along, more footprints appeared, while his shadow easily kept up with him. Thinking he was going too slowly, he ran faster and faster without stopping, until he finally collapsed from exhaustion and died.

If he had stood still, there would have been no footprints. If he had rested in the shade, his shadow would have disappeared.

You see them almost everywhere you go, it seems. On practically any sunny sort of day, you can see the Backsons stampeding through the park, making all kinds of loud Breathing Noises. Perhaps you are enjoying a picnic on the grass when you suddenly look up to find that two of them just ran over your lunch.

Generally, though, you are safe around trees and grass, as Backsons tend to avoid them. They prefer instead to struggle along on asphalt and concrete, in imitation of the short-lived transportation machines for which those surfaces were designed. Inhaling poisonous exhaust fumes from the vehicles that swerve to avoid hitting them, the Backsons blabber away to each other about how much better they feel now that they have gotten Outdoors. Natural living, they call it.

The Bisy Backson is almost desperately active. If you ask him what his Life Interests are, he will give you a list of Physical Activities, such as:

"Skydiving, tennis, jogging, racquet-ball, skiing, swimming, and water-skiing."

"Is that all?"

"Well, I (gasp, pant, wheeze) think so," says Backson.

"Have you ever tried chasing cars?"

"No, I – no, I never have."

"How about wrestling alligators?"

"No . . . I always wanted to, though."

"Roller-skating down a flight of stairs?"

"No, I never thought of it."

"But you said you were active."

At this point the Backson replies, thoughtfully, "Say— do you think there's something . . . wrong with me? Maybe I'm losing my energy" (*The Tao of Pooh*, p. 91-94).

I have to say that some Backsons play golf, because they are somehow aware of the fact that they are running around a little too much in the rest of their lives. They never stop for a second and allow their soul to catch up. They are extremely busy, and if they—out of self-preservation, or because it has been organized that way—take a vacation, their work is incomplete, causing others to bear the burden. This almost certainly has to result in a high absentee rate. It is also a social problem: Rosabeth Moss Kanter states that "workplace overload" is one of the most significant problems with which modern organizations have to contend. In my opinion this is due to the disproportionate amount of attention given to external competition and internal rivalry, which I spoke about above.

And what about you? Do you have enough time or are you too busy? The majority of the managers I come into contact with complain about not having enough time (remember the example about the chemical company in chapter 2). As I have already said: if you do not have enough time, take a break. Remember, too, that we have forgotten the art of waiting. As R. Wilhelm stated about the *I Ching*: "Power does not allow itself to be hurried through danger, it takes the time, while at the same time weakness becomes excited and loses its patience." Further on, he says, "Waiting is not hoping in vain, it contains the inner certainty that the goal will be reached." The *Tao Te Ching* puts it this way: "Composure is the ruler of hurry." And further: "If the leader is in a hurry, he will lose his leadership" (70/26).

It can be derived from all of this that finding sufficient time and rest is not a matter of technique, as many time-management courses would lead you to believe (even though they can helpful). It is primarily a matter of attitude and mentality. You must want the rest and the rhythm more than you want the achievement of results or the fulfillment of the demands that are made on you (see also Kushner). Or, you must provide your fundamental desires and longings with more energy, which, in short, is your vision, and then place your trust in the path of least resistance, as we have already seen in chapter 2. This does not mean that you will take no action. However, it does mean that you will no longer act with haste, and will have sufficient time. Your actions will be organic, in conformity with Tao. Does this sound good to you? Then you will have to incorporate your desires into your vision, and carry out the inner work that will be defined in chapter 9. This concerns what we refer to as a fundamental choice and can create a radical change in your life. You become as a child, the uncarved block. It can signify that today becomes more important than tomorrow.

Krishnamurti has a touching story about this issue. He was traveling was in a car, and in the back two gentlemen were enthusiastically discussing Krishnamurti's teachings and how we can become aware. At some point, Krishnamurti, who was in the passenger seat, turned around and said, "Gentlemen, we just ran over a goat. Did you notice?" They hadn't. What can be learned from this, among other things, is that talking is also a form of being very busy, and that being very busy is not especially beneficial to conscious living.

For managers in particular it is difficult to resist the urge to do too much when under difficult economic circumstances, or when the survival of the organization is at stake. When under external pressure, old habits emerge once more—but had they been helpful in the past? The following example shows that the situation can be handled differently.

Near Economic Death

It was the Wednesday before the Saturday of my summer vacation, 1992. I had been the director of the Centre for Energy Saving and Clean Technology (CE) for less than two years, and was actively learning how to be a director. How can you do this? Nobody could tell me. In my first year in office, 1990, we had a significant loss, and the following year the tide had not yet turned.

In summer 1992, the monthly figures remained in the red, and it was obvious that we wouldn't be able to carry on much longer. The accountant told us that "a continuation of the ongoing trends would bring the existence of the organization into peril." People who I would have liked to have held onto left, people who I would have liked to have seen leaving had to be dismissed. We had economized, devised plans, cut back and trimmed, addressed the whole network to search for new assignments. There were prospects everywhere, but all our ideas were "under discussion," "being considered," "not yet certain," or "interesting but not yet under discussion." During a sleepless night I made the decision to not go on vacation. The next morning, I told my colleague, and deputy director, who was always present in difficult times, business or personal. After our conversation, I realized that we had thought of every possible option that could be thought of and that we already had done everything we could.

My mood changed that evening; I accepted the situation and all its consequences, with the knowledge that I had done everything within my abilities. If that wasn't enough to get us on the right financial track, then so be it. I quickly decided to take a vacation as I'd originally intended. After all, what could I possibly do in the office during my scheduled holiday that I hadn't already done?

During the next two days the situation at the CE changed even quicker than my mind. There was an assignment in the post for a job which we had been chasing for months; a request from a large enterprise to advise them on their strategic environmental policy; a promise from a ministry that they would prioritize the proceedings of a number of tenders we had submitted, from which we had heard nothing for a long time; and more.

During the second half of the year and the following year we made up all the losses we had incurred.

Through this, my "Near Economic Death Experience" became a comforting occurrence that taught me to do what you have to do, and, furthermore, to accept the course of events.

Ir. J.P. van Soest, director, Centre for Energy Saving and Clean Technology

Two Comments About this Example

It could be said that this isn't so much an example of not acting, but an example of excessive action. Yet I see it as being relevant that the solution came at the moment at which the management fully accepted the situation and realized that nothing (more) could be done. I believe that this is not coincidental: solutions arise when one doesn't force them.

In addition, I know that the organization, or at any rate a considerable part of it, had an explicit vision of the desired future situation (see chapter 2, but especially chapter 9). Under these conditions, the law of manifestation works in the desired direction. This is also illustrated in the following example.

Taoist Leadership

The ideas I covered in this chapter may seem very attractive to many of you but the managers and others among you will probably object by saying that something like this cannot be realized within your own organization. And fathers, but especially mothers, will say it isn't possible in a busy family.

That remains to be seen. It is of course partly subject to the people around you. Yet inner peace is something you can create yourself. This is not always a process that occurs overnight. However, if you really want it then your inner reality—restlessness, hastiness, tension, an ongoing train of thought, insecurity, being alert, or whatever form of anxiety or fear—will shift in the direction of your vision. Meditation and Taoist exercises (there is more about this below and in following chapters) can help. However, your inner decision-making process is the primary element. The deepest decisions in your life, the fundamental choices, aren't made by you—they fall, like falling in love. This always requires that you have to sacrifice something—in this case, the desire to control the situation, or wanting to fulfill the external demands of your boss or the inner demands of your sense of duty (ten to one this is also a boss or your internal father or mother). Whatever the form, you will have to give up your attachment to your position, your possessions, your house, or your preconceived concepts. This doesn't mean that you can't enjoy everything you have—you just can't be attached to it. There is nothing wrong with possessions (except when you confuse them with people: your spouse, children, or colleagues) and enjoying them. However, there is something wrong with not wanting to let go of your possessions, because that makes you anxious and constrained, and impedes your contact with your inner peace, wisdom, and love (Tao). In fact, if you are attached to your loved ones, this impedes your love for your loved ones. According to the *Tao Te Ching* (61/17):

> The best of all rulers is but a shadowy presence to his subjects.
> Next comes the ruler they love and praise;
> Next comes the one they fear;
> Next comes the one with whom they take liberties.

The leader who is at one with the Way acts so naturally that it seems like everything he does happens as a matter of course. He does not intervene, and yet nothing remains undone. This is true efficiency, true quality. This isn't how we usually understand delegation, even though the leader who is at one with the Way will have no trouble delegating. But this is part of a more essential process: the faith that the Way will manifest itself in staff members, and that they will discover their functions in it. Once more I would like to make the comparison with the sailor on the lake. The wind and the waves are always on the side of the best sailor, and they're also on the side of the best crew. A harmonious crew sails itself. This is how the situation can be for every group. Just for the fun of it, check which processes in your own organization would carry on if you were not there.

The skeptics among you are asking at this point for real-world examples. There are examples, such as Semco, but very few of them. I can name other organizations and leaders who are on their way to achieving this. But the question as to whether it works is a typical Western question, and involves an attachment to the results. The paradox is that due to the fixation on the results, the best results are not achieved—you are actually fixating on the fear of not achieving the results. Of course you want results, but what is it all about? If you focus your energy and attention on this question, then it will be given to you. More to the point, the results will be achieved (see also the case of Jonker in chapter 7). Again, the *Tao Te Ching* has a relevant statement (1/38):

> Thus when the Tao is lost there is virtue,
> When virtue is lost there is humanity
> When humanity is lost there is Justice
> When Justice is lost there is propriety.
>
> Now "propriety" is the external appearance of loyalty and sincerity
> And the beginning of disorder.

In another interpretation of the *Tao Te Ching* propriety is translated as rites, and sometimes as rules or procedures. Both propriety and procedures represent the formal side of existence, a side that we construct, sometimes for practical reasons—in traffic, for example—but also sometimes because we (can) no longer trust one another. This may very well be inevitable, but what we, in particular as leaders, ought to avoid is giving our energy to decency, politeness, and rules instead of giving energy to what is essential. Because with politeness and rules, which overrule the essential, the Way, and integrity, we always create resistance.

I would like to conclude this section by linking it to the idea that the wise and effective leader is not busy and has no haste. This is on the one hand because he doesn't intervene, and on the other hand because he doesn't get anxious. He does what has to be done, and in particular he allows others do the things that are to be done by them. This doesn't mean that he has no function; his function is primarily to perform his own tasks in the whole complex of tasks and to form a binding or connecting energy in the background, connecting the members of the group to each other, and the whole with the Tao or the universal process of creation. You can also say that this is connection to the heart. In *Watership Down*, Hazel is a good example of this, but the remarkable thing is that in the end all leaders from *Watership Down* are Taoist in this sense.

I would like to end with two illustrations of the above discussion with a long excerpt from *The Tao of Pooh* by Benjamin Hoff.

> . . . when Pooh, Piglet, Rabbit, and Roo were playing Poohsticks. They'd dropped their sticks off the bridge into the river, and had gone to the other side to see whose stick would come out first.
> And they'd been waiting for quite a while when out floated . . .
> Eeyore. Eeyore?
>
> "I didn't know you were playing," said Roo.
> "I'm not," said Eeyore.
> "Eeyore, what are you doing there?" said Rabbit.
> "I'll give you three guesses, Rabbit. Digging holes in the ground? Wrong. Leaping from branch to branch of a young oak-tree? Wrong. Waiting for somebody to help me out of the river? Right. Give Rabbit time, and he'll always get the answer."
>
> Then Pooh got an idea. They could drop some stones into the river, the stones would make waves, and the waves would wash Eeyore over to the river bank. Rabbit thought it was a good idea. Eeyore didn't.
>
> "Supposing we hit him by mistake," said Piglet anxiously.
> "Or suppose you missed him by mistake," said Eeyore. "Think of all the possibilities, Piglet, before you settle down to enjoy yourselves."
> But Pooh had the biggest stone he could carry, and was leaning over the bridge, holding it in his paws. "I'm not throwing it, I'm dropping it, Eeyore," he explained. "And then I can't miss—I mean I can't hit you. Could you stop turning round for a moment, because it muddles me rather?"
> "No," said Eeyore. "I like turning round."

Rabbit began to feel that it was time he took command.

"Now, Pooh," he said, "when I say 'Now!' you can drop it. Eeyore, when I say 'Now!' Pooh will drop his stone."

"Thank you very much Rabbit, but I expect I shall know."

"Are you ready, Pooh? Piglet, give Pooh a little more room. Get back a bit there, Roo. Are you ready?"

"No," said Eeyore.

"Now!" said Rabbit.

Pooh dropped his stone. There was a loud splash, and Eeyore disappeared . . . .

It was an anxious moment for the watchers on the bridge. They looked and looked...and even the sight of Piglet's stick coming out a little in front of Rabbit's didn't cheer them up as much as you would have expected. And then, just as Pooh was beginning to think that he must have chosen the wrong stone or the wrong river or the wrong day for his Idea, something grey showed for a moment by the river bank...and it slowly got bigger and bigger...and at last it was Eeyore coming out.

With a shout they rushed off the bridge, and pushed and pulled at him; and soon he was standing among them again on dry land.

"Oh, Eeyore, you are wet!" said Piglet, feeling him.

Eeyore shook himself, and asked somebody to explain to Piglet what happened when you had been inside a river for quite a long time.

"Well done, Pooh," said Rabbit kindly. "That was a good idea of ours" (p. 70-75).

This passage contains all sorts of things which I often encounter in organizations: being obstructive or sarcastic, proposing a meeting when actual work is required, or being part of a management team which at its best is pointless, and at its worst makes events worse, and which also wants to take all the credit for successes. Who actually has the lead in this passage? The uncarved block.

THE ETERNAL LIFE

The aim of the Taoist is a long and happy life, after which the soul can connect with the universal soul. Happiness means inner peace and healthy body. The body plays an important role. "Hence he who values his body more than dominion over the empire can be entrusted with the empire. He who loves his body more than the dominion over the empire can be given custody of the empire" (*Tao Te Ching*, 57/13). The Taoist sees his body as being the source of all disorders, but the body can also help one to reunite with the Tao. This is apparent when one has a youthful appearance and good health even in very old age. When this happens, we are once more in touch with the cosmic energy, and the soul can find its way after death (can unite with the Tao). To reach this goal, according to Taoism, it is necessary that when an individual dies, he or she still possesses some energy. The soul needs this energy for its journey to the next destination, another world in which its development continues. (Revelations have taken place both in the past and present times from which a similar vision is apparent, also in Christian, Gnostic, and Esoteric circles. See chapter 5.) If one were to have insufficient energy, then the soul would remain here on Earth like a roaming, powerless spirit, incapable of following the Way. A terrifying prospect, the Taoist version of hell. Even if you do not believe in this, it can be extremely worthwhile to die while you still feel good. Everyone who has witnessed the deterioration of old age knows how distressing that can be, and how unhappy the person involved can become.

Taoism has developed a system of physical exercises to ensure that we feel fit and well through to the end of life (and thus maybe also beyond). The objective is to let the life energy (ki or chi) circulate freely through the body and lift any barriers. It also aims to transform the life energy, sexual energy in particular, and to direct it in an upward direction, instead of discharging it, as usually happens during intercourse. It isn't fitting within the scope of this book to discuss this further, but you can seek advice elsewhere (for example, Mantak Chia).

I firmly believe that the physical practice can provide a background for achieving the attitude of integrity and inaction I've already described. There is an obvious affinity between Taoism and yoga and they can support each other. Both thought systems are based on channels along which energy flows and on centers of energy—acupuncture points and chakras—where energy can be retained, transformed, and radiated once more. Both systems also focus on the relationship between the organs of the body and certain dispositions. Both systems refer to both positive and negative energy, and to cold and warm energy. The ultimate aim of yoga is also a healthy life and unison with the world soul (Brahman).

Even though as I said I am not going to go into Taoist practice in extensive detail, I wish to mention a few things that you can apply personally, and which in my experience are beneficial.

The first is the inner smile, an imaginary smile. You can greet yourself with an inner smile and you can convey this inner smile to all of your organs, starting with your eyes. From your eyes you convey the smile throughout your whole body. You can dwell a little longer at the organs that need it because they aren't functioning well. To finish, you must focus your attention on the area around your navel and about four centimeters below the skin. This is the spot where you can collect energy by drawing an imaginary circle around your navel 24 times; men should go clockwise and then counter-clockwise, while the opposite applies to women. I can imagine that the last part of this exercise seems less attractive than the first. It's up to you to carry this out in accordance with the rules. While the total exercise, although focused on the body, it is in fact a mental exercise, this is also the case for a major part of the Taoist practice. In addition, do not be a Backson and force this in any way. Do it in peace and tranquility.

Second, you can also apply this smile while you are walking. You can then convey it out to the world. If you then simultaneously focus on your footsteps (the contact with the ground), and synchronize your breathing with your steps (for example by taking a breath at a fixed number of steps and exhaling at a fixed number of steps), then you are doing a walking meditation (*kinhin*), also known from Buddhism. You are then walking through life with the half smile of the Buddha, which is very beneficial for inner peace. You can do this anytime, anywhere. "Why wait until you become a Buddha? Be a Buddha right now, at this very moment"(Thich Nhat Hanh).

Taoism also explains how you can deal with sexuality. Sexuality plays a significant role in Taoism. The ideal is a large amount of relaxed intercourse between a man and a woman, preferably in love, or else without love. It is important that the man learns to make physical love without ejaculating, because this is seen to be a waste of energy. It's beneficial for younger men to ejaculate from time to time; according to Taoism, the frequency of this must decrease through time for older men. However, this doesn't in the least mean that the frequency of lovemaking must decrease. On the contrary. The purpose of all of this is that the frequency and the duration of the lovemaking increases substantially. Then the partners can love as much as they want, and satisfy each other more wholly. The outcome of all of this is twofold: an exchange of yin and yang energy between man and woman (through which love will certainly develop in the form of intimacy, appreciation, and gratification), and the transformation from sexual (yin or yang) energy into an ascending life energy, which makes the connection with the Tao possible during and after this life. To illustrate this:

> The Yellow Emperor addresses a question to Su Nü saying, "My ch'i is weak and out of harmony. There is no joy in my heart and I live in constant fear. What is to be done?"
>
> Su Nü answered: "All debility in man is due to violation of the Tao of intercourse between yin and yang. Women are superior to men in the same way that water is superior to fire. This knowledge is like the ability to blend the "five flavors" in a pot to make delicious soup. Those who know the Tao of yin and yang can fully realize the "five pleasures"; those who do not will die before their time without ever knowing this joy. Can you afford not to view this with the utmost seriousness?" (Wile, p. 85).

The number five in the above passage is used in both Chinese and Indian texts and goes back to the five senses and/or the five basic elements (in India, earth, water, fire, wind, and ether; in China, metal, wood, water, fire, and earth). The *Tao Te Ching* (56/12) states that if you do not harmonize the five flavors, then "they make ones palate numb."

Being a Westerner with a scientific education, I viewed all of this skeptically for a long time. It was actually extremely helpful when I began to understand what Taoism meant to me personally—mainly, the universal process of creation, of which I am a part, and with which I can, more or less consciously, remain in touch. This impression enabled me to get in touch with Taoism, and at that point it became apparent that it holds many attractive elements, both theoretical and practical. To me, what is true or untrue in the Taoist doctrine and practice isn't important. What's important to me is that it offers so many practical starting points to live my life in the manner I wish to. For example, I've tried Taoist physical and sexual activities, and have found myself feeling well with it (although I'm certainly not a fanatic Taoist in this respect, but then fanaticism isn't a part of the Tao).

We have now reached the end of our dealings with Taoism. In my opinion, the Taoist tradition and philosophy is so rich that everybody can find something to their liking in the literature. For those who don't believe in an afterlife, I would like to close with a quotation. "Those who die and stay remembered are long lived" (*Tao Te Ching*, 77/33). In my opinion, this happens when we grow, bloom, and bear fruit, and bequeath our fruits to the world. And as far as I am concerned, this is why it all started.

CHAPTER 4

The Goddess

MOTTO: THE SPIRITUAL LEADER LETS HIMSELF BE LED BY THE
GODDESS IN HIMSELF AND IN NATURE.

*"White Chief sends us word that he wishes to buy our land.
How can you buy or sell the sky, the warmth of the land? The
idea is strange to us.*

*If we do not own the freshness of the air and the sparkle of
the water, how can you buy them?*

We are part of the earth and it is part of us . . . .

*[The white man] treats his mother, the earth, and his brother,
the sky, as things to be bought, plundered, sold like sheep or
bright beads. His appetite will devour the earth and leave behind
only a desert.*

*This we know; the earth does not belong to man; man
belongs to the earth. This we know. All things are connected like
the blood which unites one family. What happens with the earth
happens with the children of the earth.*

*One thing we know which the white man may one day dis-
cover; our God is the same God.*

*You may think now that you own Him as you wish to own
our land; but you cannot. He is the God of man, and His compassion is equal for the red man and the white. The earth is precious to Him, and to harm the earth is to heap contempt on its
creator."*

—Chief Seattle

*"The father gives the spirit, the Mother gives the body . . . we
first have to live according to the rules of the body, before we are
ready for the laws of the spirit."*

—the Peace Gospel according to the Essenes

THE RELATIONSHIP WITH THE WORLD AROUND US, IN particular with the earth and the environment, is important. We in the Western industrialized world have become a little out of touch with Mother Nature. At the same time, whether we like it or not, Western culture is becoming increasingly influential in the rest of the world. This results in alienation from the earth and the animal kingdom. Instead of living as one with the earth and the animals, and letting ourselves be nourished by them, we are beginning to exploit them more.

This process is aptly defined in the legend of the Holy Grail. The Grail, a sacred object (in some variations it's the cup which Jesus drank from during the Last Supper, or the chalice in which his blood was collected) is guarded by the Good Fisher King, who is in fact fatally wounded (he can neither live nor die). He is therefore unable to reign and the land becomes reduced to wilderness. Finally, the king is rescued by Perceval, who poses a question that heals and liberates him, and in turn the land flourishes and becomes fertile once more. In some versions of the legend the question is "What ails you, King?" and in other versions it's "Whom does the Grail serve?" The first question signifies compassion, love for fellow human beings. The second question signifies connection, as the Grail serves the whole and not only the king.

WE HAVE LOST TOUCH WITH THE GODDESS

As we can see from this story, if we lose the feeling of being linked to the greater whole we become ill, and the earth becomes a wilderness. This is strikingly similar to the Taoist view on integrity and the imbalance of yin and yang. Therefore you could also say that we have lost touch with the feminine side in ourselves, and the Perceval legend can also be perceived as a rediscovery and acceptance of the feminine side of man (see Johnson and Jung).

In this context, it's no coincidence that earth and nature are regarded as being feminine. The words "nature" and "earth" are feminine and we speak of Mother Earth and Mother Nature. In Greek mythology the deity of the earth is also a goddess (Gaia). The gods of fertility are always feminine (Demeter in Greece, Freya in the Teutonic mythology). Shamanism also regards the earth as our mother, as we saw in Chief Seattle's speech in the opening of this chapter. Therefore, when we renounce our inner feminine energy we also renounce the earth, and vice versa. We are a part of the earth, at least if you perceive this as being more extensive than the planet in a narrower sense. By renouncing our feminine energy and the earth we lose touch with our soul. I will deal with this concept more specifically at the beginning of the following chapter.

It's important that we understand that spiritual leadership is not possible without connecting to the feminine energy in ourselves and in our physical surroundings. We will symbolically call this the Goddess.

The question I would like to explore first is, How did we lose touch with the Goddess? I will then discuss how this contact can and will be re-established. To this end I would like to introduce the concept of the paradigm and paradigm shifts.

PARADIGM SHIFTS

I regard a paradigm as being a totality of concepts that are not up for debate. For example, for a long time the prevailing concept of Christianity was that around 5,000 years ago God had created Earth, and that Earth was the center of the universe and that humans were the center of creation, and that the moon and the sun revolved around the Earth, and that the Earth was flat. During the Middle Ages, this paradigm, this totality of concepts, wasn't questioned. You could see that the Earth was flat and that the sun revolved around the Earth.

Gradually, all of these concepts came up for discussion, and a large majority of us no longer support them. This type of change is known as a paradigm shift. Paradigm shifts often entail, and may possibly be the consequence of, new methods of communication and new experiences or discoveries. Therefore, when the sailors had sailed around the world, the notion that the world was flat was blown out of the water. However, the notion was under discussion for a long time preceding this, and was thus no longer a generally accepted paradigm, which in fact evoked new experiences and discoveries.

I will deal with a number of paradigm shifts in the remainder of this chapter that have resulted in us losing touch with the Goddess. A distinctive feature of the present is that a number of paradigm shifts are taking place which can re-establish contact with the Goddess. I will also deal with these. Of course, no one can predict the future. However, I will specify which of the current paradigm shifts will be influential in the near future. Understanding this history of concepts can also assist us in re-establishing contact with the Goddess, and in this way arrive at genuine spiritual leadership.

Aristotle (Beginning 4th Century BC)

My history of paradigm shifts begins with Aristotle. This is an exceptionally random point in time, since there were a number of significant paradigm shifts long before Aristotle. Unfortunately, I don't know all that much about them. But there is a more fundamental reason for beginning with Aristotle, however. Our Western civilization, which is of such vital importance to the problems presented in this chapter, has two significant roots: the Judeo-Christian tradition and the Greco-Roman tradition. Therefore it isn't such a bad idea to begin with the Greeks.

Up until the time of Aristotle, the accepted wisdom of the leading philosophers was mysticism. Their hypothesis was that a world existed which was more or less hidden behind the world of manifestation (the physical or visible world). The hidden world was either the real world, or at the very least another reality which was just as essential as the world of manifestation, for example the world of the gods or the Underworld. Plato's version of the real world is well known. According to him, the world of ideas is the real world, and the world as we know it is merely a shadow of it (like a shadow on the wall of a cave, which originates from the "real" figures outside the cave).

Aristotle was the first to consider the world of matter as a first and last reality. At any rate, he paid very little attention to a possible mystical world "behind" the world of matter. With this, Aristotle laid the foundation for our modern scientific thinking. Aristotle was extremely fascinated by the amount of detail in the perceivable world and lost himself in endless details. He considered reality as being a quantity of independent forms and separate elements. He slightly lost sight of the whole.

Why is this the beginning of losing touch with nature and the feminine principle?

In the first place Aristotle distanced himself from the world around him. He was the first truly objective observer, since prior to this the most important source of knowledge was our inner reaction to our surroundings. Thus a detachment between us and the world around us was created, which resulted in the loss of awareness of unity.

In the second place, the way Aristotle looked at the world differed from how his predecessors, in particular the Sophists, looked at the world. Before Aristotle, looking was more like "seeing": letting the world around you approach you. Aristotle looked actively—you could almost say in an analyzing, nearly hypothesis-evaluating manner. The difference is akin to the difference between yin and yang, as I explained in chapter 3. Looking is active, penetrating, analyzing, and yang; seeing is more passive, receptive, and yin. Plato, Aristotle's predecessor and master, was somewhere between these two poles. It is obvious that Socrates (the main character in the *Dialogues* of Plato) "sees": he looks through the manifestation. However, he is active and analytical in his dialogue approach. His style is much like the modern scientific approach.

All of this would be of limited significance, just an interesting development between philosophers, were it not for the fact that Socrates' and Aristotle's work and their way of thinking have had a significant impact on the Western way of thinking and are gradually penetrating society's way of thinking as a whole. What used to be self-evident, namely that there was a spiritual world and that you could only understand this intuitively, is now questioned and ultimately the reverse is accepted by significant sections of society. Inner experience is no longer considered to be a viable source of knowledge: only the objective observation counts. Intuition and mysticism have gone underground. In the Middle Ages the mystical and intuitive approach made a comeback, but after that, in the period from the Renaissance to the Enlightenment, the approach was definitively brought to a close.

This example illustrates a general phenomenon, namely that paradigm shifts often begin in the midst of a small group of philosophers and scientists. Only through the years—sometimes even centuries—does the new way of thinking become widely accepted, making the paradigm shift complete.

Jesus, the Essenes and the Gnosis

As stated, the other root of our Western culture is the Judeo-Christian culture. A significant paradigm shift took place around the beginning of this era. We all know this paradigm shift to an extent: in the form in which this is defined in the New Testament. The following Bible quotations illustrate this paradigm shift:

> "Ye have heard that it hath been said, An eye for an eye, and a tooth for a tooth: But I say unto you, That ye resist not evil: but whosoever shall smite thee on thy right cheek, turn to him the other also. And if any man will sue thee at the law, and take away thy coat, let him have thy cloak also. And whosoever shall compel thee to go a mile, go with him twain. Give to him that asketh thee, and from him that would borrow of thee turn not thou away. Ye have heard that it hath been said: Thou shalt love thy neighbor, and hate thine enemy. But I say unto you: Love your enemies, bless them that curse you, do good to them that hate you, and pray for them which despitefully use you, and persecute you."—Matthew 5:38-44

"Judge not, that ye be not judged. For with what judgment ye judge, ye shall be judged: and with what measure ye mete, it shall be measured to you again. And why beholdest thou the mote that is in thy brother's eye, but considerest not the beam that is in thine own eye?"—Matthew 7:1-3

"Blessed are the meek: for they shall inherit the earth."—Matthew 5:5

"He that is without sin among you, let him first cast a stone at her."—John 8:7

"Ask, and it shall be given you; seek, and ye shall find; knock, and it shall be opened unto you."—Matthew 7:7

"No man can serve two masters: for either he will hate the one, and love the other; or else he will hold to the one, and despise the other. Ye cannot serve God and Mammon."—Matthew 6:24

The way I see it, the intent of these passages can be summarized in two paradigms: the possibility and desirability of unconditional love, and the necessity of faith in life. I will deal with these paradigms more specifically in the following chapter, and in chapter 8 I will provide practical suggestions as to how we can make these paradigms our own, if we should wish to do so. For the moment, it is important that we determine that a paradigm shift is in progress in relation to the previous era, in particular within the Jewish tradition.

Regarding the unconditional love paradigm, the Jewish tradition itself originated from a radical paradigm shift with regard to the cultures that surrounded the Jewish population. The instruction to take an eye for an eye seems cruel, but it was a marked improvement over the endless conflict and blood feuds that had been prevalent. The concept of loving your neighbor as you love yourself is just as revolutionary. The way I see it, the awareness of human dignity makes its debut here, something which is also illustrated in the Genesis chronicles, which states that we are created in God's image and likeness and acquire the knowledge of good and evil and with it free choice. (In more ancient religions there is also a notion of human dignity, but that was either reserved for the elite—in Hinduism, for example—or less personal.)

The teachings of Jesus are something quite different. The whole notion of judging and choosing is second to love, unconditional love. It is an ideal that has inspired millions and at the same time it's an ideal that we as humans haven't yet mastered. Even still, a paradigm shift is in progress, because, although we don't conform to this ideal, there is a significant consensus about its value. I will return to this later in this chapter.

The second paradigm—the necessity of faith—also developed from an earlier paradigm shift. In the Jewish tradition, faith in life is primarily subjugation to God. Take, for example, Abraham, who had to sacrifice his son Isaac. Only after total submission to God's will does he realize that God isn't that cruel. Nevertheless, a significant conceptual shift exists in this story. Compared to the religions and faiths that had existed, God is now approachable, and can even be negotiated with sometimes. For example, this is shown in Exodus, when Moses regularly enters into discussions with God (for example about his calling) and in Genesis, when Abraham negotiates with God about the destruction of Sodom. Jonah goes even further; he rebels against the Lord and Job protests. This is a radical change. There are more gods and spirits in other religions that act randomly, and people are at the mercy of their every whim and fancy. God may well be the boss in the Jewish religion, but he also wants to be a partner—an extremely difficult combination, as any manager can confirm. But this isn't a completely successful arrangement, because in the end, Moses, Abraham, Job, Jonah, and all the others continually submitted themselves to God's will.

It is a different story with Jesus, which has more to do with surrender than submission. Let go of your worry. Knock and the door will be answered. Seek and ye shall find. The meek shall inherit the earth. This is way beyond the issue of who is the boss. It is actually a litany against fear. You do not have to be afraid, you are being taken care of. God is not your boss, but your father. As it is evident that there is pain and suffering and illness in the world, this paradigm indicates a reality, a truth, and a perception of the environment that surpasses our daily existence. Interesting: while Aristotle gave up this idea, Jesus strengthens it.

Surrender is in itself a feminine principle. However, this paradigm was only partly successful. It can be seen at best in the Christian acquiescence: the Lord has given, the Lord has taken, the name of the Lord be praised (compare with the "everything is determined" model in chapter 2). The concept that there is a God that takes care of us is generally considered to be attractive, but not broadly believed. At any rate, we do not act according to this concept. On the contrary: the general conviction is that those who don't stick up for themselves, at the cost of others, if necessary, will eventually pull the short straw. We are in fact still living in a society of fear.

However, something completely different happened during that era. It turned out that the Gospels, as we know them, were not the only version of Jesus' words and deeds. With the discovery of the ancient scriptures at Nag Hammadi in 1945 and the Dead Sea Scrolls in 1947, and with the unearthing of scriptures that were carefully hidden in the Vatican and elsewhere, other variations were exposed. I am acquainted with the Essenian Peace Gospel. This reveals that Jesus was chiefly educated by the Essenes, and may have been a member of the sect himself. The Essenes formed a group of spiritual communities that lived at the beginning of our era and were written about in the Dead Sea manuscripts. They considered their task to be the safekeeping of and handing over of the ancient tradition and wisdom, and preparing the world for a new era in which the world would be awash with the energy of Christ (the era of love). The astrologers named this the age of Pisces and, according to them, this is the reason why the fish is also the symbol of Christ. The staunch Calvinists see it differently: they consider it to be a symbol of the soul "fisher" (Matthew 4:19). Early Christian communities also used the fish to symbolize Christ and in times of persecution they even used it as a secret identifying mark. The Essenes lived in communally and in harmony with nature, and adapted their prayers, rituals, and activities to the rhythm of the daily, weekly, and seasonal cycles (see Parry, for example).

In the Essenian version of the Gospel, the body plays a much more important role than in the Gospels known to us and that the feminine principle has its own place. Besides God the Father, Mother Earth is also recognized as a goddess. Before we are spiritually developed enough to submit to God the Father we must first re-establish the contact with our earthly Mother. We can do this through a process of physical purification by allowing ourselves to be purified by "the angels of the sun, wind, and water." Baptism is the only remaining part of this in the classical Gospel. Perhaps this all sounds implausible, but I have personally experienced this purification and through this I was cured from an extremely troublesome stomach condition (within two days) that wasn't treatable with medicine.

At any rate, it's more important to note evangelistic versions of Jesus' life and preaching have been underground for centuries. Ecclesiastical and secular leaders appear to have pulled out all the stops in order to expurgate the Gospel to such an extent that the significance of a healthy body and a good relationship with nature has completely disappeared out of the whole (official) canonical version of the Bible. With the canonization of the Gospels (and Letters from Apostles) as we know them and with the conversion of Europe based on those Gospels, the feminine principle and the importance of contact with the earth has been lost (see Godwin, for example). A hierarchical religion with a dominant masculine principle replaced the earlier polytheism. The Father is at the pinnacle, followed by the Son, then the pope and then the bishop, the priest, the head of the family, and so on. These figures are all men, while the ideal woman is the Virgin Mary, "immaculate" and fertile at the same time, but not divine!

This attitude is clearly shown by the Apostle Paul. His renowned Letter to the Romans, in which he assigns total authority to the government (Romans 13), and his Letter to the Ephesians are extremely revealing. Women are required to be submissive to their men (Ephesians 5:22-23), children to their parents (6:1-3) and slaves to their masters (6:4-8). And finally concerning the men themselves, it pleased the Lord to place Christ in absolute power (Ephesians 1:22-23).

In a number of the scriptures discovered by Nag Hammadi, the feminine principle has also been allocated its own place. These scriptures are predominantly Gnostic scriptures; in other words, they make the assumption that God can only be experienced through inner contemplation (*gnosis*) and not through a priest or a bishop. The latter can only assist beginners, while the true searcher must turn to himself for advice. It goes without saying that these scriptures strongly undermine the (masculine) authority of the developing ecclesiastic hierarchy. There was a stubborn debate between the Orthodox and the Gnostics regarding the authority of the church in the second century (see for example Pagels and Slavenburg).

It's important to note that the debate was also about whether God is masculine or both masculine and feminine. Within Gnostic circles, three movements depicted God as being simultaneously masculine and feminine. In the first movement (Valentinus), God is depicted as a dyad, comprised of the archetypical Father on the one hand and Grace, Silence, the womb, or the archetypical Mother on the other hand. A second movement defines the Holy Spirit as God's female counterpart. The holy family then becomes father, mother, and child, not only on an earthly level, but also on a divine level (in the Orthodox Church, Mary has never been elevated to divine status). A modern version of this can be found in Urantia, a revelation published in 1955. A third movement defines the feminine side of God as Sophia, Wisdom. Wisdom is then the feminine divine force in which the creation of the masculine God was received (see Pagels and Proverbs 3:19 and 8:22-23).

The outcome of this debate was of significant importance to the organization of society. If God were feminine and masculine, then there would be no reason to allow only men to execute authority (such as preaching and performing sacraments). If on the other hand God were masculine then it would be possible to derive from this that the ecclesiastic and social structure of authority should also be masculine.

As we are all aware, the latter was put into practice and in this way the manner in which the New Testament is expurgated and canonized can then be readily explained. The significance of surrender is still included. However, it is equal to obedience and subjugation. The physical and sexual elements lose their sanctity. (Did Jesus live in abstinence? Very little is said about it, but it doesn't seem to suit his persona.) The Earth (the feminine) becomes a place where we are temporarily stationed and is of less value than the divine (masculine); it's more like a place where we must earn our daily bread with sweat on our brow than a sacred place of beauty that nurtures and bears us.

How can we summarize the paradigm shift that took place at the beginning of our era within the Judeo-Christian tradition? In the first place the principle of unconditional love is accepted as a principle in our society, although not integrated in our actions. Of course many of the more humane structures in our society are partially based on this principle, such as Caritas, Social Security and social legislation, and in the peace negotiations in the former Yugoslavia.

In the second place, the notion of faith in God and in life has crept into our society. However this notion has remained an undercurrent and is not yet capable of suppressing the fear of an overwhelming God, or death, or nature, or whatever: the fear which is the cause of so many individual and collective actions in our society.

In the third place the feminine principle and our contact with the earth has regressed further through the canonization of the Gospels. The Essenian and Gnostic movements and their scriptures have gone into hiding and are only re-emerging now.

In the Middle Ages, one sees that the concept of unconditional love—as well as the notions of faith in life and the feminine principle—primarily lives on with the mystics and in Gnostic Christianity, for example Francis of Assisi and Meister Eckart. The case of Eckart is especially interesting: he rose to levels of great prestige in the world of the late medieval church, but toward the end of his life he was charged by the Inquisition due to his Gnostic concepts of faith and was finally posthumously sentenced by the pope. Beyond Christianity, the feminine principle lives on in the already established nature worship, for example by the Celts. This religion also got the worst of it in the middle ages.

The Downfall of the Celts

The Celtic culture had a significant influence in Western Europe up until around 800 AD. This culture had jumped into the crater made by the Roman culture after 200 AD, when Roman power began to deteriorate.

Christianity gradually encompassed Europe from Rome, especially since the rule of Constantine the Great (306-337), who was the first Roman emperor to become a Christian, but who simultaneously established the freedom of religion. Christianity and the Celtic religion have never been able to see eye to eye. Relevant to this matter is that the Celtic religion was strongly based on the feminine principle. The mother goddess (the moon goddess, the earth) had a central position. The religious year and the rites were strongly associated with the seasons and nature (much like the Essenes). In my opinion it is not coincidental that Danaan Parry—whom I referred to earlier and who is strongly influenced by the Essenes—is from Irish Celtic descent. The most supreme spiritual and worldly management rested with the women.

The battle between the Celts and the Christians is clearly depicted in the novel *The Mists of Avalon* by Marian Zimmer Bradley. (This novel also casts an interesting light on the legend of the Grail). This novel is not an historical novel in the narrow sense of the word, but it portrays this era in a way much superior to that of any historical transcript.

It's apparent that one significant reason why the Celts were defeated was that the Christian rulers, all male, were simply not prepared to make their power subordinate to that of the female leaders, not even in the spiritual realm. This is probably not so much a cultural phenomenon, just the nature of men. We also see that power is considered to be more important than religious values. Moreover, through the elimination of the Celtic culture and religion, nature-based mysticism was lost and with it the contact with the soul.

Summing up, we can see that the process which began within Christianity itself, namely the creation of a male-dominated hierarchic principle at the cost of the connection with the soul, is now expanding across the whole of European society. This comes to form the foundation of Western culture, which has influenced the entire world in this century.

The Copernican Revolution

Copernicus (1473-1543) established that the Earth revolves around the sun, a thought that at that time was inconceivable. The prevailing world image entailed that God had created the world and that the Earth was the center of the universe. The notion that the Earth was merely a little ball, somewhere on the periphery of the universe, was unbearable. (As we know there are even fundamentalists today who maintain that the story of creation must be taken literally).

However, information cannot be suppressed. Copernicus wrote exclusively for a small group of academics. One century later Galileo (1564-1642) presented to the public Copernicus' theory, which he had solidified based on calculations and further observations. He was condemned and put under house arrest by the church. Astronomy and physics have made rapid progress since then. The universe is now seen as a great mechanical construction comprised of particles, which together form larger parts, which according to fixed rules, known as laws of nature, move in a completely predictable manner toward one another. You can imagine it as being a giant timepiece, one constructed by God and put in motion, and subsequently functioning fully autonomously (the image is from Newton).

We can hardly envision the impacts of these scientific findings.

It was now definitely established that the Earth was not flat and that Earth was not created by God as a special world, but, according to the laws of nature, was a world which had randomly developed itself at a non-specific location somewhere in the vast universe. It goes without saying that this notion caused much damage to the idea that everything is predetermined by God. The concept that events are causally determined, but at the same time occur completely randomly, gained tremendously in strength, which caused people to feel like a little wheel in a timepiece. The feeling of connection with the world around us, which was so specific to nature-based religions, was weakened further—if it had outlived all the earlier paradigm shifts at all. Also in this world image, there isn't much room for free will and free choice, for our choices are already subject to the laws of nature.

"Living"—as opposed to dead matter—means nothing special in this worldview. Living is in fact an exceptionally complex movement of matter. This has a number of direct consequences for our awareness. First, our relationship with nature changes. If nature is no more than matter, then we can use it and exploit it. We no longer have to enter into a personal relationship with it. We can experience its beauty, but it is of no real significance, since we don't view it as being the entity that can nourish us.

Secondly, our relationship with the cosmos changes. The cosmos is essentially no different than reality as we know it, only a little bigger. There is no longer room for the existence of mystery. It may be that we don't know all the laws of nature, but there is no reason why we won't eventually know them all, after which the mystery is definitely over. (A well-known representative of this concept is Stephen Hawking.)

Thirdly, our relationship with ourselves changes. If we ourselves are nothing more than a complex entity of material elements and mechanical parts, then personality is nothing more than a coincidental configuration of those elements and parts. It's like a chance pattern in a kaleidoscope—wonderful, but of no significance.

The most extreme consequence of this paradigm is that life, and thus also our lives, become pointless. No other significance can be attributed to this than it is as it is. Experience shows for most of us this is extremely difficult to accept. People like to credit a wider or deeper significance to what occurs around them. Depression or alienation can result if we are unable to do this ("Nothing left to wish for but still not happy"—Harold Kushner).

Another consequence of this paradigm is a natural tendency to fixate on the parts and not the whole, just as Aristotle did. Mechanical thought results in thinking in terms of parts. The extent of this way of thinking can be observed in modern medicine, where attempts are often made to repair or replace hearts, kidneys, or other parts of the body, but sometimes it is forgotten that a person is attached to those parts.

In the world of psychology, mechanical thought has resulted in people thinking more in terms of research results and test results rather than thinking about gaining insight and understanding of the human mind. I, personally, had the feeling that after my psychology study I had not learned enough about people; later I had to work hard to catch up.

As prevalent as these effects are, perhaps the most significant effect of this paradigm is that we tend to face the world rationally and analytically. Through this, we neglect our intuition and aren't open to the unexpected and the miraculous. We also make no contact with our surroundings at an emotional and spiritual level. We may react emotionally to nature, but we do not make contact with it. Our feminine side is neglected.

Copernicus has affected us so greatly that we can speak of a Copernican revolution or turn. This paradigm progressed even further by Charles Darwin.

Darwin and the Industrial Revolution

While much can be said about Charles Darwin, I'll keep it brief. An important proposition of Darwin's theory of evolution is that we must struggle in order to survive at both the individual and the collective levels. In this way, survival of the fittest and the characteristics of the best become the prevailing characteristics of the species. Darwin's theory of evolution is essentially a theory of progression, which states that each species either becomes progressively better or perishes in competition with other species. The whole continually progresses.

This theory provided the theoretical foundations for the already existing economic theory, Adam Smith's in particular. Smith (1723-1790) had stated that economic patterns by themselves should lead to increasing prosperity for individuals as well as for nations—but only if no intervention takes place with these laws (the invisible hand). The glorification of the market principle is based on this theory. It also laid the ideological basis for capitalism and for unbridled competition, the outcome of the Industrial Revolution.

Currently, simplified versions of the theory of evolution are common knowledge and are actively supported by almost everyone. These popularized versions require that you stick up for yourself and encourage the idea that happiness is dependent on success and social status. Do not be mistaken: variants of these theories also take on a hidden role in the anti-capitalist alternative circles. Competition also occurs there and actions—often subconsciously—are determined by the fear of not making it, of becoming an outsider, or of losing status.

The Industrial Revolution added another significant element. In an industrialized organization (a technocracy or bureaucracy) man has become a means and is no longer the end. We once created organizations to fulfill our needs and to provide more security in our uncertain existence. Man was the purpose. Now, the aim is profit (or, as with most non-profit organizations, controllability).

Man became an instrument. This is demonstrated in our language. Marxists refer to the labor factor (beside the capital factor) as a production means, the capitalist refers to the staff as "human capital" and the modern entrepreneur refers to his staff as his most important asset. This further undermines the value of people as individuals and mechanical thought becomes more deeply embedded. Man becomes a *"quantité négligeable."*

This, combined with the theory of evolution, creates the existence of a society which is based on a battle model. People fight one another unscrupulously and shamelessly: for space (traffic, for example), for prosperity, for influence, for vindication, and so on. Sometimes we do this politely, with words (De Swaan describes our society as a negotiation society); sometimes we do this craftily or violently. The world is considered to be a place of scarcity, in which there is not enough to go around. And according to the law of manifestation, which I described in chapter 2, the world will therefore become such a place. (Hans Achterhuis has an interesting philosophical consideration about scarcity and arrives at the same conclusion, following a different route, that we, as a society, create scarceness.) The paradigm shift which started with Aristotle and with the suppression of the feminine principle in the Gospel and in Christianity, and which received a new impulse from the Copernican developments, has, through these developments, arrived at a new, decisive stage. It appears that we are at the end of a period in which the yang principle has become totally dominant. We do indeed live in a male-dominated society, not so much because men take on positions of authority (even though this is the case), but because the "natural" male behavior—namely, aggressive, competitive, ego-focused, and result-oriented behavior—has gained the upper hand.

Modern Physics and Parapsychology

It can be said that modern physics started with Einstein's work. In particular, his theory of relativity (1905,1912) can be regarded as both the conclusion of the classic physics period and a beginning of a new era. Einstein was passionately engaged with the physics of sub-atomic particles and as such is one of the new theoretical physicists.

I do not feel qualified enough to explain the essence of modern physics here; it's been accomplished excellently elsewhere (Capra, Rietdijk, Van den Beukel). What I would like to convey here are, in my opinion, a few of the most significant conclusions that can be derived from the modern particle physics. I will mention three.

1. There is no such thing as independent observation. What you observe depends on what you are looking for. To put it another way, the observer influences the observed. Also: the observer and the observed are always related to one another.

2. There is a connection between elements that we cannot yet prove at a material level. The previous point illustrates this and is, among others, additionally illustrated by the fact that the two associated particles "influence" each other, even if they don't appear to be physically connected. This was theoretically confirmed by Niels Bohr (1939) and experimentally by Alain Aspect (1972). A further elaboration of this thought is David Bohm's theory of the implicit order, which has also been experimentally supported and entails that all matter particles are related to one another in a veiled manner. (This theory also supports the homeopathic potentiality theory: the fact that

specific substances are still active after the liquid in which they are dissolved has been diluted many times). This in turn links up with Sheldrake's morphological field theory, which does not only assume such a link on a physical level, but also on a mental level. Empirical evidence also exists for this theory. And, finally, the chaos theory follows this line of thought and is equally supported by experiments and observations. It shows that order can be made visible in apparent chaos, but that also in each system, order and chaos interchange with each other in time. As the pressure on the system increases, the rate of this interchange increases (Lorenz; for more on chaos theory see Gleick).

3. The theory of causality as we know it (everything has a cause and an effect), is, in two ways, apparently inapplicable in this absolute form: sometimes the apparent effect occurs prior to the cause (see Houtkooper, for example) and, moreover, the relationships between cause and effect are not deterministic but are statistic (Heisenberg's uncertainty relationship). In other words, specific causes create the probability of certain effects and specific effects form the indication for the probability of specific causes, but there is no certainty.

You can ask yourself how these conclusions in the field of particle physics apply to daily life. For me, the most significant consequence is that if the above-stated matters are valid in the area of particle physics, no certainty whatsoever exists regarding whether our traditional, mechanical way of thinking has any common validity. I think that it would be sensible to place specific "patterns," which we have always maintained as being unimpeachable, in quotes—in particular, the notion that "real" is only something you can observe or prove. "There are more things in heaven and earth, Horatio, than you dream of in your philosophy" (*Hamlet*, Shakespeare). This notion is also supported by modern parapsychological research (see once again Rietdijk and Houtkooper). In fact, in the dealings with the law of manifestation (chapter 2) I have already made the assumption that there is an unknown and incomprehensible connection between our awareness and physical reality.

Just as in the times of Aristotle, Socrates, Copernicus, and Darwin, the impact of a scientific development on common thought is apparent. It may be safely stated that all sorts of popular notions, such as New Age thinking, holism, and the positive thinking theory, could not be imaginable without these scientific developments. Moreover, in the more established areas of medicine, economics, and management we can see new thinking gaining an advantage. Once more a paradigm shift exists. In this case, the paradigm shift is not at the expense of the feminine principle; it actually supports this principle. Concepts such as connection, relationship, and uncertainty are more fitting to the feminine principles of intuition and receptivity than the masculine principles of analyzing and controlling. Is the tide turning? Could it be true that after 2,000 years of shifting in the direction of yang energy that there is an onset of a countermovement in which the yin becomes more important?

Diminishing Boundaries

This century, the second half in particular, is typified by diminishing boundaries. For example, boundaries have diminished on the physical level. Formerly, national frontiers and geographical distance also meant that communication was impeded. However, since the end of the last century there have been advances in communication opportunities across borders. I can contact the White House in America, or the Kremlin, or a remote village in Africa from behind my own desk, without the assistance of an operator. I can see on television what is happening elsewhere as if it were just around the corner. I can communicate inexpensively and quickly with the entire world using e-mail. Transportation opportunities have also advanced significantly, too. I can fly to many destinations within a few hours. Political regimes and national frontiers can still hinder me, but radio and television push their way in anywhere.

But not only physical borders are diminishing. Ever since modern anthropology brought us into contact with other cultures and since people from around the world now work together and live together, our normative borders are also diminishing. We are no longer so sure about what used to be completely true and truly correct. I'm not trying to claim that the fading of borders solely caused greater freedom and diminishing values, but it certainly contributed to it. In this way, the sexual revolution is certainly partly a consequence of Benedict and Mead's studies, which indicated that a completely different marriage, family, and sex life is possible, and in many cases not worse, or less satisfying.

Greater freedom enforces greater responsibility. We can no longer hide behind other people's opinions, or blame others if we do not like something. Greater responsibility seems fine, but many of us recoil from it. Politicians often take advantage of this. They offer ostensible security: we will take care of you because we know what is right and what is good for you all. Nevertheless, the irrepressible development toward greater freedom carries on. This may well be one of the current great paradigm shifts: that it is no longer an authority, or God, who knows what is best for us and will make decisions, but that the responsibility regarding our lives and what we make of it lies with ourselves. As such this paradigm shift is harmful to the male hierarchy, as it developed in existence for thousands of years, partly due to the typical male competitive instinct. Diminishing borders also ensures that fewer opportunities have been created for the typical male. As far as I can see freedom and responsibility are, in themselves, not especially feminine values, but because they go against the male hierarchy and culture of conflict, they create space for the feminine principle. Therefore this paradigm shift can accordingly be considered as a shift back to the feminine principle.

The Blue Pearl

1969: the first step on the moon. Seen live on television by millions of people, we were deeply struck by it. However, the question remains as to whether we realized its real significance.

When the astronauts returned from space, something had happened to them. It took a while before their doctors and psychologists, and even the astronauts themselves, realized what it was. The astronauts had changed. But how and why? As they explained, it wasn't because of the tension, the excitement, or the miraculous experience of being in space or on the moon. The actual transformation took place when they looked back to Earth while in space. And how had they changed? This can best be represented in their own words (found in Kevin W. Kelly's *The Home Planet*):

"Even before the flight, I was aware of how small and vulnerable our planet is; but only when I actually saw it from space, in all its unspeakable beauty and vulnerability, did I realize that the most important task of the human race is to cherish it and preserve it for future generations."
—Sigmund Jahan, former German Democratic Republic

"Suddenly from behind the rim of the moon, in long, slow-motion moments of immense majesty, there emerges a sparkling blue and white jewel, a light, delicate sky-blue sphere laced with slowly swirling veils of white, rising gradually like a small pearl in a thick sea of black mystery. It takes more than a moment to fully realize that this is Earth...home....The peaks were the recognition, that it is a harmonious, purposeful, creating universe. The valleys came in recognition that humanity wasn't behaving in accordance with that recognition."
—Edgar Mitchell, USA

"I saw the Earth from space—indescribably beautiful, without the scars of the country borders."
—Muhammed Ahmad Faris, Syria

"During a space flight, the psyche of each and every astronaut is transformed. You become more aware, gentler when you have seen the sun, the stars and our planet. You view all living beings with a little more diffidence and become more friendly and more patient with the people around you. At any rate this was the case for me."—Boris Volynov, former USSR

The astronauts appear to experience the Earth as a whole, a whole entity to which they feel inextricably bound and a part of. We can also experience a little of that experience when we see photos of our Earth, taken in space, especially if we lose ourselves in those photos. Many have done this and experienced unity with our planet. Just as the development of eyes was a major step in evolution, which enabled living beings to see their own kind and see themselves with the aid of artificial methods, it seems now as if the Earth as a whole has suddenly got eyes, and can therefore see itself.

It is not coincidental that this photo has been distributed across the globe and can be found on the walls of sitting rooms, offices, government buildings, and mud huts somewhere in the jungle in Africa. If the Coca-Cola logo has become the insignia of our worldwide consumption society, and is as such representative of the old paradigm, then the image of our planet has become the worldwide logo of the new paradigm. And what does this new paradigm entail? I would like to deal with that in a later section of this chapter. Before I do that I would like to state one more recent development in science.

The New Brain Research

Another interesting scientific development is the research into the working of the human brain (1). It has recently been discovered that male and female brains differ in construction and also function. As we all know, male and female differences are due to different genetic structures. The male and female genetic structure is the same, except for chromosome pair 24. Men possess an x and a y chromosome; women possess two x chromosomes.

This genetic variation causes male and female fetuses to develop differently. Not only related to their sexual characteristics, or the stature as such, but it also concerns the construction and the functioning of the brain. In an extremely complex combined action of the genes, the development of hormone production, and brain development, a situation results in which the construction and function of the male and female brains are relatively different. For example, the left and the right half of a female brain work together much more fully than in the male brain.

This and other differences are of great consequence for male and female functioning. Men are more competitive than women. They are more straightforward and more goal-oriented, and because of this more vigorous. Men are more aggressive and assertive, are quick decision makers, and are geared toward solutions. Contrary to this, women have wider views, and have a better eye for context and atmosphere. They are more focused on good relationships and are better listeners. They may not make decisions as quickly, but they are better thought-through. Men have difficulty bringing their emotional and rational sides together; women, by nature, have little difficulty with this. Women can also share their feelings better. Women are, in general, more receptive.

These differences are of course not uniformly applicable to every individual; they are generalizations. These types of variations are generally attributed to culture, but, broadly speaking, that is incorrect. They are deeper and are based on biological variations. Culture, however, does play a part in how we value the differences between the sexes.

A regrettable misunderstanding prevails here. The fact that men and women are equal does in no way mean that they are similar or the same. Nevertheless, this does get brought up often. This point of view has been used to strengthen the status of women in today's society.

However, what actually has to change is our system of values. It cannot be denied that what I defined as being the strong points of men are in fact highly valued characteristics in business and government.

In this way we create a culture in which men and women do not receive equal opportunities. This is disadvantageous, not only at an individual level, but also for society as a whole. We should switch to another culture of organizations. But then we'd also have to apply another way of working within organizations: more focus on sharing feelings, listening, and receptivity, and develop another manner of decision-making. This is a real challenge for a spiritual leader.

I'm certain that if the information from these scientific discoveries could make its way into our general consciousness, this would once more create a paradigm shift in the direction of the feminine principle.

THE OLD AND NEW PARADIGMS

Let's back up a bit. Since just before our era, a development took place in which the feminine principle in society became driven into the background and eventually became suppressed. With the assistance of Socrates and Aristotle, the sense of the mystic and the link with the invisible world began to fade. The feminine element in the Gospel was subsequently blocked out by secular and ecclesiastical leaders, although the ideal of unconditional love, of which mother love is a good example, still exists.

Subsequently the "pagan" religions, among them the Celtic religion, were eradicated in Europe, which resulted in the feminine element in religion and daily life being once more deeply suppressed. (The suppression of the shamanist native culture by the Americans had a similar effect.) A mechanistic world image was created with the assistance of Copernicus, Galileo, Kepler, and Newton, in which there was little room left over for receptiveness and the unpredictable. It's no wonder that Darwin, Adam Smith, and Marx became popular, and that the (male) battle model began dominating the world. Then in the second half of the 20th century a drastic change occurred. Developments in science, communication, and space travel resulted in more interest in the feminine principle. It seems as if a new paradigm shift is developing. What could be the elements of this new paradigm?

The Five Sides of the Goddess

For the first piece of evidence I return once more to my original idea: the Goddess and ancient Greece before Plato and Aristotle. There was not only one Goddess in Greek mythology, there were many. I will name five of the most important Goddesses and consider what they represented.

The first goddess is Artemis, the goddess of unspoiled nature, of hunting and of virginity. To me, this goddess represents passion and purity, and as such is the converse to will based upon reason and political games.

The second goddess is Aphrodite, the goddess of the natural act of creation, of the spring, love, and beauty. To me, this goddess represents playful creativity, submission, and, of course, love and beauty, and as such is the converse of striving toward position, power, profit, and efficiency.

Pallas Athena, advisor to men, represents wisdom, the converse of knowledge and analysis.

Hera, Zeus's wife, represents the warmth and intimacy of family and as such is converse to the business-like attitude in organizations and to relationships based on negotiation.

And, finally, Demeter, the goddess of agriculture, represents fertility and the harmonious relationship with the earth, our physical surroundings. She is the opposite of exploitation and achieving results at all costs.

I believe that these goddesses can offer a wonderful understanding of the values within ourselves which we will have to get in touch with and subsequently should radiate, should we wish to give the new paradigm a chance and therefore make a contribution to the health and continuity of the organizations in which we work. This does not mean to say that we have to throw our old values overboard; this remains to be seen in each individual situation.

Intuition, Love, and Unity

I think that we are rediscovering spirituality. In the prologue I defined spiritual leadership as leadership based on consciousness of unity, vision, and honesty. But I would like to define spirituality as something different. I perceive the term spirituality as being that part of our humanity whereby we exceed our own uniqueness and individuality. If we are referring to our body, our feelings, our desires, or our thoughts, then we are referring to ourselves as unique—in other words, "skin encapsulated me" (the term is from Alan Watts, quoted by Peter Russell). If we are referring to our intuition, then we are talking about our alliance. Intuition comes from somewhere (where?), or at least this is the way we see it. If we interpret love as being unconditional love, it exceeds both the distinctive and the individual elements. "Charity suffereth long, doth thinketh no evil" (1 Corinthians 13). And finally we experience unity as connection, as being a part of something. We are an inextricable part of nature, the earth, humanity, and the cosmos.

The loss of the feminine principle—or the loss of balance and harmony with yin and yang—has resulted in the loss of our spirituality. If we have lost contact with the goddesses, then we are incapable of feeling bound to God. Both God and the Goddess must reveal themselves in us—where else would they reveal themselves? However, this doesn't appear to work very well in a yang environment.

Connection became dogma, while faith became rigid religion and empty ecclesiastical rituals. Ultimately a number of us discarded those forms. In the void, we are desperately searching for new connections, a new spiritual awareness. Some of us escape in fundamentalist movements, but this is not the solution for many of us.

The time appears to be ripe for a new awakening. A new global-awareness may be developing. That the earth and everything that lives on it functions as one coherent system is generally accepted nowadays (see for example Lovelock). But there may be more to it. Maybe the earth must be seen as one single living organism, and maybe self-awareness will be awakened through this organism. This is physicist-psychologist Peter Russell's theory, a concept that may not be as silly as it initially seems.

The concept that there is a common awareness in which everyone takes part has been around for a while. Carl Jung spoke of the collective subconscious, elements of which we can find in all cultures, for example in myths and fairytales. Teilhard de Chardin also postulates a common global awareness, the development and the accumulation of human knowledge and experience, which encases the earth as a sort of atmosphere, known to him as the noosphere.

However, something new seems to be happening: the earth itself is becoming self-aware as an entity and as a conscious organism. In a way, small particle physics has fed the notion that everything is actually in coherence with everything, especially that there is a distinction but no division between the material world and the spiritual world. Furthermore, we have observed that due to the increasing means of communication, everything that is going on in the world hits very close to home and has become common property. We in fact share the same life history, in particular what surpasses our individual life history. And finally we have observed that modern symbols have become communal, from Coca-Cola to the Blue Pearl. The latter symbol in particular revives the feeling of connection and unity, as was made clear from the astronauts' statements.

How can a global awareness at an individual level, and therefore in our own personal experience, manifest itself? I think it manifests itself through the certainty that what happens to me also happens to you and to everyone else, and yes, even concerns the world as a whole. The reverse is also true. The difference between another person and me fades away.

Jesus and the Essenes taught us to love unconditionally, and we have been fretting about this message for roughly 2,000 years now. There are a significant number of traditions that consider 2,000 years as the time needed by humanity to create a new level of awareness for themselves. Astrology, for example, states that we are now leaving the age of Pisces, in which love was central, and entering the age of Aquarius, in which unity is central. This would mean that the time needed to learn that we can love one another unconditionally is almost over and we are required to enter a new learning process, namely that the other and I are actually the same, cells from the greater whole which we could call Gaia after the Greek goddess of the earth. To quote Alan Watts once more, it would signify the transition from" the skin encapsulated me" to "the connected me," in other words, from isolated individuals to an organic whole. We still consider ourselves as an entity that can be distinguished from the surroundings, but at the same time we know that we cannot be separated from it. "We came forth from Gaia, and we will return to Gaia." The Goddess (Gaia) is in fact ourselves.

Harmony and Balance

It is clear that these developments will result in the end of the suppression of the yin energy, and balance will be restored between yin and yang. This will mean that, among others things, the typical yin processes, which were defined in chapter 3, will take their rightful position in society. In order to do so, it may be necessary that they temporarily—and in this context temporarily may very well be a long time—have the upper hand. Good relationships will become more important than results. Intuition will play a more significant role than rational analysis in decision-making. Care for our human and natural surroundings will become more important than competing and winning. Harmony and peace will become more important than fighting for our interests.

Does this seem good to you? Do you believe in this? I think that we no longer have much say in the matter. If this balance between yin and yang and this feeling of oneness does not come into being, then all is not well with us. It's probably not the first time that a human race in this universe may come to an end, and it is certainly an option. But it's not too late to choose another option: in the direction of global-awareness and living at a new level of awareness.

All of us as spiritual leaders have the ability and the assignment to give direction to life, to either oppose—or not—the universal process of creation. I think our tasks are:

- To work on our spiritual abilities, intuition, love, and awareness of unity and to ensure that they become fully developed. This is possible through searching for support (chapters 5-7), self-inquiry (chapter 8), and training (chapter 10).
- To strive toward re-establishing contact with the Goddess within. This is partly a natural consequence of the learning process but we can also intensify this, by opting for it and being open to it.
- Encouraging females, in their capacity as yin specialists, to take their rightful positions in society once more, in particular as leaders, teachers, and coaches. Men may have to

take a step backwards, not only regarding their position, but also their system of values. Women will have to be responsible for this development process and come forward, but not in an aggressive (masculine) manner.

• Restoring our connection with the physical world around us and allowing ourselves to be nourished by the earth instead of exploiting it. We must regain respect for every living thing so that the parched and sick land can heal and flourish once more. Hazel Henderson, the economist, once said that as far as she is concerned the only enterprises that will survive in the long run are those that make ecological recovery (and also the personal growth of the workers) the central objective of their enterprise.

• Getting in touch with finding and implementing our piece of the planetary vision.

There are many managers and executives who accept these principles with open arms. However, they do not act on them. The principles are transformed into techniques—such as neuro-linguistic programming, quality management, formulating mission statements, positive thinking, positive discrimination, and so on—with the primary aim of becoming better managers and creating better material results. These are typical yang objectives. In this way new techniques can contribute to an increase in the imbalance of the organization, the individual within, and the world around it. Real changes have to do with a change of awareness, with more focus and care.

Respect for All Living Things

Spiritual awareness awakens a cosmic alliance that gives a totally new perspective of all living things, including the amazing biodiversity and the feeling that every form of life has the right to (remain in) existence. This respect for every living thing is probably the most important background of the vegetarian existence of many Indians.

I am no longer able to work in an area that I know is developing activities that continue to damage the environment by poisoning or burdening it in some manner. I now delve into environmental issues and have made the discovery that there are innumerable techniques that could reduce environmental burdening to a significant extent or eradicate it completely. In many cases those techniques also have a remarkably quick payout. Some others are still extremely expensive, which is primarily due to the fact that the actual costs of the traditional techniques are not calculated. In other words, in those cases the resulting pollution is passed on to society or future generations.

In a certain respect the concept of empowerment can be extended to the environment, as contamination or pollution "disempowers" the environment and respecting or recovering it empowers the environment. The uncommon vitality of nature when it gets the chance to develop freely is remarkable. Unfortunately, the sixth great extinction is in full swing, on this occasion not due to large meteorites as with the previous mass extinctions, but due to humanity, who are in general unaware or barely aware of this. The choice facing humanity is to either become a malignant tumor and to eventually perish in its dying surroundings, or to begin living with respect for and in harmony with its living nature.

I firmly believe that at the enterprise level, "empowerment" can be used in the general sense, to invite and stimulate members of staff to once more search for harmony and to find it. This is a precondition for the development and utilization of the means to deal with our natural environment in a sustainable way. The technical opportunities are already at our disposal, but can be substantially developed further. It is a matter of prioritizing.

In practice, this means that for the last few years, my colleagues and I have primarily been dealing with a comprehensive inventory of what our collective activities are doing to the environment. In the same period I have exerted a significant amount of effort into compiling relevant and useful information concerning environmental issues and conveying this to large sections of our organization. My intention is to increase awareness. To this end, I have made extensive use of the excellent publications from the World Watch Institute in Washington, including the annual "State of the World Report." There is a remarkably large interest and many have commented that they learned new things from it and have altered their perception of the world.

I believe that we should attune our business activities to the "State of the World Report." It has become obvious to me that I am only really interested in the environment. I try to not be too defensive about it, because I know that this subject is still in a very early phase and that extra effort is required.

We commenced our environmental investment program last year, which in broad terms boils down to drastic economy and efficiency measures regarding the existing processes and searching for clean processes and techniques that don't stress the environment. The environmental burdening caused by us is primarily due to energy consumption, permanent waste (including disposing of the used packaging material), and the use and discharge of water. In pursuit of this, optimal use must be made of available energy from the sun and wind, geothermal energy, hydropower, cold-water layers in the soil, and gasses that are emitted during the purification of waste water. (CFCs are to be completely prohibited by us in 2000.) Compensatory measures in the form of participation in windparks, which provide clean energy to the grid, and planting or conserving trees are to be taken for the fraction which we cannot purify. A rough calculation shows that for the remaining energy consumption (after our total electricity requirements have been covered by solar and wind energy) another 5,000 hectares of trees are required in order to neutralize the environmental impact. Up until now we generate four of the 25 millions kilowatts of electricity from clean sources and we have planted or taken on the conservation of around 1,000 hectares of trees. We are of the opinion that, if we devote 10 percent of our investment budget to environmental measures for 10 years, we are well on our way to being sustainable. With this, we mean that on balance our collective activities no longer burden the environment or remain within the so-called environmental utilization latitude. It is my personal conviction that this pursuit entails not only an extra stimulus for a significant majority of our personnel, but that we will gradually experience business and cost price technical advantages, whereas in this phase we are only sacrificing a small fraction of our profitability for this aim.

I sincerely hope that our experiment and those of other enterprises are successful, because if this doesn't work then I am at a loss as to how humanity could ever deal with our planet sustainably. My understanding of the situation tells me that we cannot possibly continue with the further burdening of our ecosystem and the increasingly rapid utilization, and in increasing quantities, of our depleting mineral supplies.

I.L.G. van Melle, president and director of Van Melle nv.

Part 2:
Instructions

CHAPTER 5

God or the Buddha

MOTTO: THE SPIRITUAL LEADER ALLOWS HIMSELF
TO BE GUIDED BY THE GREAT SPIRIT.

I believe in the sun—even when I do not see it;
I believe in Love—even when I do not feel it;
I believe in God—even when he is not present.
—Lionel Blue

WHO OR WHAT IS GOD? A QUESTION PRECEDES THIS: DOES
God exist? Yet one more question must be asked prior to this: Is there
one single God?

People have believed in gods for as long as the collective memory can remember. I understand gods as being personalities who live
in another, supernatural world and possess supernatural forces.
This "natural" belief has been deviated from in two ways. On the one
hand, through Buddhism and Taoism, which, although based on a
centrally ordained principle, attribute no personality to God.
(However, spirits and demons still play a secondary role in both religions, and great predecessors/leaders, such as Lao Tse, the Jade
Emperor, and the Buddha are sometimes worshiped as gods.)

Then the "natural" faith was deviated from through Judaism,
which explicitly states that there is only one God who rules and governs all. Christianity and Islam later adopted this view, although secondary gods have slipped in (among them the Son, the Holy Ghost,
the Virgin Mary, and Mohammed).

It is my opinion that the question as to whether God exists or not
is irrelevant for spiritual leadership. It is a question of faith, and, as
I have previously said, faith on the one hand is more certain than
knowledge of the truth (irrefutable) and on the other hand more
uncertain (always subject to doubt). Ultimately, faith is a matter of

choice: you either choose to believe or not. The proposition is made in this book that opting for faith in God (in whatever form) can assist spiritual leaders, in particular with the advancement of awareness of unity, vision, and honesty.

WHO OR WHAT IS GOD?

How can it be that while faith in God in our culture was once almost widespread, it has become so weak? I am firmly of the opinion that this is linked to two subjects which I have already covered. In the first place, if we lose touch with the Goddess, we also lose touch with God, because God and the Goddess belong together just as the sun and the Earth, as light and darkness, or as fire and water. And secondly, if we turn God into a dictatorial, dominating God, who does not leave enough space for our own responsibility and choice, then we rebel against him, because deep down we know that we were created in his image and likeness and that we therefore have our own sense of responsibility and freedom of choice. If this is not recognized—through our image of God—then we will revolt. We subsequently become afraid, because we initially assigned a jealous and vindictive omnipotent persona to him, and we must box him in with rules and dogmas. In doing so, we eliminate and finally forget about him.

If we opt for faith in God, how can we get in touch with him? Exactly the same way that we get in touch with the Goddess—we can look inside or outside ourselves. In the case of the Goddess, the way toward Mother Nature is indicated if we wish to look outside ourselves. Experience of nature can bring us in touch with the Earth and the Earth within ourselves. We then feel part of the whole, which can be referred to as Gaia. We are a living cell of her body and consciousness. We can also search within ourselves and discover the nature within us—our physical sensations, our feelings, our desires, our hurt and our excitability, our pain and our peace—in short, our soul. We feel ingrained in this existence, in the history of ourselves, our ancestors, and humanity as a whole. This is what I should call contact with the Goddess.

Contact with God is essentially no different—except that instead of looking around, I would look up. Look away from the Earth, far into the infinite universe. Come into contact with the immensity, with the overwhelming abundance and vastness. Nature can be miraculous, the cosmos can be miraculous. But nature is closer. It can be beautiful but also cruel, gentle but also violent, efficient but also incompetent, peaceful but also full of conflict.

Nothing human seems strange to it. However, the immeasurability and the experience of the universe are beyond all of our concepts. We may well believe that there may be nature and life somewhere else in the universe, but we don't experience this. By delving deep into the universe we can experience a little of the vastness and elusiveness of God.

We can also search for God in ourselves. To do this we must not search in our human history, not into the depth, because then we find our soul, the Goddess. We have to look into the void, as when we look into the universe. It is an observation of ourselves, without holding onto something. We must observe what we experience, think, and feel, but do not lose ourselves in those thoughts and feelings. We must be as uninvolved as we can be. We must remain the observer, a concept I'll explore in depth later in this book. Prayer is another way to do this, not in the form of a dialogue with God, but in the form of being completely open to God, whomever or whatever that may be.

It is laid down in the scriptures that seek and ye shall find; although true, we find what we seek. If we first imagine God, then we will also find that God. This could be called a religious projection. However, if we want God to reveal himself, as an individual character in an unexpected form so that we know for sure that we are experiencing God and not our own fantasy, then we have to be completely open minded. This isn't easy, as we are of course all completely preconditioned.

We all have conceptions and impressions about God, including doubts about his existence. However, if we are able to let go of these impressions and doubts, then we can see or experience God. (According to the Bible, in Exodus 33:20, it isn't possible to see God in this life, but he can be revealed to us through experience or visions.)

It is also apparent from this that God can present himself to us in all possible forms and manifestations. In this sense he can also be experienced in the physical world around us, although I don't feel that we specifically search for him there (as our impressions can become distorted).

The way I propose to take is the Gnostic or the mystical way. I am in accordance with those who believe that we can only experience God through direct experience (revelations), and not through Bible study or any other study, and not at all from what others say about him. This chapter should actually end here. But as it is not so easy for everyone to directly experience God, I would like to dedicate the remainder of this chapter to the ways that have helped me de-condition myself. But first a few concepts should be straightened out.

SOUL, HEART, MIND, OBSERVER, SPIRIT, PERSONALITY, GOD AND THE BUDDHA, OUR INNER GUIDE

Up until now I have apparently used these terms in a jumbled manner. However, there is a method to it, as I'll now explain.

I understand soul to be our core, formed throughout history—not the objective series of events, but our history of perception. With this I am not only referring to our history in this life, but also to all of the cultural and genetic baggage we've inherited, not only what we have experienced in this life, but also what we have experienced as a race, as humanity, and as the Earth (and also, according to some, what we experienced prior to birth in another reality).

This means that the history of our soul is also the history of our forefathers, and in a certain sense even the history of evolution and of the Earth as a whole. A distinction can be made between our individual soul and the world soul, but there is no strict separation—they share common ground.

The soul is therefore the core of our being. Soul contact tells us who our ancestors are; it brings us into contact with our roots. If we delve deeper and look behind our history of this life, then we can catch a glimpse of the world soul. We can also find our soul in what

Jung named the "collective unconscious." There are also parts of our soul that we don't wish to observe, or that we're afraid of, or that we'd like to disown. We have the tendency to suppress this aspect of the soul. Jung calls this our shadow. Our soul can also reveal itself in our daily existence, namely where our primeval humanity wishes to express itself. We can therefore find our soul everywhere: in our relationships, our families, and our friendships; in fairy tales and stories; in our work; but mainly in our inner self (see also Thomas Moore). Because the soul is so ingrained in us and our soul is so directly linked to Gaia, I am inclined to perceive our soul as an expression of yin energy. In my mind, the elements that belong to the soul are water and earth. You could therefore call the soul our source. It is of course true that if our soul is our history then through living we are expanding and developing our soul.

In language we know the expression "heart and soul." We use it when we're doing something with our whole being. The heart is also used symbolically in other expressions, such as "heartfelt," "wearing our heart on our sleeve," "heart of gold," "in one's heart of hearts," and many more. This indicates that the heart is seen as the foundation of feeling and desires. As such the heart—not the pump, but the perception of the energetic core—is one of the foundations of the soul.

Our mind represents our ability to become aware; it is our ability to think, but also our ability to become aware of our feelings. It is our ability to judge and choose, our imagination, and our fantasies. An important part of our mind is the observer: the one who can distance itself from the outside world and ourselves and then observe. I don't see the mind as our thoughts, our feelings, and so on—that is more a part of the soul—but our ability to deal with all these things. The mind by itself is empty and impersonal but it makes us human. The mind is the helmsman and the chooser, but not the only one that determines the direction.

I would like to define the spirit as the God within. The spirit reveals itself in our spiritual functioning: intuition, unconditional love, and awareness of unity. The spirit is in perpetual motion, it is an ongoing process. Just as our soul can be identified but cannot be separated from the world soul, our spirit cannot be separated from the Great

Spirit, as the Native Americans put it so well. The spirit lives in us, but is greater than we are—I believe that it is immeasurably greater. The Great Spirit is of the same rank as our spirit: Being, Becoming (1). The elements associated with the spirit are fire and air.

We are therefore a confusing mixture of soul, mind, and spirit. Personality is the factor that brings order. I understand personality as being the unique manner in which our mixture is regulated; the unique configuration of soul, mind, and spirit. It can also be thought of as the unique personal manner in which we deal with our soul, our mind, and our spirit. Personality is the part of ourselves that makes us unique, as unique as our fingerprint. Our personality is our designer and becomes visible in our style. Our personality also develops, under the influence of our mental development and the development of our soul. There are superficial parts of our personality: our habits, our acquired values and concepts, and our conditioning. There are deeper aspects, too: our desires, our deepest convictions and values, and our inner guide.

Our inner guide is the voice from within that tells us how to act. I think that there are two inner guides—the soul and the spirit. The spirit reveals itself through intuition—you must do this or that now—or through inspiration. Intuition is always very specific, both regarding time and actions. Inspiration, on the other hand, conveys the sense that the wind and the current are favorable. Your creativity then flows. You are part of the divine process of creation.

The soul also presents itself through desires or longings. Desire is always focused on the immediate satisfaction of an actual need. Longing is more focused on the satisfaction of the soul itself; it is an expression of the soul as a whole.

Let us return to our original theme: How can we experience God? Who is he, exactly?

We can experience God everywhere: in our soul, in nature, in the Holy Scriptures, in music, or in a joke, according to Lionel Blue. But the direct route is through the spirit. We can experience the God within through spiritual development and enhance the chance that we can rediscover him, no matter where, if we have lost him.

Taoism and Buddhism differ from the Jewish, Christian, and

Muslim religions in the best way to do this. This has to do with differing concepts of God. In Buddhism and Taoism, God has no personality, while in the other religions he does (see for example *The Urantia Book*). This is why the heavenly way in those religions is prayer and the possible outcome is called a revelation. In Buddhism the way is meditation and the possible outcome is enlightenment. In Taoism the way consists of exercises and a Taoist lifestyle; the possible outcome is eternal life (i.e., unification with the Tao). Buddhism equates God and Buddhahood. The Buddha is the personification of God, but only because he has achieved total enlightenment, an opportunity that is available to all. God exists exclusively within us and not outside us; whereas in Christianity and Taoism, God or the Way can be found both within and outside us.

I believe that everyone should find their own way, the way that suits them best. I also feel that it's important that you devote your whole manner of living to this search. Trial and error will clarify which method is the best for you, whether it's meditation, prayer, exercises, or something else. However, it is always necessary that you free yourself from your conditioning—everything you've learned, your thought patterns, your habits, and your values. In a sense, you will have to free yourself from your personality. Without letting go of it, the meditation, prayer, and exercises will not work (although with God everything is possible, Matthew 19:26). In the remainder of this chapter I will state a number of ways that have helped me and still help me in breaking free from these patterns. I will use the terms of God, spirit, life, and Buddhahood interchangeably.

MIRACLES

The majority of us are conditioned in the area of miracles. We're skeptical and don't believe that miracles exist. Or, based upon our experiences, we've developed a limited understanding of the world and fail to see miracles, which are not included in our worldview.

However, if you ask people if they can remember a miracle, or a moment or a situation in which they experienced a miracle, almost everyone has an answer. Many people think of the birth of their first—or a subsequent—child, but there are other replies: the sudden experience of a flower, an incomprehensible healing. Elsewhere, I have written about miracles I've personally experienced—among them the abrupt healing of my tennis elbow with the help of a healer—but here I would like to talk about what I experienced when I was writing my previous book. Just at the point when I had completed the second version of that book and had typed the last period, my computer crashed. As a result of my panic, afraid that I had lost the whole manuscript, I made another mistake, which resulted in the last version of the book being lost (all that remained was a back-up of the original manuscript). With the aid of all sorts of software, we managed to open the manuscript, but it was totally incomprehensible: it was all dots, backslashes, squares, and symbols. The manuscript was completely lost. Three weeks of work out the window! In the whole manuscript only this remained legible: "life," "surrender," and "I was sleeping."

Manifestation was one of the subjects of that book. But I had surpassed myself. I had made claim to things of which I was not completely certain. In particular, I had not paid enough attention to the fact that creation is always co-creation, a surrendering to life itself. Surrendering to one's life current is imperative in order to create the situation you wish to achieve in an efficient manner. But I had been arrogant and presumptuous. And here was the message: wake up, surrender to life! It is not your task to tell others how to create! It goes without saying that I implemented these new insights into the book (there are many more miraculous things to be told about this incident in that book as well).

I call this a miracle. Miracles help me strengthen my trust in life and to experience a little of the awesomeness of existence. They make me simultaneously happy and modest. Modest, because they remind me that there is more between heaven and earth than I can possibly imagine. Life is much larger than I am. Miracles also make me happy, because they show me that everything is possible, a thought which provides me with support and courage when many things once again go wrong in my life or in the world around me.

Miracles help us to step out of our wearisome thought patterns and to catch a glimpse of God. That is of course their purpose. At the same time I realize that we co-create the miracles ourselves (law of manifestation). It could even be said that if few or no miracles occur in your life, then this makes a statement about how you view life. You may feel that life is predictable and obeys the laws of nature as you understand them. In that case, it remains to be seen whether you get everything out of life that is available. This is a relatively mechanical and materialistic concept of reality, which leaves little space for the supernatural and the divine.

Such a concept of reality is a handicap for the spiritual leader, because it gets in the way of both awareness of unity and vision development. This view interferes with awareness of unity, because unity requires a holistic worldview. It interferes with vision development because this reality concept increasingly brings you face to face with the question of what is viable. That is not visionary thought, but a view of reality at this moment. It pulls your vision downwards and in doing so reduces creative tension, and with this the creative force.

It is therefore of paramount importance that you believe in miracles, but it's difficult if you don't know how to create them. Fortunately a do-it-yourself course exists to help you break this vicious circle—*A Course in Miracles*. This course came about because the head of a New York hospital remarked to one of his staff members, a psychiatrist, that the atmosphere surrounding the colleagues was so bad that something had to be done about it. He asked the psychiatrist if he would come up with a solution. The employee then went home, and in a trance he wrote the course.

A Course in Miracles consists of 365 spiritual exercises (one a day for a whole year), a textbook, and a manual for "teachers" (consultants, therapists, social workers, or teachers). You may of course just go ahead and do the course, but be warned: it works, but your thoughts will be thrown into confusion. Therefore you will require a fair amount of discipline. In the beginning, I couldn't recall one sentence that I had to repeat to myself on several occasions throughout the day when I was at my work and the book was at home. This is of course because the sentence contained a thought that was not in keeping with my preconceptions. The Course as I understand it is actually very simple. It's an exercise in unconditional love. Conceptually, it's very straightforward, but it's extremely difficult to grasp and put into practice.

The Course is clearly firmly rooted in the Christian tradition, as is apparent from the choice of words and the concepts used. For some people that's a plus, and for others it is a drawback. A more secular approach can be found for example in Gershon and Straub's *Empowerment*.

SPIRITUAL EXERCISES

We can advance our spiritual development through exercises. In doing so, we not only improve our intuition, our ability to love, and our awareness of unity, but we also increase the possibility of meeting God. I will provide a number of options here and in the following chapter, but you can expand on this, too.

Gratitude

Gratitude is a relatively emotionally loaded concept, because, in the Calvinistic tradition, we have to be grateful. This misuse has spread to way beyond Calvinistic circles. In my family, we were humanists, but we had to eat all our food even if we didn't like what we had on our plate, because we had to be grateful for our food. ("Think about the starving children in Africa." "During the war we were hungry.") As a child I didn't understand why I had to eat something I didn't like.

Maybe you are naturally grateful, especially when you realize the factors in your life that you can be happy about. You do not have to completely deny that there are things in your life that you aren't happy with, but this is art of your vision development.

Here are a few things that may make you happy:

- Your health.
- Material comfort. You have drinking water, food to eat, clothes to cover yourself, a house in which to live. You can heat that house and you have (hot) running water. You live in exceptional comfort. One push of a button and you have music to listen to.
- People who value you. This can be your partner, your children, and your colleagues. Maybe you have one or more friends who love you.
- Beauty in the world. You can—as a rule—experience that for free in nature, in music, in arts in general, in architecture, and in people. Yes, you can even experience beauty in things that are considered to be ugly, such as a chemical factory or a rubbish dump.
- Your talents. As Jesus said, each person always has at least one talent that can benefit others, and you can take pleasure in making it available to other people.
- Generosity and care in the world. It appears to be that the more that people act selfishly and violently, the more opposing—compassionate—forces develop.
- A good neighbor, or a devoted dog, or a nice café around the corner.

If you cannot deny that there are things in your life that make you happy, then the spiritual exercise is that you regularly stop and think about them. Gratitude will then come automatically.

Gratitude is easy to feel following a grave event such as illness, pain, or conflict. We should also be able to experience it by realizing that we have been spared one of these grave events, even though this is not always easy and sometimes feels a little artificial.

An exceptional opportunity for gratitude occurs when receiving a meal. You could then be grateful for the generous gifts from heaven and earth; for the exertions of the farmer, traders, and shopkeepers who've taken the trouble to bring this food to your table; for the chef who has prepared your food; for your employer or clients who have made it possible that you have the means to pay for the food;

and, of course, yourself, the one who has worked hard for this meal. If you share this gratitude with your dinner companions, then the meal begins on a sacred note. Of course this mustn't become an empty ritual, because it will work adversely.

And, finally, a warning: Gratitude that doesn't come from your heart can take you from the frying pan into the fire. In the words of Kahlil Gibran in *The Prophet*:

> And you receivers—and you are all receivers—assume
> no weight of gratitude, lest you lay a yoke upon yourself
> and upon him who gives.
> Rather rise together with the giver on his gifts as on
> wings;
> For to be overmindful of your debt, is to doubt his gen-
> erosity who has the free-hearted earth for mother, and
> God for father.

Becoming aware of your own generosity and gratitude are therefore very similar things. Gratitude only advances spiritual development if it is a spontaneous process. The exercise does not solely involve the summoning of gratitude, but also taking a moment to reflect on the things that you are happy with. As already stated, gratitude will follow automatically.

Grace

Grace is another word that has been abused by Calvinism. "From grace, through grace to grace…" as said by the Reformed. This means that we can receive God's grace only through prayer and then we still have not accomplished it ourselves. We are fully dependent on God. By now it will be obvious that this manner of thinking is not particularly in keeping with the concept of responsibility, which we developed in chapter 2 and which this book is partially based upon.

Grace can mean elegance, pardon, and "being in God's hand." If we feel that we're in God's hand, then these things happen automatically, in an elegant, flowing manner. If we express grace or elegance, then we can show that we possess something divine. If we make contact with this form of grace, then we become simultaneously proud and modest. Proud because we know that we are a "radiant cosmic being," in the language of the Transformation Game (see below). Proud because we are capable of expressing and have the opportunity to express the God in ourselves. Modest because we realize that something is being manifested which is larger than ourselves, and to be able to have this experience we will also have to surrender to it.

The next spiritual exercise entails that we begin to notice the grace in ourselves and in others. It is very similar to what I already discussed regarding gratitude and miracles. For example, we should take the time once in a while to observe ourselves and our surroundings from the viewpoint of grace. The next step is being capable of experiencing mercy in ourselves and others ("I am blessed").

When we have reached this point, then we know that there is a difference between the Calvinist concept of grace and what I am referring to. Grace is bound to guilt in Reformed circles. We are completely at the mercy of God. In my understanding, grace is bound to responsibility. After all, we are created in God's image and likeness (Genesis 1:26) and therefore we are also partly responsible for the creation process. Together with God we are the becoming. "Be ye therefore perfect, even as your Father which is in heaven is perfect" (Matthew 5:48). To realize this is grace and it helps us experience the connection with the universal creation process (Tao) and to find the balance between acting and being.

Obedience and Intuition

Imagine that there is a God who looks after our interests and who governs all, and that you receive an assignment from him through one-to-one contact. Will you obey him unconditionally?

This is an interesting question, because rebellion against obedience (to God, or to someone who names himself a representative of God) is often motivated by the argument that you cannot really be sure if it is truly God's voice you hear. And even though this may be true, this argument often conceals two other arguments against obedience: I will decide for myself what I do, and It isn't convenient to do what is asked of me.

The first argument places personal judgment superior to that of God (if he exists). And although it may be far from me to encourage an unquestioning following of whomever or whatever, it's imperative that we establish that the argument boils down to pride. Now, as far as I am concerned, in the moral sense there is nothing really wrong with pride, but pride urges you to become deaf to the assistance and help offered to you. You know best. You are not open to the forces of life itself, which may possibly carry you to your destination and happiness. Effectiveness and efficiency are in any case not possible without these forces, just like the sailor in the example I provided in chapter 2.

The second argument—that what is asked is inconvenient—boils down to attachment to comfort. There is also nothing morally wrong with this, either—my father always said: who does not search for comfort is lazy—but comfort is often not in our best interest. We often hear an inner voice that tells us what we should do, but we do not have the nerve, or we do not want to. For example, we do not give up our job, even though we know that the time is right, or we do not give our true opinion because we are afraid to put our neck on the line. And we are, at a later point, surprised or incensed when are dismissed or when our opinion is not considered. These examples show that in practice, obedience very often boils down to obeying our inner guide. At the same time, this also means that we do not comply with what is expected of us, or what another external authority instructs us to do. True obedience liberates us instead of constrains us, as stated in the converse sense by Jacques Perk—"True freedom listens to the laws."

The spiritual exercise regarding obedience helps us learn to distinguish between our inner guide (which can be our desires, our longings, or our intuition) and our standards, our attachment to comfort, or our apparently reasonable reasoning, which is often based on fear.

Actually, only intuition should be obeyed unconditionally, as the voice of God—or Life, if you wish—speaks through this. You can only learn to make this distinction in practice. However, there are a few guidelines:

- You do not make a decision that is based on intuition; it falls. It seems stronger than you are.
- Pure intuition is always specific: it describes the following step precisely, as well as when to take it (almost always immediately).
- Pure intuition is paired with inner conviction, a sure knowing—this is the way I have to do it. If this conviction is lacking then this is not intuition, even though it may be what you have to do. You cannot reverse this preposition: we can talk ourselves into conviction without intuition.

These are only guidelines: practice will be your teacher. If you often ignore your intuition, then through time it will no longer communicate with you. If you follow your intuition, then it will become increasingly clearer and you will be able to appreciate the value of your decisions based on intuition. This, however, does not mean that the decisions based on choice cannot be just as valuable.

Letting Go

We attach ourselves to all sorts of things—to our habits, to specific concepts, to what we regard as good and bad, to our position, to our dignity, to money, to sex, to our possessions. Most of all we attach ourselves to our loved ones. However, all attachments result in constraint. All attachments are limiting and lock us into our conditioning. Even attachment to our loved ones limits our love.

Therefore it is good to practice letting go. This creates more space for our spiritual development. We may once again be capable of hearing the voice of God, or developing our own Buddhahood, in that space.

The majority of us should start small. Give something away which you are attached to (but do not attach to receiving gratitude). Get rid of a habit. Attempt to let go of a conviction.

For example, I have given away all of the books I thought I wouldn't read again, even though even if I got ill I might get the time to do so (I gave away all except a few which are precious to me for other reasons). Even now the rule still applies that my books may only take up a certain amount of space on the bookshelf—therefore, if I buy or receive new books, I have to get rid of old books. You can do the same with clothes, old papers, cassettes or CDs, and photo albums. As Lionel Blue stated, "Someone told me he liked my tie—red roses on blue silk—and I was proud of it. I hesitated, maybe all of half a second (I was after all still only human), and then I took the tie off and put it into the man's hand. Maybe an exaggerated gesture, but there is no end to the Spirit."

The most difficult thing to let go of is what we are attached to in our relationships—our precious habits (including the sexual ones). And, finally, we must let go of the other person. We shouldn't abandon them, but we should allow them to be completely free. We want to love the other dearly, even if they do not do exactly what we would like them to do, or even if they wish to do something we think isn't good for them. Parents, do you recognize this dilemma in relation to your children? But consider this from Kahlil Gibran's *The Prophet*:

> Your children are not your children.
> They are the sons and daughters of Life's longing for itself.
> They come through you but not from you,
> And though they are with you, yet they belong not to you.

Lastly, we have to let go of our own soul. If there is anything we are attached to, then it is our own soul (Thomas Moore). This is apparent from the way we cling to the past and why we wish to keep everything (photos, letters, and so on).

The most extreme form of attachment is addiction. Many of us are addicted to something, perhaps our morning cup of coffee, a toothbrushing ritual, reading stories to our children—whether they like it or not—a sport, specific privileges in our work situation, and so many other things. Some of us are seriously addicted to alcohol, drugs, sleeping pills, gambling, acting the victim, to idols (this is why God categorically forbids the making of and worshiping of carved images), and to a specific fantasy perception of reality. You name it, we can be addicted to it. Addiction is a terrible thing, as it makes us constrained and irresponsible. An addict cannot be a spiritual leader.

The first step in the next spiritual exercise is to face the naked truth in such a situation and to realize that there is a power greater than ourselves (this is the first step of Alcoholics Anonymous' 12-step program). Then the desire for a free and responsible existence must be allowed. The realization will follow automatically that you need something that is more powerful than the addictive substance if you want to get clean, and that is God. Knock and the door will be opened. It all sounds terribly simple and it is. However, it is extremely difficult to adhere to.

Leaders can be addicted to their position, and also to the patterns they have developed in their relationships with their staff. In order to become a true spiritual leader they are required to let their staff be free. A few directions:

• The use of the possessive pronoun should trigger a red light for the spiritual leader; for example, "my staff."
• The same is true for transitive use of language. For example: "I motivate my staff." I is the subject, motivate is the verb, and staff is the object. Conclusion: the staff is turned into a thing. Letting go means realizing that you cannot motivate another person, cannot change, cannot control, cannot protect, and cannot force. You cannot even instruct them, as I explained in the first chapter of this book. The only thing you can do is communicate with them, which entails that you listen to them and that you want the other person to see the real you. I will return to this point in chapter 7.

For leaders, oftentimes the most difficult thing to let go of is attachment to success and results—and, consequently, the notion that we have to act in order to achieve results. But nevertheless, letting go of this attachment is a prerequisite to reaching spiritual leadership. This in turn is necessary if we wish to achieve what we feel is the essence in the long term.

Beauty and Craftsmanship

In our dealings with gratitude we touched on beauty. However, this is such an important subject that it deserves a separate section. In my opinion, learning to see beauty and wanting to create beauty are important factors in your spiritual development.

As I already stated, you can experience beauty in nature, in music, in the arts in general, in architecture, in people, and even in things that are considered to be ugly, such as a chemical plant or a rubbish dump. I have personally experienced beauty in plays. Three examples stick in my mind:

> • In Arthur Miller's *After the Fall,* the second wife of the main character (modeled on Marilyn Monroe and at that time played by Myra Ward), said with endless sorrow in her voice: "I am but a joke."
> • In the dialogue from the end of Edward Albee's play *Who's Afraid of Virginia Woolf?,* Martha makes one last desperate attempt to get her husband, George, back into the game:
>> Martha: You don't suppose, maybe...
>> George: No.
>> Martha: Yes. No.
>> George: All right?
>> Martha: Yes. No.
>> George (singing softly to her):
>>
>> *Who's afraid of Virginia Woolf*
>> *Virginia Woolf*
>> *Virginia Woolf*
>>
>> Martha: I am George.
>> George: Who's afraid of Virginia Woolf?

Martha: I am George, I am.

(George nods, slowly: silence; cast)

CURTAIN

• At the end of Anton Chekhov's *Three Sisters*, the husband-to-be of the middle sister is killed and this sister tells with sorrow how she imagines her life in front of her, the way it will continue in its monotonous fashion (as it already has up until that point).

I give these examples to show that beauty can reveal itself at unexpected moments. I think that in these cases I was touched by the combination of total honesty—both in the text and in the performances—and the professional skill of the actors.

True professional skill and craftsmanship is a combination of a refined technical proficiency and personal mastery. It is not merely technique. The personality of the professional or the craftsman is always present and this personality is in continual development. We can perceive a glimpse of God or Buddhahood in true expertise. This is why it is always exquisite and touching, whether it is concerning a carpenter, a car mechanic, or a musician.

We can also be craftsmen in our relationships and in our leadership. This means that we have to contribute all of our talents and develop them. Then we can experience beauty in our relationships and in our cooperation. Conversely, being open to beauty in our personal and work surroundings brings out the best in us. Beauty can reveal itself in a different form. It is, as stated by Robert Pirsich, not so much the quality of the things and people around us, but the relationship we enter into with these things and people (see also Krishnamurti). Seeking beauty is thus developing beauty in ourselves; this is why it assists us in finding the way to God or Buddhahood.

Forgiveness

The final spiritual exercise I'd like to discuss with you is the exercise of forgiveness. Maybe you have nothing or no one to forgive. If so, you're the exception.

The majority of us believe that all sorts of bad things have been done to us, or that we've done bad things to ourselves. Forgiveness is the notion that in the most essential sense this is not at all true. Of course we have been through all sorts of things and they may have been extremely painful, which may very well have influenced the way we think and act, but our being has not been irreparably damaged. I understand our being as "I will be who I will be," our Buddha, or the God from within. In reality nothing has been done to us.

If we are capable of perceiving forgiveness in this manner, then we can also understand why forgiving is such an effective spiritual exercise and helps us with our spiritual development.

Forgiving is not excusing something. Forgiving isn't understanding why the other person—or one's self—did something. Forgiving is also not pitying. These things can create a little space in specific circumstances and allow forgiveness to become a little easier. However, the best spiritual exercise is to try to forgive. Say to yourself, or a stand-in: I forgive you, mother, I forgive you, father. I forgive you, sister—or brother, or son, or daughter, or partner, or teacher, or friend, or colleague, or boss. I forgive you, men, I forgive you, women, I forgive you, God. I forgive you, Hitler. I forgive myself, I forgive my past. Or try asking: can you forgive me?

And when you say this you will naturally feel whether this is right or not. You will naturally feel what is left in the form of judgment, rancor, grudging, rage, hatred, or revenge. You will naturally feel that you first have to let go of these feelings, for example by expressing them—maybe not to the person concerned, as this often incites new destruction—or by crying about it. And you may feel that you would like to forgive, but that you are not yet able to. Or you sense the stubbornness, or moral justification, which makes it impossible for you to forgive. And there is nothing wrong with this, if you are aware that this is an obstacle in your spiritual development, and especially for the development of your ability to love unconditionally.

Whatever the case may be, if you feel you are really ready to forgive, then do it. The sign that you have actually truly forgiven is the extensive relief you will feel—a weight of a thousand years can be lifted from your shoulders. As the Transformation Game puts it: "I forgive myself, I forgive my past, I forgive everyone, I am free!"

The Transformation Game

I have referred to the Transformation Game on a few occasions. It's a board game, designed by Joy Drake in Findhorn, in which you symbolically live your life, and the goal is to acquire insight into yourself. It's also an oracle in that you can ask for clues regarding a specific problem. The game is played at various levels or phases: physical, emotional, mental, and spiritual. Roughly speaking, these are the aspects of human functioning: your body (and the material matter), your feelings, your mind, and your religious awareness. You can play the game for yourself or with friends, but you can also play it under the guidance of a specially trained "facilitator." I always recommend doing this before you play the game alone, because you will better equipped to decide how strongly you believe in the game (2).

The Transformation Game is a view into both the soul and to the spirit. Where the emphasis lies depends on the question you ask the game and at which level you get a reply from the game. Among other things, the game provides a better understanding of the processes and concepts stated above. Furthermore, it provides insight into the issue of free will: what it is and what is its position in relation to the divine.

The Genesis story tells symbolically how we lost our innocence and replaced it with the knowledge of good and evil, our ability to choose. As a consequence, we are now free—we're even free to dismiss or revolt against what God has in store for us (or if you wish to put it less personally, against Tao, the flow of life, or the universal process of creation). We often do this, sometimes subconsciously. This results in us no longer submitting to the creative process, and losing our personal creativity. Thus there is a sort of contrast between free will and creativity (see also Raphael, *The Starseed Transmissions*).

The Transformation Game allows us to practice using our free will and provides feedback. In this way, it can provide an insight into the relationship between free will and creativity and teach us to deal with it in a more conscious manner. Another significant aspect of the Transformation Game is that it shows that an attitude of being at the service of ourselves and others aids us on our spiritual paths.

Service

What is service? Is it something like carrying out repairs free of charge or supplying parts? Or is it something like being helpful to the customer? The latter comes close to how I understand service. Service is perhaps Mother Teresa's activities in India and also Nelson Mandela's activities in South Africa, at least at the time this book was written (1994/1995). But service is also doing the dishes with a smile without expecting anything in return, or listening to a friend who is sad.

The old concept of servitude is the closest to how my idea of service, but this concept has also been corrupted through Calvinism. Service has nothing to do with humility and even less to do with subservience. It is also not "doing your duty" or providing a service in order to accrue so-called dues, or something in return the next day. Service is giving unconditionally—to yourself, to others, or to the world—just because you like it, or out of love, or because it is as natural to you as breathing. But for some people, service is a spiritual exercise. This is also expressed in the ancient Indian Sanskrit word for service, *seva*, which also means loving, cherishing, honoring, and worshiping.

If serving others doesn't happen automatically, how can one do it? I would suggest to begin small and do what you like doing—not to ease your conscience, but because it feels good to do something for yourself or someone else. It is important to note that the same applies to service as to love: serve another as you would serve yourself. You cannot be of service to another from within if you don't take good care of yourself.

If you do something out of guilt or a sense of duty, ask yourself: if I didn't have to do this, would I? Sometimes you would and if so, forget your duty and do what you thought you must do, for your own pleasure. Guilt is never constructive, and guilt-fueled actions always have a negative effect, however concealed. Visiting your mother out of guilt, or because it would be mean not to, is not taking your mother seriously and this always causes hard feelings. Guilt is always veiled aggression toward yourself and the other person.

Service makes us become a little bit like God or the Buddha. To leaders, service means at the service of. It is a good counterweight against the awareness of a hierarchy, which always threatens to sneak into a situation of leadership, and which, in itself, gets in the way of spiritual leadership. A wonderful example of service is Jesus, who washed his disciples' feet. "If I then, your Lord and Master, have washed your feet; ye also ought to wash one another's feet. For I have given you an example, that ye should do as I have done to you" (John 13:14-15). Nicely said, but never do it only because that is how it should be. I can tell you, from personal experience, how nice it is, when the reciprocal, strengthening process of service gets started within a community. I will return to this in chapter 7.

Service also means, to a leader, being a coach and a teacher. This means intending that your staff develop themselves to their own personal level of competence and surpass their own limits. This also means that you, the leader, must be pleased when they discover the area in which they can surpass you. They must be taught to solve their own problems, and not be unfairly criticized. Heartfelt appreciation is also a form of service.

It goes without saying that an attitude of service that spreads through a company or a service institution benefits the service of the company in the usual sense of the word. I will even go one step further—good service and long-term success are not possible without "service." Unfortunately, if you strive toward service for that reason, it won't work. The only good motives for service are to care for yourself, out of love for another, or because of the pleasure you gain. Even the search for God is not a good motive, if it is the sole one. To use the words of Paul Duke from Chemlawn: "Our people first, our customers next, and the thing will work" (Nayak).

Masters and Avatars

According to some traditions it isn't possible to find God or Buddha without a personal master. I do not agree. I believe that everyone can become blessed in his or her own way and that the way can be different for each person.

This doesn't mean that masters can be of assistance. But we have to make a distinction between a master with whom we have a personal master-to-student relationship and the masters we can encounter all around us and in ourselves.

Let's begin with the latter. Naturally we all have sources from whom or from which we can learn. This begins with our parents, and continues on with the teachers at school, our friends, our colleagues, our children, film and pop idols, political and spiritual leaders, books, films, plays and, last but not least, ourselves, our soul, and our inner guide. In this sense we always all have masters.

The external master with whom we have a personal connection supplements the matter that he teaches us. This may be the love he radiates for us, or the natural authority that he has over us. Or he may be giving us specific advice and assignments. It this situation, our task is to find the balance between surrendering to our master and being true to ourselves. This is an exceptionally difficult issue, as good masters sometimes say things or instruct us to do things that do not suit us and can result in resistance. It's difficult to distinguish whether our resistance has to do with resisting growth, fear, or apathy, or a healthy critical judgment.

In the end our heart has to decide. Experience shows that there are just as many people who have damaged themselves by blindly following their master as people who have made it needlessly difficult for themselves by not trusting a master. One thing is clear: spiritual growth is not possible without some sort of surrender, if not to a master, then to our inner process. We are unable to be in charge of or control our own growth, although part of ourselves may wish to do so. Surrender to a master can assist in this. I wonder how long it would have taken, before I had found myself again, if I had not at some point in my life unconditionally surrendered to my master. The divine can be experienced in a good and meaningful master-student relationship.

The importance of a master is also that he reminds us of the fact that our power and position are merely relative. This is, in particular for a leader who wishes to be spiritual, an extremely sound thought.

The word avatar was included in the title of this section. Avatars are masters who are said to be—or they themselves say that are—

"totally realized." This means that they don't have to go through another learning process in order to realize the divine within themselves. They are already God, like Jesus. They are here and have remained here with the sole purpose of assisting others with their development process. It has been ascertained that these types of people are present in this day and age, have a special charisma, and are a blessing for the people around them. The latter feel supported and established and rediscover the happiness, direction, and purpose in their lives. It is also a fact there are always people who are less susceptible to an avatar's influence, or are more attracted to one avatar but not to another.

How do you recognize an avatar? Although some avatars can perform miracles, especially in the field of healing—but you and I can also do this occasionally—this is in fact not the essence of their identity. Your spiritual development—nothing else—is significant to them. Healing and miracles are merely aids to assist your further. If healing is the sole aim, then we are more than likely not dealing with an avatar but with an "ordinary healer," which can also be extremely beneficial.

Recognizing an avatar is in fact a double-edged sword, just as with beauty or quality. Beauty and quality are not so much characteristics of objects or processes, but they say something about our relationship with objects and processes: we assign beauty or quality to them. It is the same with avatars: we recognize an avatar when we are in a relationship with a fully realized person, a relationship that we experience with certainty, as in a relationship with a "God-sent" person, a representative of God on earth. This is why there is much truth in the expression: you won't find an avatar until the time is right—and when the time is right the avatar will find you.

OUR PIECE OF THE PLANETARY PUZZLE

We've just discussed how we can once more—or more deeply—get in touch with God. In the previous chapter we dealt with how we can regain contact with the Goddess. What is the relationship between these two processes? Where do God and the Goddess meet up? Where does God, figuratively speaking, fertilize the Goddess?

I believe that this occurs in a global vision. I use the word vision in the same manner I used it in describing the law of creativity: the image of what we want to aim for, what we want to achieve. I will elaborate upon this in chapter 9, when I'll discuss how we can develop our personal vision and how we can reach a collective vision following our personal vision.

The ultimate collective vision is the global vision, what we, as the total human race, wish to achieve. It is obvious that an explicit, collective global vision is out of the question at the moment. Our destiny, what we want to make of this world, is not clear-cut. However, multiple visions for the world do exist. Everyone has his or her own concept regarding an ideal world. The case is rather that the individual visions for the world are not brought together and developed into a collective image that can be shared and to which everyone can say: yes, that is also my vision. At the moment there are as many different visions as there are people.

On the other hand, such a global vision is closer than we think. As long as we don't make it too intricate or become distracted by what we think is viable, there seems to be much more unity in our visions than is apparent at first sight. For example, almost everyone wants a world in which there is enough food for everyone. Almost everyone wants a world in which there is enough space, not only for us but also for our children. Almost everyone wants a world of peace, health, prosperity, and abundance. But our opinions about how to achieve these visions differ. In addition, we tend to defend ourselves, if necessary with violence, from those we suspect are trying to take from us what we've achieved. However, underneath this, many people still want the same things: happiness for ourselves, our loved ones, and our offspring. And we also want this for others, even if this is only because we realize that our happiness is under threat as long as not everyone has it.

Why is the global vision the place where God and the Goddess meet up? Because I believe that the world vision has two sources. On the one hand the world vision comes forth from our collective requirements and desires. As such, it emanates from our soul and our collective soul is the world soul. As soon as we have converted our collective requirements and desires into images of what we want to achieve, these images become part of the noosphere: our collective knowledge and concepts world (Teilhard de Chardin).

On the other hand our global vision emanates from our collective destiny. The countless esoteric scriptures state that we have a destiny, which, in reality, we have already been allocated to and which we can recognize or at any rate surmise by listening to our spiritual source (Raphael, *The Urantia Book*, Teilhard de Chardin, the Point Omega, the Seth books, Russell, and of course the Bible book Revelations, to name but a few). This destiny reveals itself in words or images that come to us through our intuition or inspiration, or through a directing force we can observe within ourselves. It feels as if this force is actually given to us from an external source. Each individual's vision of the world is the product of the gathering of his or her personal needs and longings on the one hand and on the other with his or her spiritual source. Here, something is conceived and born—which accounts for my fertilization analogy. Soul and spirit come together—yin and yang come together—and the result is something new. To put it in Taoist terms: two become three.

This process occurs with everyone more or less consciously. In this way three becomes "the myriad things," to express it once again in a Taoist manner. From these thousand things we can then once again arrive at one global vision. With this, God has then fertilized the Goddess.

To become a true spiritual leader, we must become aware of these processes. A prerequisite of this is that we give this process the benefit of the doubt and appreciate its necessity and desirability. Our heart must be in it. We must care what happens with the world; we must put in an effort to find our piece of the planetary puzzle ourselves (the term is from Danaan Parry) and we must want to carry out that part through our attitude, our words, and our deeds.

The "must" in the previous sentence is not a moral or ethical must, but a conditional one. We as a group, and also as individual beings, can influence where the world is going. We can choose to be a part of the problem or a part of the solution. If we wish to be the latter, then we must search for our puzzle piece and our contribution. Then we must search for both our visions and our talents (see chapter 8). Then we can do nothing other than take our spiritual leadership upon ourselves.

These processes occur automatically if we are in direct contact with the God in ourselves and with the Great Spirit. There were many aids included in this chapter for stimulating our experience of this contact. This is nothing new to those who are already aware of this knowledge. If you have experienced God, then you know you have experienced God and this gets you in motion automatically. You can allow yourself to be guided by God and seek refuge with the Buddha. Then as a leader you are led.

However, for those who aren't so certain and want to have something to look forward to, I can safely say that no matter how many varieties of experience there can be, this experience always involves the experience of awe and silence. Consider the description that I used at the beginning of this chapter: directing your view toward the skies. In this context the astronauts' experience in the previous chapter is extremely illustrative. But also allowing the feeling of awe or permitting the feeling of silence and emptiness can result in a direct awareness of God. You may have experienced something similar. My request is that you don't let this slip by, but that you cherish and remember this experience and remain open to it. Then your spiritual leadership will develop as a matter of course.

CHAPTER 6

The Teachings

MOTTO: THE SPIRITUAL LEADER ALLOWS HIMSELF TO BE INSPIRED THROUGH ONE OR MORE RELIGIOUS TRADITIONS.

"Wholeheartedly also I take my refuge in the Dharma . . . which is the abode of security against the rounds or rebirth."
—Shantideva, Bodhicaravarta

AS IS APPARENT FROM THIS QUOTE (FROM THE SEVEN-fold puja, the worship service from the Western Buddhist Order), people always have been supported by the teachings of the great religions. If we don't have a personal master, or if we've lost the inner way, or if there is no community that cherishes and supports us, we can always fall back on the teachings. However, even under more favorable conditions, teachings can assist us with our spiritual development and thus onto the path of spiritual leadership.

The teachings of the great religions always have two aspects: a wisdom side and a moral side. They make a statement about how life—the world—works and how we ought to behave. Both sides can develop into a dogma, the sacrosanct truth. The devil of the dogma always comes with the Beelzebub of intolerance, creating our potential to smash each other's skulls in the name of the truth.

The moral dogma always involves guilt and penance, making us feel that we aren't good enough, and, combined with the "knowledge" of the vindictive God or negative karma, can result in a fear which, suppressed, can create an unyielding attitude and intolerance. The circle is then fully closed. Islam and Christianity in particular exhibit this unyielding attitude, but no religion is completely free of it.

If, on the other hand, we are capable of considering the teachings as a source of inspiration and a helping hand, enabling us to deal with life better and to advance our personal spiritual development, then there is a treasure trove of wealth hidden in the sources of tradition. This enrichment of our daily life costs nothing.

In chapter 3 I drew from such a source: Taoism. In this chapter I will tap into two other sources: the Judeo-Christian tradition and Buddhism. I will also illuminate an aspect of yoga, namely, the teachings of the chakras. These choices are totally random. They're partially inspired through practical considerations because they're the traditions in which I am knowledgeable, and partially through tactical considerations, because Buddhism and Christianity are readily accessible and in my experience directly apply to leadership.

This isn't a book about Christianity, or about Buddhism. As with the other chapters my orientation is leadership. I am like a baker who argues the point of biology (say, the genetic structure of wheat or yeast), or like an engineer who talks about management, or as a minister who talks about psychology. I am a business consultant, psychologist, and psychotherapist who talks about spiritual matters. I am no expert in the field of religious teachings. But as a layman, just like you, I can draw on the teachings when discussing my leadership and yours.

The intention of this chapter is not to provide an introduction of any type of teachings, but an introduction that may encourage you to learn more. According to the Jewish tradition, learning has always been the core of religious life. In this aspect, the Jewish tradition is exceptionally practical and creates awareness that this is a miraculous universe and that our purpose here is to co-create it.

THE JUDEO-CHRISTIAN TRADITION

Both Judaism and Christianity are based on the Bible (the Jewish tradition solely on the Old Testament). Throughout the centuries, the Bible has been studied, guidelines for moral and practical actions have been derived, and endless discussions and battles have taken place, unfortunately also on a physical level. I am no theologian or scribe and I have no comprehensive knowledge of even a fraction of all the scriptures. Therefore, I went directly to the source: the Bible. Returning to the source is always the best option, if the opportunity is present to do so.

The Bible is a compilation of stories. In this sense the Bible is both extremely modern and classic. Stories are always used to convey something tangible. As is commonly known, many of the stories in the Bible didn't take place as stated, and many people—but not everyone—are in agreement about this. However, many of the stories contain messages. They narrate, in a symbolic manner, what has occurred or what life is all about, or they provide symbolic guidelines for our actions.

Take, for example, the creation story. This did not happen literally, of this much we are certain. It is not even an analogy of the actual development of the world. But recent studies show that it provides an accurate, albeit styled and closed, description of how the Earth recovered after the disaster which took place following the Cretaceous Period, after the immense collision with an asteroid around 66 million years ago (Tollman). There is a direct link between the creation story and the flood story—and also the story of the fall of Sodom and Gomorra. Conceived in this manner, the story shows that light and life are stronger than chaotic darkness and death. Such a story can provide hope during difficult times. Sunshine follows rain. A simple piece of proverbial wisdom, but important when you're completely down.

I will now randomly extract items from Bible stories to demonstrate the significance of the Bible in our daily lives and for spiritual leadership.

The Fall of Man

"Evil is nothing but energy flowing backward rather than forward."—Shirley Maclaine, *Dancing in the Light* (1)

"Evil is only the lack of consciousness of God...the lack of spiritual knowledge."—Ken Ryerson, as quoted by Shirley Maclaine

I have already remarked that it's improbable that—remaining in the symbolic language of the Bible—God didn't know that we would eat from the Tree of Knowledge. Didn't he deliberately tempt us by explicitly forbidding us to eat from it?

We are created in God's image and likeness and we are conscious of good and evil. This is apparently intentionally so. The significance of God's set up is that we can no longer blame God that he has saddled us with a conscience. We did this ourselves, did we not? However, upon closer inspection, more much more significant ideas can be derived from this story.

Where there is a rule there is a violation. Therefore, we ought to deviate from the rules as little as possible to possess "good," constructive, responsible, and creative behavior. In fact, rules shouldn't even be necessary. After all, we possess the knowledge of good and evil. Our inner voice should therefore be capable of determining what is correct behavior and what is not. Indeed, rules can be thought of as obstacles. They ask for violation. We apparently possess a sort of congenital, inherent craving for freedom.

So why in the name of God do we have rules? First, for practical reasons. Consider for example traffic regulations. What's distinctive about this type of regulation is that it isn't emotionally loaded. Whether you abide to these rules or not is, at the most, morally tinted. In addition to practicality, we don't trust ourselves. *Ad absurdum* this was implemented by the orthodox Calvinists, who posit that humanity is incapable of any good and is solely predisposed to all evil. They also derive this from the fall of man story. However, to me, this only shows that we have lost our innocence and with this direct contact with God. However, not innocent is completely different from guilty!

I must admit that this lack of trust in ourselves is also nourished through other aspects of the fall of man story—for example, through the retributions pronounced by God. As he states elsewhere: I am a jealous God. In all honesty, this isn't the God in the Old Testament that appeals to me. I think this must be another god incorporated into the Bible.

This lack of trust in humanity is justifiable when you take a look around. We humans continually do things that are detrimental to our faith in ourselves and to our faith in our own conscience. Maybe we do have a conscience, but do we heed it? At any rate, in this way we find ourselves in a vicious circle: our lack of trust in ourselves results in more regulations that we rebel against and which results in more violations, which in turn results in an increased feeling of guilt. This is difficult to live with; therefore we suppress these feelings and become unable to listen to our conscience.

Where did this cycle begin? I think that it started with a relatively innocent confusion, just as children can become entangled in a situation that's way too complex for them. For example, many times children encounter more options than they can deal with—too many toys, too much freedom. Compare this to God in the fall of man story. We as a race have become confused, and, like children, become short tempered, unruly, and unstable. We're separated from God.

So what is the significance of free will? I believe that it's nothing more than the ability to choose to surrender to the life flow or not, to submit to this universal process of creation, and in doing so whether to work with it or oppose it. This is in fact the choice between good and evil. In order to make this choice knowingly, we have to experience a certain freedom; we must want to and be able to experiment. We must also be able to make a wrong choice and make mistakes. In my opinion, the ability and the need to make mistakes could be called the original sin—a non-biblical concept, by the way. Mistakes are just the creation of situations we didn't wish to create at all. This shows us that the gift of free choice is at loggerheads with the efficient creation of the divine—a conclusion we've already arrived at in chapter 5.

The story of the fall of man gives rise to this type of speculation. This story offers a totally different approach to the traditional one of guilt and retribution. Sin, to me, is nothing more than waste—waste of talent or energy. It is part and parcel of life and nature, in the terms of the previous chapter. It belongs to the soul. Sin results in pain and sorrow. However, it is a learning process through which we can learn to create along with God. Sin is not blameworthy. It is the price we pay for our freedom.

Currently, there is much talk of the significance of ethics in management, government, and politics. This can sometimes lead to a strong ethical and normative approach. In this manner, actual values become rigid regulations, which, consequently, are violated. In my opinion, this is not the way. For me, true moral action is conscious, with an understanding for the other person and in touch with our inner decision-maker. This inner decision maker doesn't have a standard solution, but a specific solution to each situation. On the face of things the decision maker may appear to be inconsistent, as he opts for this in one situation and in another situation for that. Yet if you truly act in accordance with the decision maker then the general concept will become clear: creativity, spiritual growth, and love. The last word is taboo in the world of politics and management, but let's discuss it anyway.

The Great Commandment

"You shall not go up and down as a slanderer among your people: and you shall not stand against the life of your neighbor; I am the LORD. You shall not take vengeance or bear any grudge against the sons of your own people, but you shall love your neighbor as yourself: I am the LORD."— Leviticus 19:16, 18

"You have heard that it was said, You shall love your neighbor, and hate your enemy. But I say to you, Love your enemies, and pray for those who persecute you. . . For if you love those who love you, what reward have you? . . . You, therefore, must be perfect, as your heavenly Father is perfect."—Matthew 5: 43-44, 48

"So faith, hope, love abide, these three; but the greatest of these is love."—I Corinthians 13:13

While Buddhism and Taoism are outstanding examples of the wise religions, Christianity is the religion of love. At least, that's its intention.

What is love? "Love thinks no evil" (I Corinthians 13:5). Love is seeing beyond the behavior, through the outer form. It is making a connection with the core of your being, or the being of another. It is also claimed that the correct translation of Leviticus 19 is that you shall love your neighbor, who is just as you (Whitlau).

That is why love is all about the awareness of unity and the courage to take a true look at oneself. Love exceeds our individuality and earthiness; a Christian would say it's a gift from God (that also explains "I am the Lord"). It makes us perfect.

When I was still a practicing psychotherapist, my first impression of some clients was that they weren't likeable. I once had a client who did things that bothered me. However, when I was able to gather the courage and conviction to listen to that person, to open myself up, then eventually the other person allowed their inner side to be seen: their vulnerability, their hurting, their—sometimes damaged—hope and trust. Later on, in my role as a business consultant and trainer, I encountered people whom I had difficulty with initially. But every time, once personal contact had been established, my original reservations were no longer present. Then there is love. Love is present when our cores meet each other. Rajneesh Chandra Mohan (Osho) states the following:

> Love is very rare.
> To meet a person at his centre is to pass through a revolution in yourself, because if you want to meet a person at his centre, you will have to allow that person to reach to your centre also.
> You will have to become vulnerable, absolutely vulnerable, open.
> It is risky.
> To allow someone to reach your centre is risky, dangerous.
> You never know what that person will do to you.
> Once all your secrets are known, once your hiddenness becomes unhidden, once you're exposed completely, what the other person will do you never know.

It helps to realize that the danger is in fact imaginary, that we are invulnerable, as I explained in the earlier section about forgiveness. This can be extremely difficult to comprehend, as it isn't in line with our interpretation of life as we have experienced it up until now. Love can blossom between ourselves and our partners, our friends, and our families, but in fact it can also occur between everyone. This is how Jesus enhanced love: love thy enemy. This is possible and it will be wholesome to ourselves and to the world around us. There is a soul in each and every enemy, and we can love it. It is of course not so difficult to love someone we like, or someone who does pleasant things, but do we still love the person if they do something else? Or is our love bound to conditions and therefore limited? The trick is to love the one who doesn't comply with our conditions. This is why it is so important not to judge (Matthew 7:1-5 and John 8). We can be judgmental about behavior but we shouldn't judge the entire person. Love is no respecter of persons. This suddenly reminds me of a Lionel Blue joke. It goes as follows:

A Nazi said to a Jew: "The Jews have caused all of Germany's problems."

"Yes," said the Jew, "the Jews and the cyclists."

"Why the cyclists?" asked the Nazi, not understanding.

"Why the Jews?" said the Jew.

Ever since I heard this joke, I try, in an impression of Lionel Blue, to add the thought " . . . and the cyclists." This shows me the absurdity of it all. This jokes shows that love isn't all that easy. Krishnamurti says: "So when you ask what love is, you may be too frightened to see the answer. It may mean complete upheaval; it may break up the family; you may discover that you do not love your wife or husband or children—do you?—you may have to shatter the house you have built, you may never go back to that temple." And Gibran says in *The Prophet*: "For even as love crowns you so shall he crucify you. Even as he is for your growth so is he for your pruning. Even as he ascends to your height and caresses your tenderest branches that quiver in the sun, so shall he descend to your roots and shake them in their clinging to the earth." Here's Krishnamurti again: "If you have not got love—not just in little drops but in abundance—if you are not filled with it—the world will go to disaster." Unfortunately, the trouble is that if we wish to generate love as a means to avert evil, it won't work. We can only love for love's sake, if it comes from our natural desires, if our soul allows itself to be fertilized by the Spirit.

This is why love is so threatening—it is limitless, immeasurable, and overwhelming. This can be perceived with a primitive form of love, such as falling in love-sickness. Love can turn your world upside down. It incites you to behavior that sometimes is completely inconvenient. Our attitude toward love is often ambivalent: we do and don't want it. We also often attempt to tame love by attempting to attach ourselves to the other person and subconsciously or consciously make agreements regarding our behavior. This results in fixed behavioral patterns and routines in the relationship. But that is the beginning of the end of the love. This is why letting go, as defined in the previous chapter, is a precondition for blossoming love.

Love is also very often interpreted as a commandment. In my mind, this isn't a very productive approach. What happens if we don't carry through? We experience a sense of failure, or even worse, we feel guilty. In my opinion, it's much better to perceive love as an ability we all possess; we all long for its realization and we are all afraid of it. The ability to love can become blocked, through fear or an unhappy past. Nevertheless, it can always flourish. We can do this by incorporating it into our vision. (I will indicate how this can be done in chapters 8 and 9.)

It can also be derived from the above quotes that you cannot love another more than you love yourself. The way to love is therefore not through sacrifice.

Apart from the more "technical" approaches in chapter 8 and 9, the way to love is through forgiveness. It's also the case here that you cannot forgive the other person until you have first—or at the same time—forgiven yourself (A Course in Miracles). That's why the Lord's Prayer also states: "Forgive us our sins, as we have forgiven those who have sinned against us." I have always understood this as "help me to forgive myself, so that it becomes possible for me to forgive others."

Perhaps I have made love seem very heavy and difficult, but it isn't. The following quote from Phil Anderson illustrates this point well:

One day a young manager was informed that if he wanted to have a successful career then he would have to exhibit more leadership qualities. He attended a number of courses, he sought advice from a number of organization advisors and senior managers of successful enterprises. However he did not succeed in discovering what leadership is.

At a loss, he decided to travel to India to visit a guru, renowned for his wisdom and insight. He asked the guru if he could tell him what leadership actually was, in order that he would be able to exhibit more leadership qualities and have a successful career. The guru nodded and said that the manager would have to return with a follower, otherwise he could not explain it. The manager asked if it could be one of his colleagues, however the guru shook his head. "It has to be someone who truly follows you." The manager departed feeling confused.

He returned a number of years later, this time with his three-year-old daughter. And he went on to explain to the guru: "You asked that I bring a follower with me, and no matter where I go, she follows me."

The guru smiled, sat the little girl on his lap, and said: "And why does she follow you?"

The young manager thought about this for a moment and said: "I think that it's because she loves me."

The guru nodded and asked: "And why does she love you"

The young manager thought about this for a little longer and than said: "I think it's because I love her."

The old guru smiled, returned the child to her father and shook his hand. "You already know all I can teach you about leadership" (*The New Leaders*, May/June 1992).

I feel a certain affinity with the little girl, and with the young manager and the guru. In fact this passage says it all. Love is the most powerful leadership there is and it is the divine way to spiritual leadership. But, since for many of us, the direct way is the most difficult, I will carry on with this book nevertheless.

Where Is This God of Yours Now?

Maybe you are familiar with the story of Job, but I'll recount the story for those who are less well-versed in the scriptures.

Job was an extremely pious and noble man who lived in the country Uz. God blessed Job with many possessions and a large family. The Prosecutor said to God, "It's no big deal that Job is so pious and generous. Take away all of his possessions, and then you'll be surprised." So God permitted that Job's possessions be destroyed by storm and fire in which all the members of his family perished, except for his wife. Job tore off his clothes when he learned of this disaster, but he didn't abandon God. "The unnamable has given, the unnamable has taken away, he shall be blessed." At this point, The Prosecutor said to God, "Big deal—if he loses his health then he'll change his tune." So God permitted The Prosecutor to afflict Job with tumors from head to toe. "Where is this God of yours now?" asked Job's wife, but Job uttered nothing negative.

Alone, Job sat down at the garbage dump, where he was visited by three friends. When they saw him, they burst into tears. They spent seven days and seven nights silently by his side because they saw that his sorrow was immense.

I'd like to make a comment about this point in the story. Such wonderful friendship! Such compassion! Just being there, for days and nights, without trivializing what mustn't be trivialized. How often do we encounter such friendship and helpfulness in these hurried times? How quick with words are we nowadays.

Getting back to the story, while his friends were visiting, Job cursed the day he was born. His friends attempted to convince him that he had in fact brought his misfortune upon himself. After all, God doesn't punish without reason. Job must have sinned, otherwise this disaster would have not happened to him.

In chapter 2 we have already comprehensively dealt with the

world concept on which this is based. Here, though, I want to stress the arrogance of his friends. How pretentious to say that they know how the world works—what brings God to his actions—and that therefore Job had sinned! This part of the story confronted me with my own self-importance and pride as a father, psychotherapist, and consultant.

Job doesn't buy it either. "Nonsense," he cries out in despair. "I've always behaved correctly. I cared for my family and my friends; I felt compassion for my loved ones, I have paid my tithes and more; I was always there for those who needed me. Nonsense, that I must have sinned. Is it a crime to be rich and in material comfort? If I have sinned then it was unknowingly. I did everything within my capabilities." His friends weren't convinced, though. They stubbornly clung to their opinion (this is known as dogma).

Instead of leaning on his friends, Job turned to God himself. "What did I do wrong that you punish me so? I find your policy obscure. I call to you, but you give no answer when I stand still in anticipation of your attention. Instead of this you show no compassion—in fact, you knock me down with full force."

Note that Job is also wrestling with the theory that he's being punished for his sins. But instead of adhering to this theory, he protests against it. He finds God and life itself to be unfair.

The unnamable replies, "Where were you when I created the Earth? Did you create it? Who do you think you are, that you think you can understand my motivations and can call my policy obscure? What do you know?"

God's reaction here is difficult to comprehend. It seems like a debating trick. God is on the defensive; this isn't a model of open communication, a style of communicating that we'll cover in chapter 7. (There is also a later addition in the Bible book Job, in which God goes a lot further: Job literally becomes crushed by God's authority.) I assume that this text is more likely to be from the person who wrote this story than from God himself. God has no need for tricks such as this. What he is actually attempting to convey is that Job does not yet have the understanding to be able to precisely comprehend what the problem is: his insight is lacking at a spiritual level. Job understood God's words in this way. He finally said, "Indeed, I spoke because I didn't understand it at all. It is way above my head, it's incomprehensible. I had heard of you through hearsay, but now I have seen you with my own eyes. This is why I take back what I said. I am sorry." I don't believe that God judged Job's words harshly, but the Bible doesn't express an opinion about it.

To summarize, the book of Job teaches us that the point and direction in life can be found, even though we cannot comprehend it. It also teaches us that it's beneficial to remain true to yourself and not to let yourself be talked into things because of the opinions of others (which is, of course, not the same as not listening to someone else). And, finally, it teaches us that our emotional rage and our protests are useful and can bring us into contact with God. However, it also teaches us that it isn't useful to be impeded by this protest—ultimately it's better to trust God (or the Buddha in us, or life), even though it seems unjustified (we will deal with this in more detail in chapter 8). Righteousness is an earthly concept that merely forms a distorted reflection of the divine concept of justice.

Do Not Worry
> The LORD is my shepherd; I shall not want.
> He maketh me to lie down in green pastures;
> He leadeth me beside the still waters.
> He restoreth my soul . . . .
> Yea, though I walk through the valley of the shadow of death,
> I will fear no evil . . .
> —Psalm 23

The Sermon on the Mount (Matthew 5-7) is one of the most beautiful passages in the Bible. I believe that what's brought together in one speech, in a few pages, is unsurpassed. I would, with pleasure, like to write a book about this passage alone, but here I will single out a few aspects. First, the pronouncements about worry. Here is the famous quotation:

Therefore I tell you, do not be anxious about your life, what you shall eat, or what you shall drink; nor about your body, what you shall put on. Is not life more than food and the body more than clothing? Look at the birds of the air: they neither sow nor reap nor gather into barns; and yet your heavenly Father feeds them. Are you not of more value than they?

And which of you by being anxious can add one cubit to his span of life? And why are you anxious about clothing? Consider the lilies of the field, how they grow; they neither toil nor spin; yet I tell you, even Solomon in all his glory was not arrayed like one of these.

But if God so clothes the grass of the field, which today is alive, and tomorrow is thrown into the oven, will he not much more clothe you, O men of little faith?

Therefore do not be anxious, saying, What shall we eat? or, What shall we drink? or, What shall we wear? For the Gentiles seek: all these things; and your heavenly Father knows that you need them all.

But seek first his kingdom and his righteousness; and all these things shall be yours as well.

Therefore do not be anxious for tomorrow, for tomorrow will be anxious for itself. Let's the day's own trouble be sufficient for the day.

Although this is an exceptionally well-known passage, it's often misinterpreted or forgotten. It cannot be derived from this that you have to take no action: not to sow, to reap, to work. and to spin. What is stated is that no matter what, God will take care of you. No matter what, God will provide the nuts, even though he may not crack them open. It also states something that's more significant than material matters: the search for "His Kingdom and His Justice." I understand this as follows: If I strive toward what is truly important to me and let myself be carried by my desires for this—love, justice, peace, prosperity for everyone, or whatever you wish to add to this—life will take care of me. In other words, you can trust life—even if you do not strive toward justice. Life—or God if you wish—provides you with what you need.

In this context, what precedes the section I just quoted must also be examined. This passage states that you cannot serve two masters, as you will either love the one and hate the other, or you will attach yourself to the one and feel contempt for the other. "Thou cannot serve God and Mammon," and in my opinion Mammon represents money, position, power, status, or something along those lines.

But is it so wrong to strive toward wealth or prosperity? This depends on your intention. I think that it will only become a problem if you wish to obtain wealth (or anything else) at the cost of someone else. Rich people appear in the Bible on various occasions, even in Jesus' circle, who are exceptionally positively portrayed: Abraham, Job, Joseph of Arimathea, the wise men from the east, and so on. Jesus' message is that attachment to possessions or position is damaging to yourself and to others. It creates dependency and hinders your energy, which is required to focus on that which is actually wholesome. This reminds me of the story about the rich young man who asks, "Teacher, what good thing must I do to get eternal life?" I would tell him to become happy, but Jesus replied something to the effect of "If thou wilt be perfect, go and sell that thou hast, and give to the poor, and thou shalt have treasure in heaven: and come and follow me." But when the young man heard that, he went away sorrowful, for he had great possessions. Jesus them spoke the famous and memorable words: "Verily I say unto you, that a rich man shall hardly enter into the kingdom of heaven. And again I say unto you, it is easier for a camel to go through the eye of a needle, than for a rich man to enter into the kingdom of God." What he says next is also interesting: "When his disciples heard it, they were exceedingly amazed, saying, 'Who then can be saved?' But Jesus beheld them, and said unto them, 'With men this is impossible; but with God all things are possible'" (Matthew 19:16-26).

The message here for the leader is that it's important to recognize what (my, our) life is all about. Moreover, there is a force that is greater and more powerful than we are, which will eventually lead us to our individual and collective destinies. Spiritual leadership is therefore spiritual following, as I have previously stated. Efficiency and effectiveness can only be achieved if we are in harmony with life, the Way, the universal process of creation, God; if we are able to create and play together with this force. If we can experience and realize this, then we're no longer afraid and have the urge to do well and be successful. We are then capable of being simultaneously distanced and feeling involved. We no longer have to arrange the situation to suit ourselves, and the pressure in our lives disappears. I will return to this in chapter 8 (see the core beliefs section).

"And in praying, do not heap up empty phrases."
—Matthew 6:7

> O Great Spirit . . .
> Let me walk in beauty...
> Make my hands respect the things you have made and my ears
> sharp to hear your voice.　　　　—from an old Native prayer

Praying is dialogue with God. It is listening, "whether I may also hear it." Being open, so that Life—God—can communicate with us. It similar to meditation, which I will deal with later.

Praying can also be talking. I would like to discuss the fundamental Christian prayer with you, the Lord's Prayer, and hopefully I will make it appealing to non-Christians. It is the prayer taught to us by Jesus and which he highly recommended (Matthew 6:9-13).

> Our Father who art in heaven,
> Hallowed be thy name.
> Thy kingdom come,
> Thy will be done on earth, as it is in heaven.
> Give us this day our daily bread.
> And forgive us our debts, as we forgive our debtors.
> Lead us not into temptation, but deliver us from evil:
> For thine is the kingdom, and the power, and the glory, for ever.
> Amen.

"Our Father who art in heaven": we turn our eyes upwards, toward what is greater than us, with the intention of discovering inspiration and support. Praying is more like striving toward the ultimate than digging to the deepest (this is more like soul research, as I will discuss in chapter 8).

"Hallowed be thy name": with this we declare that divinity exists in what is valuable and precious, or in what we stand up for (fight for), or in anything that gives our lives meaning and significance. Someone who doesn't believe in God could therefore say that Life itself is divine.

"Thy kingdom come. Thy will be done": With this we declare surrender and obedience. Not *my* will be done, but *thy* will be done. There appears to be a higher principle in life than my will.

"Give us this day our daily bread": We only ask for what we need now, and we declare faith in tomorrow. We ask only for necessities, not for possessions, wealth, or anything else, and with this express what is essential to us and what is not. This is therefore not desire.

"And forgive us our debts, as we forgive our debtors": With this we make ourselves open in order to forgive ourselves; otherwise, we cannot even receive God's forgiveness. This is therefore the way to dispose of guilt. This also clears the way to forgive others and to take our place in the world lovingly.

"Lead us not into temptation, but deliver us from evil": This assists us in keeping an eye open to what is important: God or Mammon. It reminds us of our freedom of choice and invites us to discover our essential purpose. It is also a request that we do not waste our talents (sin). It activates our moral function. When I think of temptation I always think of addiction, everything we're attached to: coffee, cigarettes, alcohol, drugs, possessions, sex, or whatever. "Lead us not into temptation" can also be interpreted as a prayer for mastery and freedom of our own lives.

"For thine is the kingdom, and the power, and the glory, for ever": This not only expresses surrender, but also hope and faith in a better world.

The Lord's Prayer will probably benefit our spiritual development if we regularly recite it as an automatic ritual, but it will become much stronger if we experience it consciously. To do this we must endorse it—maybe not totally rationally, but on a spiritual level. It helps to ponder it on occasion. It could be summarized as: surrender, trust, forgiveness, freedom and choice. I could not phrase the foundations for spiritual leadership better (2).

Remember the Sabbath to Keep It Holy

I would like to conclude my discussion of Christianity with something it has inherited from Judaism: the day of rest, the seventh day of the week.

The dedication of a fixed day in the week for rest and celebration is a true achievement. In biblical times the concerns for daily existence were in general much more significant than they are now. There was always work to be done, and people very often a struggled against deficiency and deprivation. Despite this, on one day of the week no work was permitted, and that day must be sacred. This entails that we stop and reflect on what life has given us. It is a day for gratitude, contemplation, and celebration. It is a day during which we must realize that there is more to life than our daily bread, such as beauty and generosity. It is a day in which we can become aware of our connection with the earth and with the Spirit. This does not have to be a solemn, gloomy affair, as some orthodox circles would lead us to believe. On the contrary, the Sabbath is a day of peace and relaxation, but also reflection, and to create the space for this, we can't be preoccupied with what we have to do. I personally attempt not to work for my daily bread on the Sabbath day. Study and spiritual exercises are all right, and can be combined quite well with celebration. The Sabbath is the day during which I nourish myself, the day that I stop for a moment to allow my soul to catch up with me.

It's also good to devote a little time during the Sabbath to doing nothing. How often do you actually do nothing—truly nothing—at all? Not even relaxing in front of the television, having a chat, or leafing through a magazine. Not even meditating, praying, or taking a nap. Only seeing and being, lying down, sitting, standing, or walking. It is fine to curb the flow of activities once in a while. The flow of thought may then also be able to stop and we can rediscover the peace in ourselves and be filled with the awe which life creates in us.

In the Western world, the Sabbath has degenerated to, on the one hand, a day of enforced and absolute rest and, on the other hand, a day filled with meaningless fun. There is of course nothing wrong with fun, but fun without spiritual content is very shallow. Instead of peace, boredom is possible and to keep it at bay we require increasingly more distractions. It's no wonder that in the Western world we have the tendency to throw the whole Sunday celebration business out of the window and to switch to a 24-hour economy.

This degeneration of the Sabbath threatens the most unique achievement of the human culture. Once more we are in danger of allowing Mammon to gain precedence over Spirit. In this context, it's sad to see that the most significant opposition to this is not based upon preserving space for spiritual development, but on the desire to maintain our established rights (like free time on Sunday or the right to be paid double for work on Sunday), which I consider to be just as much a defense of Mammon.

The solution isn't to create a free day in the week for all and sundry, a different day for everyone. If this were so then we would miss out on an opportunity to bundle our collective energy in a natural manner and to focus on celebration and the realization of spiritual values. In my mind, we'll need this energy to secure the yield from the Sabbath celebrations we require at an individual and global level.

In the Bible it is taken one step further (Leviticus 25). It states that every seventh year should be a Sabbath year. And after seven times seven years, the fiftieth year should be the Sabbath of the Sabbaths, a jubilee year. Once again, the meaning of these years is contemplation and reflection. The *Course in Miracles* states that a life without meaning incites fear. And that is the purpose of these moments—the rediscovery of the meaning of life in general and of our lives in particular. Currently, it isn't realistic—it wasn't in biblical times, either— not to work during these years. However, it is possible to insert a period of reflection every seven years to ask: where am I, what am I doing, do I give to life all that I can give, do I learn what I must learn and do I do what I must do? Am I actually achieving what I really desire to achieve? If you are open to your inner perceptions, then you will notice that your body and spirit do indeed require a period of reflection every seven years. If you skip it you will become bad tempered or lose your enthusiasm or zest for life. Your health can also be in danger. These periods are moments of re-orientation. If we don't focus enough attention on them, then all too often a crisis occurs, sometimes apparently caused by the situation, but nevertheless always caused by the manner in which we react to them.

All of this is even more important for the jubilee year. I am of the opinion that we, during or around our fiftieth year (3), should incorporate a long period of withdrawal from everyday life. One year would be ideal, but not everyone can do this. It's interesting that, in the biblical definition of the jubilee year, all of the slaves were sold or liberated and the land was also sold and returned to the original owner. "The land shall not be sold for ever: for the land is mine, for ye are strangers and sojourners with me" (Leviticus 25:23). In my mind the modern significance of this is to attach no value to possessions, as wealth does not rightfully belong to man but to life itself. The jubilee year is an opportunity to let go, to distance oneself and to renounce oneself and in this manner clear the way for the next level of spiritual development. In this context, I'd like to note that in Buddhism has a tradition in which a man who turns 50 leaves his family and his wife behind to subsequently devote himself to a life as a roaming monk—as the Buddha himself did—or to life in a monastic order in which spiritual exercises and meditation are central. An example of a modern manager who took a six-month jubilee can be found in the sidebar titled "God Stand by Me."

I would like to conclude this discussion of the Sabbath with a few words about retreats. In the Buddhist tradition, people periodically withdraw in a monastery for a retreat, a period of meditation and study, to achieve peace and to distance oneself from the maelstrom of life and in this way re-establish the contact with their inner silence and with the esteem for life. This tradition existed previously in Catholicism. It is my firm conviction that we must reinstate this custom. Many opportunities for this exist, from a lonely trek through the desert or the wilderness, to fully guided weeks in monasteries, or of all modern variants of these.

This means two things to the spiritual leader. First, a spiritual leader must give significant form to the Sabbath celebrations—each week and every seven years—in his or her own life. If he doesn't, he should consciously realize and ensure that he must in another manner—regularly, weekly, and daily—create an opportunity to contemplate and find silence. Second, if a spiritual leader participates in a public debate concerning Sunday rest or the sabbatical leave, he should ask himself: what do our soul and spirit actually require? The answer to this question will determine our standpoint and our practices regarding the celebration of the Sabbath.

THE BUDDHIST DHARMA

"Dhammam saranam gacchami (I seek refuge in the teachings)"—mantra

I have read much about Christianity. This is not the case with Buddhism. I have primarily acquired the knowledge I wish to share with you from the Buddhist practice (retreats). The Buddhist teachings, as I will explain here, are mainly based on what I learned from my master at that time, Sangharaksita, head of the Western Buddhist Order (4).

The Four Noble Truths

The basis of the Buddhist teachings *(dharma)* is formed by four theorems, the so-called "four noble truths." They are:

1. Pain and sorrow are inextricably bound to life. Suffering is a natural part of life. You could even say that life is suffering. Indeed, it can't be denied that pain and suffering are an integral part of our life. If it isn't a part of our own lives, then it's a part of the life surrounding us. We can shut this out to a certain extent, but in the end we will be troubled with it once more, at the very least in the form of a vague, half-conscious feeling of unease.

2. The cause of this pain and suffering is our desires. Whether we are aware of it or not, our needs, our desires, and our longings are the driving forces behind our actions and cause continual suffering. But our desires and needs can conflict. For example, we primarily want to take care of ourselves and to share with others as well. We want to

God Stand by Me

It is January 2, 1996, the year that I turn 50. Therefore, last year I completed seven times seven years of my life. This is to be my sabbatical year. I have worked for almost 14 years on the board of directors of KPMG Management, the last six years as executive chairman. I started my career with KPMG 25 years ago and have been employed for 28 years. Many years ago I had planned to take a period of contemplation before the age of 50. Of course in making this choice I allowed myself to be influenced by anthroposophist, Christian, and Kabalistic concepts about life phases. But I was much more influenced by what I saw around me. Many men in high positions reach their peak between the ages of 40 and 50. Some people experience an indefinable feeling that something's not right in their lives. On the outside everything is looks great, but on the inside they know they're entering a phase in which they will function with an energy which is completely different to what took them to the top. Those qualities were intelligence, the ability to multi-task, initiative, and determination. This was the energy of the nobleman, the strategist, or the crown prince who must fight to prove that he is the best so that he may become king.

Many managers do not understand that they must develop other qualities before their fiftieth birthday to remain creative and productive for the rest of their lives and to be an example to others.

It is the norm in many enterprises that the executives may, and in the majority of cases must, leave between their fifty-seventh and their sixtieth years. I have often seen men who were unaware of the fact that they were entering a new phase after the age of 50 adopt the attitude that "I've managed quite well for the first 50 years, I'll manage the last few years as well." Some of them desperately hung onto their acquisition of power, status, and money. Some experience a sort of despondency. What often happens is that one postpones everything that could provide a little happiness in life. They have—and I have, too—done this all their lives. They believe that real pleasure takes place during the weekend, and if not, then during vacation. But the true sabbatical never happens: reflection on life, which prevents life from being no more than survival. For I was able to survive: the survival of the fittest. Now I want to be fit for my future.

I stepped down as executive chairman, as chairman of our European consulting organization, and as a member of the international steering group that manages the KPMG global consulting activities. I will also shortly step down from the board of consultancy organizations (ROA). No more stripes on my shoulder. I'm confronted with the question, Do people respect me for who I am or what I am? But above all I must ask myself how I can prepare myself for the coming 15, 20, or 30 years of my career. Retirement is a strange phenomenon for people in creative and intellectual professions. Have you ever seen a poet who laid down his pen after his seventy-fifth birthday? Does a judge lose his wisdom after he retires? I do not wish to work an 80-hour week for the coming seven years and then fall into an abyss at the end of it, a social grave by way of preparation for the real grave. I want to live now.

During my whole life I have had difficulty with putting ora et labora—prayer and work—into practice. The time for contemplation, meditation, "learning" was too short in relation to the time I allocated to work. I want to give my work the quality of life. To this end I take the time for reflection, deepening, awareness. It will be about discovering Essence, that is, Being. The form is relatively unimportant; this normally follows when the essence is found or is approached. I am going to attempt to find the way from the inside to the outside. To this end it will be necessary that the ego which must mask the lack of self-respect be tracked down and where necessary to be resolved. I will have to examine my shadow in order to understand my projections.

Slaves regain their liberty in their fiftieth year. Will I manage to disband my slavery? God stand by me.

J.W. Ganzevoort, director, KPMG Management Consulting nv.

be prosperous and we also want to be liberated. We want to achieve a certain result and we also want to just do what we feel like doing. However, the root of the problem lies deeper. Each new fulfillment creates a new need. Therefore, we are never satisfied. And when a specific need is satisfied and we experience satisfaction or happiness, then we want to hold onto it or to continually equal it. But life changes and develops continually. New experiences will always be different to previous experiences. If we measure our previous examples against what we now experience, then we will always be disappointed. Nevertheless, it is in our nature to do so.

Also from this we can see that it at the very least contains many truths. Whether all of our pain comes from our desires can be disputed, but the reverse—that our desires are the cause of much suffering—as far as I am concerned is beyond dispute.

3. We can escape these troubles. This opportunity lies in achieving enlightenment, a state of understanding through which we can withdraw from the cycle of desire and pain. This therefore shows that Buddhism, just like Christianity, is a faith of salvation. In Buddhism, though, we aren't dependent on an external source of mercy, but rely

on ourselves. In addition, salvation can be found here on Earth, and in Buddhism this also means eternal life (5).

4. The way to enlightenment is via the eightfold path. The eightfold path in turn indicates how we can escape our troubles. The eightfold path consists of a number of phases and at the same time a number of activities. The interesting thing about the path is that you can, in principle, travel along it in both directions. It is recommended in practice that you exercise all steps simultaneously. The eightfold path also contains a specific system of ethics. I've found that the eightfold path is an exceptionally practical guide, whether you wish to achieve enlightenment or not. The principles of the eightfold path in themselves can be worth pursuing, both for ethical reasons and for effectiveness and efficiency. In my opinion the eightfold path is Buddhism's most important contribution to the spiritual leader.

The Eightfold Path

> Hear them!
> Form is no other than emptiness.
> Emptiness no other than form.
> —The Heart Sutra, translated by Philip Kapleau

The eightfold path is known as the noble eightfold path, which means that it is the regal path to ultimate insight. I will now proceed to successively deal with the eight steps. The use of the word "right" in the consecutive steps indicates that there is a "right," effective, and efficient manner of achieving enlightenment. Although the path in itself provides ethical guidelines, the word does not refer to "morally right." The word "perfect" could also be used.

1. The Right View

We have an incorrect view of life. We perceive the world of manifestation, but this isn't the true world. We do not see open-mindedly; we attach significance to everything in accordance with the way we are conditioned. The true world is a world of emptiness. The right view is to know this and to experience it.

There are four levels of emptiness.

1. Being free of conditioning. This means being free of opinion, judgment, and observation patterns. For example, we cannot see a tree for what it actually is because we always supplement the image of a tree with our previous experiences with trees and our thoughts concerning them. We associate all sorts of things with them, such as: a tree is wood, a tree provides shade, a tree has roots and cannot walk, a tree is beautiful, a tree is healthy, a tree is dying, a tree has no soul, a tree has no spirit, and much more. But we do not actually know if all of this is true. We do not see open-mindedly but our view is colored by our knowledge and experiences. Krishnamurti states: thinking is always old and this is also true of our views (this is also an important principle of *A Course in Miracles*).

The above can also apply to a chair, a person, or a situation. We are unaware that we always supplement, always think, and always observe according to a fixed pattern. We continually attach significance to things based upon our conditioning. The right view is free from our conditioning, free from the unreal.

2. The second level of emptiness is being free of our non-conditioned attitude, being free from what one could call reality, such as our peace, our sorrow, our pain, our fundamental requirements, or our body. If we experience that all of these actual affairs are in fact merely phenomena and that we are not our sorrow or our body, for example, then we experience emptiness (in chapter 8 I will provide a good exercise for this). The second level of emptiness is being free from the real, the experience of "nothingness" (6). The Buddhist calls this "nirvana," a state of complete rest and peace.

3. The third level of emptiness is freedom from the distinction between the conditioned and unconditioned, between the real and unreal. We realize that this distinction is merely a theory and although a theory is temporary, as in the previous levels, it can fulfill a useful function—after all, there is nothing more practical than a good theory—but a theory is of course never reality itself. It is a model of it. When this distinction has been omitted, there are no longer any

boundaries: everything and nothing becomes the same. This is what I previously referred to as awareness of unity.

4. The fourth level is the level at which we are also free of the concept of "emptiness" itself. The whole category of emptiness no longer holds any significance.

We will become aware that with this, the right view in essence has become the same as the right meditation (step 8). This supports the thought that the eightfold path can in principle be traveled in both directions. Another way of defining the right view is the preliminary acceptance of the four noble truths and the realization that the first two truths in particular are related to the fact that we are unable to experience emptiness. This entails that we recognize the suffering in our own lives and that we do not shut out the suffering around us. I say "preliminary acceptance," because according to Buddhism we can only experience the truths as being incontrovertible when we have won the ultimate insight.

My own experience shows that exercising the right view, in particular with the first two levels, creates a new distance, which can be extremely beneficial to our effectiveness. In the words of Edu Feltman, we no longer make ourselves interesting, and we become less interested, even disinterested. We no longer posses the attitude, with regard to reality, that we want to finish everything or change everything. The paradox is that through doing so we gain more influence. However, what is much more important is that we achieve inner peace and compassion through this. We become more "being" and less "doing." This is extremely beneficial to our energy management and our health.

2. The Right Intention

The right intention concerns the resolution to want to escape from suffering—not through denial, but by recognizing it and reacting to it with the fixed determination to win enlightenment. In the *hināyāna* ("small vehicle") Buddhism—the most ancient Buddhist teachings—

this means being fully focused on personal development toward enlightenment. In the subsequently developed *mahāyāna* ("great vehicle") Buddhism, this also means being open to the suffering of others. I will base the following on the latter school. The right intention means that you make a choice, that you mobilize and direct your energy precisely in the manner defined in chapter 2: by incorporating the aim of ultimate insight into your vision. It also entails that we no longer provide energy to what gets in the way of achieving this vision. This means giving up our desires and all that stems from them. This of course does not mean that we must suppress our needs and desires. They would only become stronger and, besides, it's impossible to do so. But this means we must continually ask ourselves: what's really at stake for me? In this case that must be the values and the mental attitude that lead to enlightenment. (Note that the choice is not dissimilar to what I defined as the choice between God and Mammon.)

And what are these values and state of mind? I'll list a few here.

• Generosity. This doesn't always have to relate to large things. It can also be admitting to being wrong, helping with the dishes, or whatever. It is an awareness that life is not about give and take, but about giving and receiving. A specific form of giving is hospitality, or opening the doors of your house.

• Love, best defined here as the wish that all is well with another person.

• Compassion. This can take on the form of tenderness, care, concern, or interest. It is the manner in which love manifests when another has pain or sorrow. It isn't pity, because pity involves a certain sense of superiority (feeling sorry for the other; unless you actually take it literally: *com-patior*, co-suffering). This is the opposite of indifference, which can be conceived as a form of cruelty.

• Selflessness. This is, in a way, at odds with the previous point, as concern entails bonding with another person and selflessness means completely letting the other person free. The apparent contrast between concern and selflessness can be bridged by realizing that you and the other person are in fact on, a crucial point for spiritual leadership. A possible aid is the realization that you and the other person are in the same boat.

• Joy. But also being happy with the joy, happiness, and prosperity of another.

• Patience. The realization that life cannot be molded to your wishes.

• Dedication to and faith in your own development process. This can also include the recognition of another person as a teacher, even though he or she isn't perfect (the judgment of this is for that matter not the right view). It also means recognition and respect for those who have been on the journey longer, and, in Buddhism, it also includes respect for those who dedicate their lives to the teachings.

There are a number of religious values and actions in Buddhism that are also included, such as:

• Honoring the Buddha as the honored guest in your life
• Seeking refuge in the Buddha, the teachings and the community
• Confessing mistakes (deviations from the path)
• Requesting assistance from the master: the realization that you require help

People in the West often do not consider these actions to be attractive, and too often a link is made to orthodox Christianity. But Buddhism places less of an emphasis on guilt and repercussions; it is, in fact, an optimistic religion. Many of the religious actions are also significant when they're detached from the specific religious context. Honoring then becomes honoring Life itself; seeking refuge then becomes seeking support by a master, friends, colleagues, books, etc.

These exercises do not work if you do them out of guilt or duty. They only work if you freely choose to do them. This results in the projection of a great exemplary effect and force. They are extremely stimulating and are almost contagious, although it cannot be denied that they are resisted by those who, often from subconscious pain, guilt, or fear, cling to their striving toward power or possession or position.

Exercising these values creates an atmosphere of care and respect, resulting in people being prepared to actually listen to each other and work together. The sidebar shows an example of how spiritual leadership can manifest itself in "managing values."

Managing Values

When I became executive chairman of KPMG Management Consulting I devoted all of my energy to formulating a strategy. Since I didn't want to slight my predecessor, I didn't create too many new policies. Therefore, forming the strategy wasn't difficult. Expanding on existing policies and initiating some new ideas was sufficient. The strategy paper was put together relatively quickly with just a little brainstorming one day at my desk and a few additional meetings. I was slightly disappointed, though, because I thought that laying a new course would be my greatest task ever.

After a year or so it became apparent that our structure had had its day—too many cutbacks, not enough synergy, many disputes about competence. Therefore I started to work on developing a new structure with my managers. This was a difficult task, as it involved significant internal displacements and intense talks with management. We devised a new personnel policy, developed a quality program, improved our management information, moved into a new building, and upgraded our international activities.

It became increasingly obvious that devising all of these things wasn't the work of genius; although the implementation of these plans was a little more difficult, the most pressing problem was influencing the behavior of the staff. No matter what we changed and improved, specific behaviors repeated: petty-mindedness, insufficient cooperation, clashing agendas, and competition. These problems cannot be resolved with procedures, structures, or systems. However, one thing I did know was that our organization was strongly focused on values. Matters such as integrity, discretion, trust, and collegiality were supplied right from the start. In the majority of cases these values were only implicit, due to the fact that they were too obvious. What you ought to do or not do was apparent from the behavior

---

of long-time employees. What's more, thanks to a merger in the mid-1980s, a book of commandments had been drawn up which contained a sort of code of conduct. In practice, not a lot was done with it. The only remaining option I could think of was to preach.

I did this enthusiastically. I tried to make use of every opportunity: lunch every month with the new members of staff, a monthly management lunch, Christmas drinks, a New Year's gathering, anniversaries, farewell speeches, and especially, my monthly column in the personnel magazine. I found my pieces quite moralizing, until a readers' poll showed that they were the most well-read and highly valued portion of the magazine. Soon afterwards, I asked a communications expert if my moralizing was acceptable. He said only: you are here for the morals! I truly understood what he was trying to say.

Of course, values must be reflected in the work, in the review and reward systems, and in the customer and assignment evaluations. But the most important thing is that managers continue to convey the message of our values.

There are some requirements. First, managers must—of course—behave consistently with what they say. They must walk the talk. This can only take place when values aren't commanded from on high, but when they arise from inner reflection. Values are mainly created through transference from parents and other people, but they also come from people who are developing their awareness, then evaluated and altered at the moment when the individual realizes that these values are right. Only then have they become an integral part of one's thinking and doing.

Another prerequisite is that deviating behavior is immediately dealt with. Not in the judgmental sense, but as an observation that doesn't cause defensiveness. The directness and immediacy of the observation is essential. Dealing with behavior and the underlying values in formal situations (such as in one's performance review) has less impact, as oftentimes the feeling is no longer present. If evaluation and reward are intertwined and at stake, true learning is difficult.

Let me conclude with one more thought: it's only logical and that you acquire new insights regarding values. But you must talk about it. Then you must show that you have learned. This makes life much easier for others.

J.W. Ganzevoort, director, KPMG Management Consulting nv.

3. *The Right Speech*

A man I know finds himself in a meeting room at the very edge of speech; he is approaching his moment of reckoning and he is looking for support from his fellow executives around the table. Strangely, at this moment, no one will look at him. The CEO is pacing up and down on the slate gray carpet. He has asked, in no uncertain terms, for their opinion of the plan he wants to put through. "I want to know what you all think about this," he demands, "on a scale of one to ten."

The CEO is testy; he makes it plain he wants everyone to say "ten," and damn whether they mean it or not. He is just plain tired, after all this time, of people resisting his ideas on the matter. He glares at them, he wants compliance. My friend thinks the plan is terrible and there is too much riding on this solitary ego; everyone in the company will lose by it. He is sure also, from talk he has heard, that half the other executives is the room think so too. As they go around the shamefaced table, the voices of those present sound alternatively over-confident, or brittle and edgy. Most say "ten," one courageous soul braves "nine and a half," and my friend is the last to go. He reaches his hand toward the flame, opens his palm against the heat, and suddenly falters; against everything he believes, he hears a mouse-like, faraway voice, his own, saying "ten."—David Whyte, *The Heart Aroused*

The right speech here complies with four conditions:
- It is honest
- It is loving
- It is supportive
- It promotes harmony

Honesty doesn't mean being careless or causing unnecessary pain. But it doesn't mean absolute honesty, either. On the contrary—honesty can mean that my truth doesn't have to be identical to yours. We can see things differently. In fact, that is the consequence of being honest and loving. However honest we are about our own truth, we still must show some consideration to other people; otherwise, communication is impossible. Paul Simon has a well-known song called "Tenderness," with the following lyrics: "What can I do? / You don't have to lie to me / but there is no tenderness beneath your honesty."

When there's no tenderness, I cannot hear you. That is why I plead for "mild honesty," which is completely different from disguising the truth or being vague.

One's intention determines whether or not the speech is right. If the intention is to be right or to score points, or to strengthen your own position, or even wishing to convince, motivate, or change another person, then this is not right speech. The intention can only be wanting to have contact with or to support the other person. This of course does not mean wanting to sort it out for them or wishing to comfort them too quickly. We all have our own responsibilities and have the right to our own feelings and to solve our own problems.

In David Whyte's example, there is no honesty whatsoever. But note that being completely honest isn't the only alternative. One could say something along the lines of: "I'm having a hard time giving an honest answer. I think you'd rather hear me agree with you and not hear what I actually think. And I also fear for my position if I give an honest answer." In this way communication is taken to another level. It could be supportive at a more essential level—provided the intention is pure. This example displays once more the importance of honesty and the courage to connect to one another, as I have already stated in the prologue.

In the following chapter I will return to the communication aspect of right speech.

4. The Right Action

When we in the West speak of right action, we initially think of actions that are morally correct. The Buddhist doesn't think in this manner. Right action is sensible, proficient action, and wrong action is action without insight. The words sensible and insight are of course defined in terms of the previous steps in the path. You could also say: right actions express the right view and the right intention.

There are five Buddhist precepts regarding the right action. The acceptance of these is a prerequisite for calling yourself a Buddhist. There is, however, a large variation in compulsory levels at which these precepts are imposed. For the majority of Buddhists, the precepts are more like recommendations that you would follow as a matter of course if you had won perfect insight. They can also help you win perfect insight.

These are the five precepts:

- To abstain from harming living creatures. Some Buddhists interpret this to mean that they must become vegetarian.
- To abstain from taking, or not giving. Life for a Buddhist is therefore not giving and taking, but giving and receiving. Note that this is also a precept against exploitation of humans and nature.
- To abstain from sexual misconduct. The Buddhist comprehends this as acts that are disrespectful toward others: rape, adultery, incest, and sexual acts that involve elements of violence. Marriage is monogamous, but divorce is certainly possible. Likewise, Buddhism makes no statement about birth control. Abortion and euthanasia are, according to some Buddhists, contradictory to the first precept.
- To abstain from speaking untruths. This is nothing more than a repetition of the third step in the eightfold path.
- To abstain from all forms of intoxication. The

assumption behind this is that alcohol and drugs—and for some Buddhists cigarettes and coffee—hinder the attainment of perfect insight. This results in total abstinence for some Buddhists, while for others this is merely a call for moderation.

In my experience these precepts form good guidelines for daily actions, not only because it feels good to live life according to them, but because they invite you to think about their meaning and significance, and with this your personal growth process. It goes without saying that they can only work if you opt for them freely and with flexibility.

An interesting question is why the precepts are formulated in such a negative manner. I think it's because they indicate limits. They are much like warnings to a small child about activities that endanger his physical and mental well-being. We have not yet reached spiritual adulthood, so therefore we must determine a number of clear limits for ourselves.

For leaders, the precepts also form a good guideline for the community. It is exceptionally fascinating to see how many of the ethical discussions in politics and business boil down to a discussion about these precepts. I admire an ethic, developed two and a half thousand years ago, that can be so useful in today's world of technology and rationality.

5. The Right Livelihood

Livelihood here means the manner in which we earn our money—or, more inclusive still, the manner in which we provide ourselves with the means to exist. Here I would also like to include domestic work. Volunteer work is, in my opinion, also included here, if we are simultaneously receiving social security (if not, then it is covered by the previous step in the path).

The previous steps are primarily about a transformation of ourselves. This step deals with a transformation of society. What is right livelihood?

A quote from Kahlil Gibran:

Work is love made visible.
And if you cannot work with love but only with distaste, it is better that you should leave your work and sit at the gate of the temple and take alms of those who work with joy.
For if you bake your bread with indifference, you bake a bitter bread that feeds but half man's hunger.
And if you grudge the crushing of the grapes, your grudge distills a poison in the wine.
And if you sing though as angels, and love not the singing, you muffle a man's ears to the voices of the day and the voices of the night.

When do you feel love for your work? I think when it complies with the following conditions.

1. If your work provides you with the opportunity to express and develop your talents. I think that it is our destiny to make our talents available to the world and to develop them in the world. Only then do we feel fulfilled and content. This is why we are often touched by good craftsmanship, whether it is by a carpenter, a musician, or a teacher. Craftsmanship, being the combination of great knowledge and proficiency with personal involvement, is always moving. Beauty is always expressed in it.

2. If your work contributes to making the world a little better, a little more perfect. You can only feel love for your work if you can feel love for the result of it. And you can only feel love for the result of it if you have the feeling that it is of significance to others, or society or the world as a whole.

It seems as if leaders, politicians, and managers continually forget that involvement and lasting intrinsic motivation can only be achieved with the right livelihood. Subsequently, books have been written on how to get people politically involved or motivated. I believe they're all nonsense. There is a lot of truth in the Christian saying that idleness is the parent of vice, but also in the statement that dull or destructive work can never be truly satisfying. Instead of being infinitely occupied with the issue of motivating people and getting them involved, we should focus more on how we can create a beneficial working situation for ourselves and, what's more, how we can stimulate others to do the same.

One last comment: "Thy shalt not live on bread and water alone." We touched on this principle in the dealings with the Sabbath, but it's also valid here. No matter how well the time for work is spent, it is important that time remains for spiritual development, for meditation or another form of spiritual practice. I'd also like to add that right livelihood is focused on the realization of non-material values. Another link with the previously defined Christian approach can be seen here: you cannot serve two masters, God and Mammon.

6. The Right Effort

The right effort means the continual striving toward perfect insight. As such it is part of each and every step of the eightfold path. But as a specific step it entails the prevention and elimination of thoughts that hinder the winning of insight and the advancement and preservation of the thoughts that promote this. It is comprised of the following aspects:

- The prevention of ineffective thoughts. The means to do this is the awareness of how your thoughts occur to you—as a result of what you observe, or from experience. This is therefore the function of the observant sentry (see also the following step of the path).
- The elimination of ineffective thoughts. Buddhism distinguishes five obstacles on the way to enlightenment, all of which can cause ineffective thinking. They are: desire (see the four noble truths); hate, which can result in persecution, violence, or war; restlessness and fear, which also result in haste and anxiety; inertia, laziness, and indolence; and doubt and

indecisiveness. But how can these obstacles be removed? There are four ways of doing this. 1. Consider the consequences of the obstacle. 2. Consider what the opposite is, focus your attention on it, and cultivate it: generosity instead of desire, love instead of hate and so on. 3. Pay no attention to it. 4. And if all of this does not help, find out where it originates, allow the associated feelings to be expressed (preferably to an understanding person), and then let go of them. Never suppress the obstacle, because then you supply it with energy. And if this doesn't help? Seek refuge with the Buddha, or what is known in the Christian doctrine as prayer.

• The advancement of effective thoughts. An outstanding means for this is meditation: concentrating and letting go of all thoughts and perceptions. Meditation can be defined as an intended exertion, but also as a spontaneous result of our spiritual life. In that case this is the eighth step of the path.

• Maintaining effective thoughts. It's very easy to slip back into a state of ineffectiveness. Therefore, discipline and regularity are required; you can choose to focus on what you want at a set time and to affirm the effective thoughts.

7. The Right Attention

"Most of us walk through life inattentively, reacting unthinkingly according to the environment in which we have been brought up, and such reactions create only further bondage, further conditioning, but the moment you give your total attention to your conditioning you will see that you are free from the past completely, that it falls away from you naturally."—J. Krishnamurti, *Freedom from the Unknown*

We are now dealing with one of the core concepts of Buddhism: mindfulness. Mindfulness is the total awareness of what is happening now, what the issues are now. The absence of mindfulness comes from forgetfulness, absent-mindedness, mistakes and poor concentration. In organizations this represents inefficiency and a lack of quality. At an individual level this represents a stagnation of spiritual development. Attention always results in awareness at the following levels:

1. Awareness at a spiritual level. This means truly seeing things instead of projecting our conditioning on them (see also the right view).

2. Self-awareness. This means:
   - Awareness of our bodies, posture, and movements, as well as what is taking place inside our bodies. In order to become aware of this we must slow down the pace of life and stop and think every now and again. In this context, it is interesting to compare a Japanese tea drinking ceremony with a Dutch business lunch, or a morning meditation with driving through traffic.
   - Being aware of (all) our feelings. This also requires slowing down and becoming introspective.
   - Being aware of (all) our thoughts. This doesn't mean being caught up in our thoughts, but taking the time to examine our thoughts.

3. Awareness of other(s). This means actually seeing the other person (not sticking our perception on the him or her), truly listening (listening with your heart), and being truly open. I will return to this in the next chapter.

4. Awareness of God or the Buddha. If we do not directly experience this in ourselves, then it helps to remember and reflect on the words and deeds of the Buddha or Jesus. A more direct way is experiencing emptiness, the first step of the path.

I find this step of the eightfold path to be one of the most essential and practical steps. It requires that you commit yourself to living at the highest possible level of awareness, an attitude of continual researching and observing without allowing it to be affected by your preconditioned thinking.

In practice, this step results in insight and wisdom. It appears that, in practice, it is easier to view another with preconditions than to observe with no prejudice and total acceptance: first yourself and then another. The leader's task is to lead the way in this and to supply feedback in an open manner. I will deal with the last point in the following chapter.

This step doesn't request exclusively intellectual decisions; it requires complete effort. To once again quote Krishnamurti: "If you see the danger of your conditioning merely as an intellectual concept, you will never do anything about it. In seeing a danger as a mere idea there is a conflict between the idea and action and that conflict takes away your energy. It is only when you see the conditioning and the danger of it immediately, and as you would see a precipice, that you act. So seeing is acting."

The motivation behind this step is being alarmed about yourself, others, and what we are doing. This is an important motivation which, as a rule, is hidden behind spiritual leadership.

In the example on the next page, Gerda Voorbij defines how she views spiritual leadership in practice. We can recognize various steps of the eightfold path in the elements she states, namely, the right intention, the right speech, the right effort, and the right attention.

8. The Right Being

The Buddhist understands this as the state of samadhi, a term older than Buddhism itself and one that even occurs in the Vedic tradition, which is the basis for Hinduism. The literal meaning of the right being is the perfect state of being. Buddhism has less to say about what this is than the way toward attaining it. The Buddhist claims that the perfect state of being, just as with the Way in chapter 3, cannot be grasped with words. You can only know what it is when you have experienced it. This seems obvious. For example, we can only know what pain or an orgasm is after we have experienced that sensation. Talking about such things beforehand merely provides a vague indication.

This is also the case with samadhi. Nevertheless, a number of elements can be identified.

Does the Spiritual Leader Do Things Differently?

The essence of spiritual leadership is its inner approach. A spiritual leader does not do other things, he does the same things but with a different inner approach. But what is that? The true spiritual leader will find it difficult to answer this question, simply because he is the way he is and does not believe that he does things differently. In my encounters with people in whom I recognize aspects of spiritual leadership the following qualities strike me:

- Mindfulness: they give me the impression that they are giving me 100 percent of their attention, even at unannounced moments.
- Transparency: conversations are always transparent—open, honest, free.
- Discipline: these leaders continue to study, meditate, and adhere to their practices.

Because of these qualities, they seem confident and they don't make me feel dependent. Therefore, less energy is wasted on fear, doubt, or lack of clarity.

Spiritual leadership elevates people to what they really are and is decidedly efficient and effective. And above all it makes people happy.

Gerda Voorbij, former executive director, Voorbij Groep, Wilnis, director Kikai bv.

First, samadhi has the experience of the void of voids, as defined in the right view. Form is a void, void is form, to once more quote the *Heart Sutra*. Samadhi corresponds with nirvana: a state of nothingness. Nothing and everything are in fact the same.

Second, samadhi is a direct experience with a connection to the All, the Way, the divine. We feel that we are a part of God, as Meister Eckart would express it. We are the Buddha, as the Zen Buddhist would say. We are one with the Way, as the Taoist would put it. Samadhi is, in short, the most essential form of awareness of unity so clearly experienced that we are now certain that everything and everyone is one entity. Because if we are one with the All, then everyone else is too, and that means that everyone else is also one with us. This is known as perfect or ultimate insight or enlightenment. When we've attained this state, we no longer have to convince ourselves or anyone else. We express this awareness naturally through our words, our silence, and our deeds.

Samadhi is also a state of inner peace and tranquility. We no longer have to go anywhere; we are already there. This is often paired with a state of bliss. In some traditions this bliss is considered to be the essence of samadhi, but yet it is not. We can achieve this bliss without achieving total samadhi in the strict sense. This could be called euphoria or ecstasy, which can be achieved through mantras or other forms of concentration or contemplation, and even through the use of some drugs. According to some, this is a good step on the way to total samadhi, and according to others it isn't, because we hold on to the feeling of utter bliss, which could hinder the perfect insight.

With this we have reached the end of the eightfold path, a path that gives meaning to our existence and creates excitement and inspiration. As I stated, if we could agree on the importance of our spiritual development, many motivational and quality problems would be resolved. This of course results in the question of how we, if we choose to do so, can influence others without becoming annoying. In my opinion there are two solutions to this.

1. Practice what you preach (walk your talk). We can only urge others to become spiritually developed if we do this in our own lives.

2. Create open communication.

We have seen that the Buddhist teachings along with Christianity provide clear indications for our spiritual development. It advances awareness of unity, vision, honesty, and courage and as such is helpful for the spiritual leader. Your background and personality will influence which tradition appeals to you more. I'd like to emphasize that the traditional teachings are more practical than we think and that achieving spiritual leadership without the assistance of an existing spiritual approach is not so easy. It is as if you have to re-invent the wheel—it isn't impossible, but it's inefficient. On the other hand, knowledgeable readers will realize that my interpretation of the teachings is very personal, and that is exactly what I recommend: use the tradition, but not as a fossilized dogma or ritual. Allow yourself to be inspired through it, but integrate the traditions with your own personal religion. There is nothing as practical as a good theory and I'm filled with respect and admiration when I see how good these centuries-old theories are, even if we do so little with them. If we were to take these theories more seriously, then I believe that many everyday problems would be resolved at last—at micro-, meso-, and macro-levels.

THE SEVEN CHAKRAS

The chakra theory originates from the Indian yoga tradition, which is considerably older than the *Bhagavad-Gita* (circa 400 BC), the most ancient written tradition that includes a definition of the yoga concepts.

The chakra theory posits that there are seven energy centers in our body, sort of energy intersections, each of which controls a part of our mental and physical life. The term chakra originates from Sanskrit and literally means wheel or disc. These centers function at birth (or even prior to it in the womb), but develop during our lives. According to theosophy and anthrosophy this occurs in periods of seven years. Each seven-year period is controlled by the development of a chakra. Moreover, through predisposition or through specific occurrences a chakra can become more or less blocked. Blocking results in a disruption in the functions controlled by this chakra. Up until recently the chakra teachings were no more than theory, but that's beginning to change. Now, what was accepted in the Eastern and Western mystics for centuries—namely that compaction of energy occurs at seven locations in our body, concentrations of thermal and electro-magnetic energy—can be proven. This however proves nothing about the relationship between these concentrations and the functions of our organism.

As far as this is concerned we must primarily rely on the intuitive ancient tradition. The following is primarily based on Alice Bailey, quoted by Lansdowe, on Peter Goldman's teachings, and on my own personal experience. I present the teachings of the chakras, because these teachings can support your own personal spiritual development and the development of yourself as a spiritual leader. A concise overview of the seven chakras is given below, the most important psychological functions they control, and the sensitive age period for each chakra in which they undergo an additional development.

The root chakra. This is located at the base of the spinal column, or also in the perineum (although according to some authors the chakras are located just outside the body). This chakra controls our relationship with the physical surroundings—primarily the earth and nature and the world of objects, but later it encompasses the world of money, possessions, and position. The root chakra is focused on survival and on safety, earthiness, strength, and certainty. It develops mainly between birth and age seven (when you learn to live in the world) and between the ages of 28 and 35 (the period of career and making a family, when you conquer a position in the world) (7).

The spleen chakra. This is located in the lower abdomen, roughly four fingers below the navel, at the back of the body. This is the chakra of our feminine and masculine identity and also the chakra from which we experience our individual power (literally: indivisible, whole; derived from the Latin *dividere*: separate). This chakra could also be called the core of our being; it's where the life energy is collected. When we act from this center we experience autonomy and a natural self-confidence but also softness, sensitivity, and tenderness. The spleen chakra is the center of our yin energy, our feminine sexual energy. Together with the root chakra this controls the female sexual activity. This center is also developed in the initial seven years of life and subsequently in the period between the ages of 14 and 21; for females also in the period between the age seven and 14.

The solar plexus chakra. The solar plexus chakra is a nerve matrix at the level of the stomach. The chakra is located behind this, at the back of the body. The solar plexus chakra is the foundation of the basic emotions such as rage, sorrow, pleasure, and desire. It also controls our intellectual development. Furthermore it is the foundation of the yang energy, our masculine sexual energy. When functioning from this system we experience passion and fanaticism, but also intellectual clarity and pureness of sensation. Together with the root chakra, this controls sexual activity in men. This chakra primarily develops between the ages of seven and 21.

The heart chakra. As the name states, this chakra is located at the level of the heart, at the back of the body. It is the chakra of connecting with and being involved with others. It is also the chakra of attachment (inability to let go). It can also be the chakra of fanaticism, but on the other hand it is also the chakra of motivation. Furthermore, the heart chakra is the foundation of all feelings that deal with relationships, such as affection, care, love, hate, jealousy, and compassion. Together with the root chakra it is the foundation of competition. A well-functioning heart chakra represents a rich emotional life. It develops in particular between the ages of four and eight, between 14 and 21, and between 35 and 42. (In practice this often goes amiss with men in today's society, which results in a midlife crisis.)

The throat chakra. This is situated behind the throat, at the back of the body. It is the chakra of vision and creative energy. It is the chakra which transforms a reproductive force (such as reproduction) into a productive force. Furthermore, it is the chakra of communication. If it functions well, we feel productive, creative, and capable of conveying our ideas to others. It develops during the initial seven years of life and then once more between the ages of 42 and 49.

The forehead (third eye) chakra. This is the only chakra located on the front of the body: just above the eyes (the third eye). It is the chakra of intuition and telepathy or parapsychological capabilities. It is the chakra of wisdom. It often develops early in various life phases, but also between the ages of 49 and 56.

The crown chakra. This chakra is often located above the head, at the spot where a baby has its fontanel (think of a saint's halo). It is thought that the life energy (or the soul) enters the body here and exits again at death. This is the chakra of universal love, cosmic awareness, and perfect, final insight. This chakra develops at the end of one's life, but there are also sensitive periods during childhood, puberty, and adolescence.

This is of course a very general description of the seven chakras. Development can take a different course for each individual. However, a basic understanding of and sensitivity to the development of our chakra can assist us in not striving toward things for which we are not yet ready. In this way we avoid striving to become holy before it is our time. "Man with head in the clouds cannot keep feet on the ground unless he is very big man," according to the ancient Chinese proverb. On the other hand, we can ascertain which chakras are blocked by closely examining what we lack in our lives regarding our emotions and perceptions. If you wish to learn more, there are many books that are devoted to the chakras. Generally, yoga exercises support the development and opening of chakras and there are specific exercises for specific chakras. Taoist and Hindu exercises can also help.

I have benefited from a series of five Tibetan exercises, which, to me, combine the bioenergetics developed in the West, condition exercises, and yoga (see Kelder).

In this context, I must add a few words about testing and initiation (inauguration). We have just seen that personal development takes place in phases. The transfer from one phase to the next does not always occur without difficulty. Known examples of this are the sexual awakening at around 14 years (concerning in particular the spleen chakra and the solar plexus chakra), the midlife turning point around the age of 42 (the heart and throat chakras), and the spiritual awakening at around the age of 56 (the forehead and crown chakras). These are periods of uncertainty and possible crisis. Existing behavioral patterns are no longer sufficient and new forms have not yet presented themselves. These are also periods in which specific chakras begin developing, in particular in connection with each other. This often occurs in fits and starts, which can result in a temporary imbalance in the organism, which manifests in physical symptoms such as depressive feelings.

People who are attuned to nature often have special initiation rituals around these periods. There are always two phases—a test phase and a ritual phase—in which the actual initiation takes place. The existence of these customs eases the transition, even if it is merely to help make a difficult situation comprehensible. The collective character of these rituals also summons the supportive energy from the community. The rituals are often linked to seasons, allowing advantageous circumstances to be created for the transition.

These days, we often have to do this without such collective rituals. This doesn't mean that personal growth doesn't turn into a test, but life itself puts us to the test. This can take on the form of a complete inner process (such as feelings of doubt, uncertainty, fear, or emptiness), or it can manifest itself through outer structures that crumble. For example, we are fired or we get into a rut in our relationships (compare also Wessel Ganzevoort's contribution earlier in this chapter). It helps to recognize this process so that we identify what is wrong and are no more anxious than is necessary (8). If we get through the test, then we are ready for the initiation.

I would like to conclude this section by linking the chakras with the functions of spiritual leadership.

- The root chakra: being able to perceive reality, being realistic, being concerned with the interest of individuals (safety, security), wanting to achieve a personal concrete and tangible result, and aggression.
- The spleen chakra: natural self-confidence and faith in oneself, understanding the necessity of independence and autonomy, the ability to delegate, perception of the feminine (receiving, tenderness, good atmosphere), and the ability to be a good listener.
- The solar plexus chakra: being open to emotions, being analytical, and having passion and zeal.
- The heart chakra: care and personal attention to others, sensitivity to group processes, development of good relationships, and attunement to group results.
- The throat chakra: vision, creativity, imagination, and communication.
- The forehead chakra: intuition, wisdom, and the ability to allow oneself to be inspired.
- The crown chakra: love and awareness of unity.

This summary can be used to indicate where your strengths lie and where the gaps are. Then you can examine the gaps to determine whether they can be altered and also if they are part of your current life phase. You can also find out who in your workplace is connected to certain chakra abilities and if they are able to express them. Think back to the characters from *Watership Down*. The main source of the power of the group was that each member of the group fulfilled his or her own leadership function. Bigwig acted mainly from his root chakra, the solar plexus chakra, and, later, from the heart chakra; Blackberry from the solar plexus and the throat chakras; Fiver from the forehead chakra; and Hazel from the spleen and heart chakras, and, later, the crown chakra. You can carry out a similar exercise with the members of your own work group, and also discover which functions are being insufficiently fulfilled in your team.

With this I have reached the end of the chapter about the teachings. I would now like to now turn to the third source the spiritual leader can draw upon (besides the Buddha and dharma): the community (the sangha).

CHAPTER 7

The Community

MOTTO: THE SPIRITUAL LEADER ALLOWS HIMSELF TO BE
NOURISHED BY THE SPIRITUAL COMMUNITY WITH THE AID
OF OPEN COMMUNICATION.

"Most conflict is a cry for intimacy. Go for the intimacy."
—Danaan Parry

THE NEED TO BE A MEMBER OF A GROUP IS MILLIONS OF
years old. As we all know, we are descended from the apes, and apes
have been living in groups for 20 million years. Our forefathers,
humans and anthropoids, have been doing so for a million years. The
problem with modern groups is that they are either too large or too
small. The family unit is the most significant source of group mem-
bership. We are all aware that the family is, besides being a place of
safety and security, also a source of frustration and neurosis.
Furthermore, the family is becomingly increasingly dysfunctional,
partially because we allow economic situations to take control—we
aren't prepared to scale down our consumption level—and partially
because it no longer seems to be the place where we can develop into
liberated and responsible human beings. It no longer fulfills our actual needs.

All sorts of groups try to fill in for the family unit: the clique, the
gang, the school, the church, the association, the corporation, and the
state. There are a number of reasons as to why none of these groups
fulfill our fundamental group requirements. One main reason is that
many of these groups are too large: we don't know all of the members.
Another fundamental reason is that the objectives of many of these
groups are not exactly in keeping with our fundamental requirements.

But what do we need from our community? I will deal with this below, as well as why groups are always a source of insecurity and can only function well when they are also a spiritual community; or at any rate are part of a spiritual community. After exploring my definition of a spiritual community, I'll then explain why communication is the best way to transform a group into a spiritual community. And finally, I will deal with a specific practical issue, namely that of public participation and democracy.

THE GROUP AND GROUP NEEDS

There are three fundamental needs that we attempt to satisfy within a group:

1. The need to belong, which is a profound, almost instinctive need. We have all experienced a member of a group being shut out (this often takes place in the classroom). This is an emotional experience, and one of the worst things that can happen to a child. If we witness it we feel compassion, but if we don't offer our help—and we often don't have the courage to do it because we're afraid we'll also become outcasts—we feel guilty. We then do everything in our power to ensure that we are not shut out ourselves. We conform, typically when non-conformist actions will endanger our position.

Group experiments have been carried out that indicate just how strong the conformist force really is. Salomon Asch's experiment is renowned. In it, a group is shown two lines, A and B, and A is slightly longer than B. Only one member of the group is a guinea pig, while the others are in on the plot. If all of the group members say that B is longer than A, then more often than not the guinea pig conforms to the majority. But no matter what he says, he will fall prey to great inner stress and confusion.

We must not imagine being shut out as always being a physical thing. In society, in corporations, and in work teams, we have all experienced a member of the group being physically tolerated, but in fact ignored. Does this sound familiar?

Identifying the motivation behind this action is an interesting question. Paradoxically, it's always the—often subconscious—fear of being shut out oneself, a fear which may be based on previous experiences (for example, within the family). It may also be a bid to create unity and at least temporary security. By focusing on a common enemy—the group member who has been shut out, the scapegoat—the remaining members can close ranks more tightly. However, the price is high: fear also creeps in alongside the apparent unity as the members realize that what's happening to the scapegoat now can happen to them tomorrow. Trust disappears and conformism increases. A group like this isn't a good breeding ground for creativity and cooperation.

2. The need for autonomy. We all like to be, to a certain extent, the master of our lives. We want a certain freedom and room to play. But this is of little use when we have no one to play with. We also want to have a certain power in a group situation and don't want to receive orders about how to act.

This need for autonomy often takes on the form of competition. This need for competition and autonomy is also millions of years old and may be related to hormones. There is a pecking order in almost every social group of animals or humans. This need is also a source of insecurity. If you're at the top of the pecking order, sooner or later you can be knocked off your throne. Lower down the pecking order the danger is that we lose our freedom—not so much physical freedom, but intellectual freedom. Are we able to determine our own working tempo, our own contribution, our own style, and our own friendships and relationships?

3. The need for intimacy. The word intimacy is almost a taboo. Nevertheless, it represents our needs more precisely than the words "personal contact." I understand intimacy as soul-to-soul connection, from core to core. We desire this strongly; we cannot do without it, but at the same time we are scared to death of it because intimacy means openness and surrender, openness toward each other and also toward our own inner world.

If we aren't open to ourselves, then we can't be open to someone else. If we are unable to fully express ourselves we'll be unable to fully receive or surrender to the other person. Surrender means trusting ourselves, because when it happens we never know what will occur.

Intimacy leads to unpredictability—especially regarding relationships and experience. In that sense it is similar to passion, the energy behind our motivation. We tend to control it, just because we don't like its unpredictability. However, without intimacy and passion our lives become empty and unfulfilled. We then become discontented, which manifests in overt or veiled destructiveness.

As a reaction to our ambivalent attitude towards intimacy, a group often creates a sort of intimacy. This often manifests as gossip, talk in the hallways, a sort of worked-up feeling of us vs. them, being falsely "nice" and over-friendly to each other (not daring to tell each other the truth). It appears that our need for intimacy is satisfied at no risk, but that is a fake. This form of intimacy is in no way whatsoever true connection. Instead, it's inadequacy posing as intimacy, which actually stimulates fear and aggression, if not directly, then at least indirectly.

We attempt to satisfy certain fundamental needs within a group. William Schutz has placed these needs in a diagram (see figure 7.1; group assumptions are the answers provided by the group to the questions below).

In the diagram, In-Out relates to the need to belong, Up and Down to the need for autonomy and power, and Nearby-Far Away to the need for intimacy.

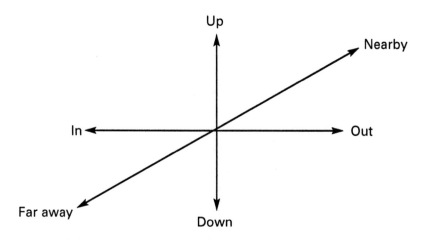

Figure 7.1 Group Assumptions (W.G. Schutz)

A group is safe only if all the members are in agreement about all three dimensions, in the sense that there is clarity about and a general approval of the answers to the following questions:

1. Who belongs to the group?
2. Who is in charge here?
3. How personally do we interact with each other?

Approval must come from every member of the group and be given with heart and soul, although it doesn't have to be explicit. If this requirement is not met—and it usually isn't—the group is unsafe and it does not fulfill our needs. Consequently, it is also not as effective and creative as it could be. In this case, no synergy or a limited synergy occurs, meaning that the added value of the group does not exceed that of the individual. Often the group has all sorts of damaging effects, such as a reduced productivity. In the 1930s, George Homans' research found that if a group sets strict group values as an unnatural means to create group coherence, these values can run counter to the individual's, group's or organization's interests. Something similar to this can be seen in negotiation processes between groups and in labor disputes.

A lasting fulfillment of our group needs can only be developed in groups with a spiritual core. In order to explain this more specifically, I will now deal with the concept of spiritual community.

The Spiritual Community

A spiritual community is a group with four specific characteristics.

1. There is a common purpose; if not explicitly spiritual then it possesses a spiritual aspect. Common in this context means that the purpose is shared by all the members of the group. Although it is a group purpose, everyone considers it as being his or her personal purpose, too. In other words: the purpose is based on a vision and the common purpose is based on a common vision.

A spiritual aim is defined as: the spiritual development of the members of the group and of the non-group members, and the expression of the insights thus achieved in daily practice. There can also be other purposes, such as communal activities, caring for the members, the development of policy, the production of goods, or providing services, but the spiritual aspects must always be an explicit or implicit part of the objective. A spiritual community is a group whose members have, as a common vision, a form of awareness of unity.

2. The members of the group live as consciously and independently as possible. They strive toward knowing themselves and acquiring an understanding of their behavior and interactions with one another. They strive toward a life that is as mindful as possible. This naturally requires courage and honesty. Shankarashita once used this definition: a spiritual community comprises individuals; whether the members are individual or not determines whether the group is a spiritual community or not.

This implicitly means that a spiritual community cannot develop between people who:
- Believe that their current personality cannot be changed ("That's just the way I am")
- Who perceive their conditioning as being all-important
- Are not prepared to connect to the spiritual purpose of the group; they are usually skeptics
- Are dependent on moral rules and perceive the rules themselves as an objective instead of a means.

3. There is a culture of open dialogue in the group. This entails that breakdowns in communication are noticed immediately and discussed (meta-communication). I will deal with this in more detail in the following section.

This entails further that the group members refer to "I" when they talk about themselves and not "you," "we," or "one." It is especially fatal if a group refers to "we" when there is no "we." That is false intimacy. "We"—a sense of unity and solidarity—can only develop if the members of the group have the courage to speak for themselves and not to mask any possible disagreements. In a spiritual community "I" precedes "we" and not the reverse.

4. The dominant culture in the group is one of service to others. This entails supporting one another in the purposes stated in the above in points 1 and 2, with loving confrontation and feedback

(which I'll discuss shortly). It also encompasses care for each other's spiritual and physical well-being. Ultimately, service within the group automatically results in service to the outside world. Nevertheless, each person has his or her own responsibilities.

In a spiritual community, the values of awareness of unity, vision, and honesty are central. These are also the values required for spiritual leadership. This means that leadership in a spiritual community can only be spiritual leadership.

In this context, it must be stated that a spiritual community is not a sect. As a rule a sect is in no way a spiritual community, nor are the majority of modern churches. In this sort of situation, authoritarian leadership is normally present, which results in dependent individuals, the supremacy of moral regulations, and defensive communication. A spiritual community can overlap the group in which it is formed, or can form the core of a larger group (1).

Groups are necessary. But to prevent groups' damaging effects—which lead to inefficiency, poor quality, and destruction—there must be a spiritual core. A leader can personify this core. But a spiritual core group—a community—is stronger. This community can gradually add more members.

I discussed this process in connection to *Watership Down*. The spiritual core was initially limited to Hazel and Fiver. However, new members were included gradually—Blackberry, Holly, Bigwig, Bluebell, Silver, Hyzenthlay, and others. Their spiritual purpose was both the personal development of the members and the creation of a society based on love instead of conflict and fear.

More companies now realize that you cannot live on bread alone—or profit. This applies not to individuals but also to the company as a whole. If spiritual development isn't incorporated into the company practice and if spiritual values are not linked to the company objective or the product, then lasting enthusiasm and motivation within the company are impossible. What we're now seeing is that some companies bring in spiritual activities to improve efficiency and quality, which explains the increasing interest in ethics in business. However, this doesn't mean that there is a collective spiritual purpose. Good examples of this include McDonald's and Shell, which were threatened by the anti-racism and environmental movements, and reacted with ethical and mission statements.

We can only promote spiritual community development if we truly want to do so. We must opt for the values of the community—unity, openness, independence, care, honesty, and courage—because we consider life as being not worth the effort without them. There are also examples of this in business life: The Body Shop, Chemlawn (VS), or Semco (Brazil). Companies in the Netherlands are also taking steps in this direction; these include Van Melle, SHV, and Centraal Beheer, although they would not portray themselves in this manner. This of course does not mean that these companies are "good" and that the others are "wrong." This is in fact irrelevant. Every company can make mistakes or be temporarily very successful, but this is irrelevant, too. I believe that companies that strive toward being a spiritual working community out of their own accord contribute more toward the welfare of their staff and society as a whole. It's highly probable that this also means that these companies are engaged in developing a more sustainable form of organization and manufacturing.

But how do we create such community? First, by incorporating the image and concept of this community into our personal vision. An explanation of how to do this will be given in chapter 9. Second, through stimulating self inquiry. In doing so we promote the condition stated above under point 2 (autonomy) and a strong longing for the spiritual community will develop organically. I will deal with this more thoroughly in the following chapter. Third, we can promote the development of this community through the introduction of transitional rituals. For example, applying the chakra idea to spiritual leadership functions. Last, we can do this through open communication. My interpretation of this is explained in the following section.

The example below is a good illustration of these points, especially the dinner with the partners as the transitional ritual.

Avant la Lettre

"I never knew I had it in me."—Ollie B. Bommel/Marten Toonder

It all started quite innocently.

Around 35 years ago, after I had been partner in an extensively developed pension and insurance consultancy firm, I received an inner sign that the time had come for me to stop rushing. It was time to seek my own truth. I roamed Europe, stopping every so often in the Netherlands to fulfill my family duties and to earn enough through freelance work to stay alive.

And then I got a new start in the business world. I wanted to do things differently after these sabbatical years. I had gained the vague idea that an enterprise could be more than just an institution in which the owner rounded up people to earn money. It could be more like a sort of community of people who work together in a business context, but where production, turnover, and profit are no longer the actual objectives. The business could be a means to grow together and individually toward an optimal personal development.

But how could this be achieved? I knew that it had something to do with true concern for one another and also unity. And I needed help to do this.

Take note: this was in the beginning of the 1970s and there was as yet no New Age or training culture. Therefore, I ended up at a traditional psycho-technical laboratory. I was lucky. The man I had a meeting with, understood exactly what I meant. He told me that he couldn't help me, but referred me to the "Center" in Amsterdam: a center for "personal growth." This was very innovative in the Netherlands at the time. A staff member there listened attentively to my idea about doing something together with "my" people—I had, in the meantime, started my own business which had started to grow and flourish. This staff member said: "A wonderful idea; however, I think that you have to do something about your own personal growth first.

Lesson #1: I had to work on myself first, because what we refer to as spiritual leadership begins with ourselves.

In this situation, a true Rotterdammer like myself, would say: "well, let's do it then." I immediately enrolled in a three-month learning course to learn about myself. This meant gatherings for group discussions and exercises each weekend and a few evenings per week for the duration of three months. Then I learned lesson #2. Working on your personal growth and development is an ongoing, lifelong process. This often means that in the initial years one requires assistance from others in a group form or with the support from experts in the field, until you come to terms with what you're doing and are able to manage the ongoing learning process alone.

A few years later, while I was on a flight to London to participate in a training group, I met a fellow traveler who had the same aim. We started talking and thus began a friendship with the author of this book, in which we have regularly stimulated one another with working-on-yourself ups and downs.

Thus, I am not alone. Lesson #3: Once you have made the decision to work on yourself and on leadership, then you will certainly meet someone else along the way with whom you can hang around: support and be supported, confront and be confronted, laugh and cry. Just as you find leaders you also find co-students.

But how did I map out my business policy further based on this ideal? In all honesty, I didn't. Only later did I come to realize that this is in accordance with the law of manifestation. I had a credo: Business is not in the first place about production, sales, or profit; business is in the first place about people. And that manifested itself through the powers of the law of manifestation. A few of the characteristics:

1. The leadership structure in our business was horizontal. This meant, among other things, that everyone was involved in policy meetings one way or another. This created continual total openness regarding financial and other matters. This openness resulted in hidden conflicts being rapidly brought to light so that they could be resolved. For those who believe that a horizontal structure is only possible in small enterprises: read: P Fentener van Vlissingen: Ondernemers zijn Ezels ("Entrepeneurs are donkeys," unfortunately not translated).

2. The policy of openness and involvement resulted in the salary scale not becoming the determining factor for motivation and input, but the mutual bond and the team spirit instead. One of the team members who had at one point refused to take on another job elsewhere for a higher salary said: "it's all so much more human here."

3. As a result of the involvement of the staff members we developed such a good product and reputation that actively seeking out customers was no longer necessary. Of course not everything was perfect, but almost everyone in the company was aware that something unusual was happening. I overheard one of the older staff members saying to a colleague: "I have had a lot of employers but I never knew that a business could be managed in this way." At this point, I became aware for the first time that I was engaged in a new type of leadership. Indeed: "I never knew that I had it in me."

4. External assistance also played a significant role. Four or five years after I had visited the "Center" for the first time, we were ready for a workshop dedicated to personal growth. I had laid down the condition that this workshop could only take place if everyone was prepared to participate in it. Now we were ready. It was a fantastic experience that intensified the mutual bond. The concluding dinner, which the partners were also invited to, was a commemorative occasion. And once more I learned a few lessons:

Do not concern yourself with whether they are "ready for it." Each individual gets what is in it for him or her. Nothing more, nothing less.

No true miracles take place in such a workshop [that remains to be seen—EvP], but the effect is usually radical. For some, it had an influence on their life for a long time afterwards and genuinely enriched their lives, also their private lives. For others the workshop was just a very special, unique event; a wonderful memory later on; nothing more, nothing less. [Nevertheless, the seed has been sown, who knows when it will germinate?—EvP]

If you were to ask me: what specific action did you take, and can you provide a few examples of how your decision-making was affected in certain situations through that "spiritual" thing? I may be able to do that, but I don't want to, that isn't what spiritual leadership is all about. It is more that the underlying conviction plays a role in the daily contact with the people around you and always influences the outcome of this contact. This book is more about spiritual leadership as a conscious choice, than a book which supplies a formula for managing to deal with that difficult dismissal, or the staff member who expects a promotion, but isn't ready for it. A manager who has a little decency, or sense, will handle situations such as these with care.

I have often thought: what a shame that only after I had withdrawn from business did I begin to clearly see that what I was striving toward was "spiritual leadership." Partially as a result of this I missed the opportunity to consciously convey the essence of that leadership to others. Sometimes life gives opportunities. It provides me with a feeling of satisfaction that, as the supervisor of a business and a development project, I still have the chance to do so.

Aa. Jonker, former director-owner of a pension and insurance consultancy firm

Collaborative Communication

"I always say that a tortoise can live for a hundred years because he is so well protected by his shell, but that he only makes progress because he dares to stick his neck out."—Richard Semler

"Listening and then speaking is learning."—SHV corporate philosophy

When I enter a company as a consultant, one of the standard complaints I always hear is "nobody listens to us." Yet another complaint is: "We never hear anything or are informed about anything. 'They' do as they please without taking us into consideration."

When I present these complaints to management, I get the following defense: "We do listen to 'them,' but 'they' just can't get their way all the time." I also hear: "How can they claim that they're not informed? We tell them everything but they don't read memos and forget things."

Innumerable books have been written about communication. I wish to keep it simple. In the above scenario information is being confused with communication. Information is dispatched from both sides—but it isn't always received. This happens because the information doesn't suit the recipients. How does this happen?

Like me, you've probably known the answer for a number of years. I received a model from my colleagues, Danaan Parry and Jerilyn Brusseau, a number of years ago (see figure 7.2), which summarized the answers in entirely new manner. Since then, I've begun to realize how difficult it is to truly communicate openly. Open communication is a learning process that never ends and has layers upon layers.

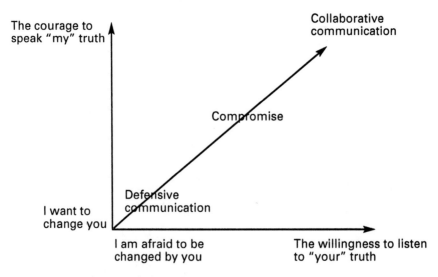

Figure 7.2 Collaborative communication

The effectiveness of communication depends on speaking and listening. Let me begin with speaking. Very often our intention when we speak is to influence another person. If you think about it, you'll realize how often we try to achieve something by making someone else do something or think something or change his or her behavior or opinion. But we know that this isn't possible. We cannot change another person: he is the only one who can change himself. Nevertheless, we keep trying. Most communication is a kind of civilized battle to get our own way. This applies to discussing, presenting, selling, convincing, arguing, advising, negotiating, expressing pity, judging, interviewing, etc. I often say that we invented discussion when we became too civilized to smash each other's skulls—and from that viewpoint it is a significant advancement. If two people—colleagues, a boss and a staff member, or couples, for example—come to me because they have problems, it's always the same old story: "We could get along if only he did not…" If only he would listen to me, if only she could understand my situation, if only he was home more often, if only she viewed things in proportion, if only he was less bad tempered, if only he was a little less authoritative, if only he was a little smarter, more diligent, conscientious, responsible, friendly, more aggressive, braver, quicker, more meticulous, more sensitive, more sensible, fatter, thinner, more attentive, whiter, browner, more feminine, more masculine, younger, older, wiser… The cyclists cause all the trouble.

This manner of speaking is known as defensive. Of course you don't do this often, but everyone else around you—including myself—does. The attitude behind it all is that I have the monopoly on truth. My view is the best and the most correct.

However, there is another manner of speaking. The intention behind it isn't to change the other person, but to let oneself be seen. I would like you to see me as I truly am, including my opinions and ideas. However, I am aware that my truth is not *the* truth. Everything I write in this book may be untrue. Because I do not know the truth—perhaps the truth doesn't even exist—then we can only partly know the truth. Maybe the truth is like a big jigsaw puzzle. I have a piece, but you do, too. I am also unsure about the best solution, even though I often think I am certain of it. But above all else, I would like to express myself. The only thing I ask of you is that you listen to me—nothing more and nothing less. And if you are unable or unwilling to do so, then that is too bad. I can hardly force you to.

This manner of speaking is known as open speaking: speaking aimed at developing contact and cooperation, instead of protecting one's position.

The same distinction can be made with listening. There is one manner of listening which is based upon the fear of being changed by the other person—defensive listening. There's another manner of listening which is geared toward truly hearing the other person. The latter type requires a commitment, because we may hear things we don't like or things that hit a sensitive chord or are painful. We may hear things we totally disagree with or threaten us.

In a group, we refer to this manner of listening and talking as dialogue or sharing, as opposed to discussion. There is time for dialogue and discussion in a group. But many groups seem to misunderstand the distinction between the two and spend the majority of their time discussing, even though a dialogue would be much more appropriate. Dialogue is of paramount importance when dealing with a problem and with opinion forming; discussion is only important for accentuating arguments or when making a decision relating to opposing interests. Discussion is a veiled form of battle. There is nothing much wrong with it, as long as we view it as a game. Dialogue, on the other hand, is not about winning or losing.

If people are experiencing problems with one another, then it's difficult to truly listen and speak collaboratively. This is why it isn't recommended, in situations such as these, that you put each other to the test. Speak for one minute and ask the other person to repeat what they have heard you say. If you think that you have conveyed it well, then give the other person their minute before you proceed.

Many of us go through life without ever being truly listened to, not even for a minute, not even as a child. Someone else—typically the parent—always interprets, interrupts, or doesn't give the child time. This is why many of us are wandering around, desperately searching for someone who will allow us a minute, only one, to be truly heard. Unfortunately, this cry is often misunderstood, as it is often defensively conveyed. As a result you are also no longer able to listen yourself and the circle is complete.

The tragic nature of the above must not be taken too lightly. Hours are wasted, conflicts are fought, people are injured, misunderstandings are created, and mistakes are made through miscommunication. This costs billions and causes untold misery. Exaggeration? Take a look around you. Maybe you are one of the fortunate exceptions. But just how certain are you that you truly understand your boss, your partner, your colleague, your daughter, your son, your mother, your father, your friends, your representative, or your voter? Are you certain that they understand you? For as long as we believe the misconception that there is only one truth, we will continue to make life difficult for one another, and the gaps between women and men, Protestants and Catholics, Jews and Christians and Muslims, blacks and whites, the poor and the rich, Germans and the Dutch, Russians and Caucasians, natives and foreigners will exist and result in violence and war.

It is my deepest conviction that almost everyone has learned to communicate defensively but that we are all capable of learning how to communicate more collaboratively. We merely have to become aware of how we communicate now and ask ourselves if we wish to carry on in this manner. If not, then we have started out on an adventure which, as with all adventures, has its ups and downs, but which will ultimately bestow the greatest reward: true contact, intimacy. And with this, the way is clear for spiritual leadership.

Meta-Communication

A common objection to the model above is that it takes two to communicate collaboratively. What do you do if the other person doesn't want to communicate collaboratively and remains defensive? Upon closer inspection, you'll find that this objection is defensive, because the underlying intention is that the other person must change and become more open. You can always begin collaborative communication at any given moment and situation. Whether you choose to do so is another matter. But if you yourself remain defensive, then collaborative communication will never arise. Attempt to communicate collaboratively yourself, and this is an invitation to the other to also become open. Maybe he will accept the invitation, maybe not. In the latter situation, you haven't gained any ground but you haven't lost any ground.

Fortunately, there are processes that support the development of collaborative communication. The first process I'd like to discuss is meta-communication: communication about communication.

We can—in a collaborative manner—define how we have experienced the communication process up until this point in time. For example, we can say something along the lines of: "I've noticed that we're running around in circles and that I'm becoming increasingly frustrated. Shall we examine what's wrong?" The model in figure 7.3 can assist with this.

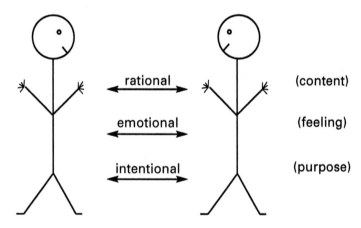

Figure 7.3: Levels of communication

Communication takes place at three levels: the rational, emotional, and intentional levels. On the rational level we deal with "content": the matter in question. Feelings—about the business, each other, or ourselves—are dealt with at the emotional level. The intentional level encompasses the open or—on occasion also to ourselves—concealed intention behind communication. Reasons to communicate are, for example, to complete our work, to share someone's company, to gain assistance, to trip up someone, to relieve discomfort, or because we care about the other person.

A negative intention occurs when the overt intention doesn't tally with the (conscious or subconscious) hidden intention. For example, a discussion may be carried out to reach an agreement, but the hidden intention is to outwit another party. This is also known as a hidden agenda. More than one intention simultaneously play roles in any given situation.

All levels and all intentions are incorporated in each communication, whether we are aware of it or not. Problematic issues or blocks can occur at each level, which often become apparent at another level. However, problems can only be resolved at the level at which they occur. In this case, resolving means talking about the issue. You then talk about the manner in which the communication takes place—meta-communication.

Meta-communication can also be defensive or collaborative. However, if it is collaborative, then it can be a tool to make communication collaborative. Here's an example of collaborative meta-communication: "I've noticed that I entered into this discussion with the surreptitious intention of getting my own way, while I'm pretending that I'm considering what the best solution is. Sorry—I don't want to do this anymore." Here's an example of defensive meta-communication: "You're being very sensible, but I think you just want to get your own way."

Schutz's model can also aid meta-communication, in this case relating to the group process. Meta-communication can be a comment in the manner of: "This discussion makes me feel unpleasant. It seems to me that we're occupied with safeguarding our own positions within the group while we pretend to be talking about the matter in question. At any rate, that's what I'm doing." Such a statement requires a certain sensitivity for group processes and the courage to express this sensitivity. However, this can be learned (see following chapters) and it is worth the effort—at least if one is striving toward a true spiritual working or living community.

Feedback

There is another tool for the advancement of collaborative communication: feedback. There is a feedback giver and a feedback receiver. The information provided by the feedback giver comprises how he perceives the other person and the feelings this evokes.

Feedback is an excellent tool for achieving open communication, but it must fulfill certain conditions.

For the giver: follow these suggestions.

- Be straightforward. Feedback must be direct, specific, and concrete. Vagueness has no use and can even be confusing. Either give a concrete definition of the behavior or a precise description of the impression or feeling the receiver creates.
- Do not rehash the past. The feedback should be given as quickly as possible after the situation being analyzed.
- Feelings are facts. If they reveal nothing about the feedback receiver, then they at least make a statement about the giver. It is of paramount importance that they be expressed; otherwise, they'll obscure the feedback.
- Watch your intentions. The giver's intention must be either geared toward the advancement of collaborative communication or toward supporting the receiver. Feedback must therefore be given out of love, or at least respect. In no circumstances must it be used to dump one's feelings on the receiver or to run down the receiver.
- Feedback is not criticism. Criticism always involves judgment. Judgment, in working situations, should be restricted to assessing performance on the basis of clear criteria. There is no space whatsoever outside working situations for judgment. This of course does not mean that the behavior of each person must be accepted. Boundaries can be set without judgment. After all, what do we actually know about the other person? Very little. It's difficult to overstate the disastrous effect of judging in organizations and in society. It creates insecurity and leads us into open and veiled battles with no hope for forgiveness and love.

• Feedback is an observation, an impression, a feeling—not an explanation or a psychological analysis. Explaining, analyzing, and psychological reasoning make the provider seem superior, and it makes the receiver feel small and creates resistance. "I'm bothered by your being irritated" is feedback, but "You seem to be touchy, do you have problems at home?" is an explanation. "You get angry with me really quickly. I must remind you of your father" is psychological reasoning, not proper feedback.

For the receiver, it's important to listen with an open mind, listening, and yet again listening. Feedback is like spiritual food and if it's to work then it has to be handled just as ordinary food: chew on it, taste it, swallow it, digest it, and only then excrete what you have no use for. You don't have to agree with the feedback; its value can only be assessed later. Thus, take it in. Listen, let it sink in, meditate about it. It was given to you for a reason. Each reaction to feedback, except for "thank you" or "I heard you" should be seen as a defense against feedback. This also includes explanations ("that's because…"), denial ("as far as I'm concerned you've got it wrong"), and giving feedback to feedback ("yes, but you…"). These statements will hinder profound contact and obstruct the learning experience. Even expressions of sorrow or remorse are only of value at a later point in time, after the feedback has been digested.

If these conditions for good feedback have been achieved then it is not only a tool for achieving collaborative communication, but it's also a prerequisite for a spiritual community. A spiritual working or living community without integrated feedback is virtually impossible, because without feedback, the communication will sooner or later become defensive. Too many problematic issues will accumulate at an emotional level. When this happens, the intentions of the group members will also become insufficiently pure. But this can be reversed: a group or organization with a feedback process that's integrated into daily practices is a spiritual community, or well on their way to becoming one. This is because the natural effect of a good feedback process is that it results in collaborative communication, which automatically leads to spiritual development.

Conflicts

I define a conflict as any form of disagreement, disrupted relationship, or battle that cannot be resolved. Conflicts are one of the most valuable things a group or an organization can have, as it is always a form of intense involvement. A conflict often contains an enormous quantity of accumulated energy and life. This doesn't alter the fact that chronic and unswerving conflicts can have an extremely destructive effect. They cost a lot of energy, time, and attention, which is then unavailable to be put to use elsewhere. Oftentimes, though, it's better to avoid conflicts by applying collaborative communication and utilizing the energy that would be locked into the conflict for something more worthy. If conflicts have arisen, then it is sensible to value them and subsequently learn how to manage them. Because if we, in our relatively peaceful situation, do not succeed in managing our own conflicts, why should we expect the same of the Yugoslavians, Palestinians, Israelis, and the Northern Irish?

Conflicts can be prevented by:

1. A group or an organizational culture that's geared toward a win-win situation. Better still, a culture in which a win-at-all-costs attitude is replaced by different values such as enjoyment of work, care and respect for humanity, personal development, the meaning of the work, unity, and honesty.

2. Meta-communication and feedback.

3. The creation and utilization of the prerequisites for listening while, at the same time, the renunciation of defensive communication.

4. Spiritual leadership.

5. The lack of games and manipulation, and the goals of maturity, responsibility, and freedom. I will deal with this in more detail in chapter 8.

The application of all of this puts us well on our way. However, if conflict does occur, then it has to be discussed. Below you'll find important conflict-management principles that were developed by Danaan Parry for major conflicts such as those in Northern Ireland and in Israel-Palestine, but can be applied to the more everyday conflicts within your group.

Ten Conflict Management Principles

1. No single conflict is permanently resolvable without 100 percent effort from all concerned. If I am totally present with my mind, heart, and soul, then wonders can take place.

2. Assume that one single truth does not exist, or that we are only capable of partially knowing the truth.

3. There are always win-win solutions. Win-lose is in fact lose-lose. This knowledge can stimulate us to be creative. Thus, each conflict is an opportunity for creativity.

4. The presenting problem is usually not the original source of the conflict. To resolve the conflict, we must go to the source and be willing to go way down to the depths. If we don't then it will only become toxic once again, just as would happen with a tooth that was filled, but wasn't fully cleaned out. Gentle healers make rancid wounds, as the Dutch proverb says.

5. In each conflict or opposition of interests, masculine and feminine behavior come into play. Awareness and acceptance of this contributes to the resolution of the conflict.

6. Both parties feel threatened during conflicts. Thus we are unable to begin an actual discussion before we have created a safe space. This can be seen as physical—a room where it is safe and pleasant—but also in a more mental way by starting with a safe subject or shared activity.

7. A conflict can only be resolved if both parties are prepared to communicate collaboratively. However, collaborative communication cannot exist if certain conditions have been laid down (for example, "I'll be open if he promises to be open"). To create open communication, one party begins, either by speaking (about themselves), or by listening (truly wishing to hear the other). This means that we have to abandon the belief, albeit for a moment, that the other person is an enemy.

8. Water can grind stones and is stronger than fire. "The gentle forces are sure to win in the end" (Henriette Roland Holst). Soft is strong. But gentle is not weak (see point 4). In this context it means patience, compassion, and feeling.

9. Behind almost every conflict lies a longing for intimacy. We can hear this by hearing beyond the words and listening with our heart. This is why a good conflict resolution results in deep contact: we have weathered the storm together.

10. There is no conflict resolution without conflict.

The life force of a group or a spiritual community depends on the extent to which the group is capable of resolving conflicts. This can even be reversed: if a group has developed a strong ability to resolve conflicts, then it has also developed the ability to communicate collaboratively (also on a meta-communication level) and it will develop automatically into a spiritual community. This releases the energy required to work efficiently on each common group purpose, whether it's spiritual (geared towards spiritual growth) or not.

Men and Women

The conflict between the sexes is a remarkable form of conflict. It seems as if it's in our genes. On the one hand, we're fascinated by and feel sexually attracted to the opposite sex, while on the other hand we don't understand one another. This is because men and women function differently, but this alone isn't so great a problem. However, this lack of understanding has degenerated into a power struggle, which in the formal sense of things was won by men, as power struggle is more in their nature. This of course resulted in women, as a suppressed group, going underground with their aggression, which has in turn resulted in their becoming more indirect, more veiled, and even meaner.

The battle between the sexes has been ongoing since (almost?) the beginning of time. There is no single culture, as far as we know, that is completely free from it, although cultures vary significantly in the extent to which this struggle and discrimination manifest. This age-old struggle is reflected in what could be termed the "soul" of humanity and has amplified the existing biological differences between the sexes.

This is the reason why the conflict between the sexes, consciously or subconsciously, is part of our emotional and mental baggage, even if we haven't experienced it personally to any great extent. We have internalized this conflict: it lives in us. The ideology about the parity of the sexes, in which parity is often confused with equality, often serves the purpose of denying this conflict. Of course we want to deny this conflict, as it is exceptionally painful.

This conflict is the driving force behind, or contributes to, many other conflicts—including conflicts between men and those between women. When we aren't aware of this basic conflict, then the veiled form manifests in all sorts of other battles. The disastrous consequences which can result from this can be seen it chapter 4 but we can also observe all sorts of conflicts in daily life, major or minor.

As I have already explained, there is no way to avoid conflict. This means our only option is to become aware of our own part in it. This doesn't have to be active discrimination or violence. It can manifest in a much subtler manner—through language, or some misunderstanding, or assuming someone isn't suitable for a particular job, or judging, or wishing to change the other person.

A spiritual community can only continue to exist if this conflict is identified and worked out. This is also the case for spiritual communities that are comprised of only one gender. In a way, it's more difficult for same-sex communities to resolve the conflict between men and women. Yet, as it also manifests itself in same-sex groups in other conflicts and misunderstandings, then in principle it is possible.

The challenge for the spiritual leader lies in noticing this wound and not trying to get around it (2). The spiritual leader is only capable of doing this if he (or she) admits his own pain and responsibility in this conflict so that he no longer has to use defensive communication. Collaborative communication with yourself and another person is also a way to rise above this conflict. In doing so, we also have to learn to deal with the sexual energy. This doesn't mean it should be suppressed, although controlling it may be worthwhile as you'll see chapter 8, because then it can become stronger (which, admittedly, can be fun), but because it can also become more aggressive. Rather, dealing with sexual energy means that one should find a form that's acceptable to all parties concerned. If we can achieve this, then life becomes richer and more stimulating and the sexual energy then becomes available for our personal growth and creativity.

The outcome is a deepening of the spiritual community: both within the group and with our partners in life.

Involvement, Authority, and Motivation

"I always end up laughing when I hear directors bragging about how much involvement they permit. They say: 'I want everybody to feel that they are involved. So, I call everyone to me and I listen to what they have to say and only then do I make a decision.'

"What is known as 'participating management' is often nothing more than 'consulting management.' This is nothing new. Managers have been consulting their staff members for centuries. Just how progressive do you really have to be to ask someone for his or her opinion? And to listen to that opinion—well, that is at least a start. But only when the bosses stop making decisions and allow their staff members to deal with things themselves will an enterprise be enabled to be jointly managed by staff members and bosses. And this is true participating management, not merely a lip service to philosophy."

—Richard Semler

A spiritual community is impossible if the members do not feel that they're making a contribution to the community. They want to contribute to activities have an influence on the purpose, values, and regulations, on the manner in which members deal with each other and in general on the working or living conditions. People who do not desire this can, in accordance with the previously stated preconditions, be a member of a group, but not of a spiritual community.

Having an influence doesn't necessarily mean that you wish to help determine the course of events. If you have become a member of a group because the purpose or specific activities appeal to you, you of course no longer need to say anything about that. Having influence also doesn't mean that you want matters to be dealt with in a specific manner. It does mean, though, that you feel that you are truly being listened to and that you are truly being heard, even if you don't get your own way. It means that you feel that your voice counts. In practice, it naturally means that you, every now and then, can perceive the effects of what you say and do.

For the leader—which means every group member who exercises influence—this signifies a great challenge. It means that he or she must be prepared to share power and give up control. It sometimes even means that the leader must manage the execution of decisions he doesn't fully support, put his viewpoints and his position up for discussion, and has the courage to be led. In short, the spiritual leader is the opposite of the CEO we encountered in the previous chapter who only wanted total agreement. Hazel from *Watership Down* is a good example of such a leader, as is Richard Semler from Semco.

There may of course be boundaries that shouldn't be crossed. However, it's important to examine the origins of these boundaries. Will the spirit—or the personality, ego, or dignity—be trampled on? Many rigid attitudes are masked by invoking the common interest— "But if we do that, we'll all suffer because it isn't in our best interests!" This may be true at times. However, it is in fact often (also) a rationalization of the supposed self-interest. In my experience, if boundaries are truly based on our spirit (the Great Spirit, the God in us), then they will never evoke resistance. This is known as natural power, or natural authority.

There is an exception to this rule—namely when a leader asks too much of group members. Then all types of irrational, violent reactions can occur, varying from rebellion (as in *Watership Down*) or mutiny, and, in extreme cases, murder and manslaughter (Jesus, Martin Luther King Jr., Gandhi, or the Kennedys). These so-called crucifixion processes also take place to a lesser extent in the form of denunciation, gossip, passive resistance, or sabotage.

Every person who speaks openly from his or her heart will always evoke a certain level of resistance. This is because the people being addressed then have to investigate their own heart and soul, which can be very painful indeed, and can result in challenges, which are in no way whatsoever convenient—especially when the person being addressed is not used this kind of introspection.

Therefore the spiritual leader always finds a balance between authority and surrender, exercising and sharing influence, taking the initiative and letting go, involvement and distance. A lasting equilibrium—which will lead to development of a spiritual working or living community that functions effectively and creatively—can only exist when each of the group members has found the balance between, on the one hand, freedom, the desire to take part in decision-making, and autonomy, and on the other hand renouncing, being flexible, and respecting leadership. This is also valid for the political community, the community formed by citizens, politicians, and authorities.

Only under these conditions can something like intrinsic motivation occur. Only under these conditions will the members of the group feel so involved that they continue to give their best to the group. Their own personal needs and longings then correspond with those of the group and they can develop and make available their individual talents within the group.

This is, of course, desired by everyone. But then again, if we truly want it, why does it occur so rarely? I think it's because we rarely want to make the effort to achieve this ideal situation. Because we aren't prepared to give up security and possessions. Because we are afraid of disappointment. And because we think this goal is unrealistic. This may very well be true, but the question as to whether something is realistic or viable is irrelevant; what we desire motivates us to act.

One final comment. Influence, space, and involvement are not things that can be given to members by the leader, because if he does, he will remain the influential person on a meta level. After all: he gives the influence—so he can also take it back. But the leader can allow himself to be influenced if this doesn't challenge his own boundaries. And what the group member can do is claim influence and space by taking it. If you don't, then you can't complain that someone doesn't give it to you. In short: if you do not fulfill your own leadership function, then you cannot accuse another person of poor leadership. Many group members are afraid of the repercussions of sticking one's own neck out. However, this does not mean that you don't have any personal responsibility. If you allow yourself to be stopped by sanctions, then you are complying with the leadership.

The history of democracy is a good example of these processes. In the past, parliaments have only acquired sustainable power when they claimed it; power was never awarded by a ruler (although there are examples of this which have been temporarily effective). It is interesting to see how nowadays, the Russian, Japanese, American, and European parliaments are involved in a power struggle with their rulers.

In a spiritual community acquiring influence does not have to involve battle. If the leadership is spiritual and the members do not oppose it but stand up for themselves, then there is no battle. A gradual distribution of the leadership then occurs. If, on the other hand, the group is not spiritual, then the group members' desire for influence inevitably results in a power struggle.

I will return to this subject again later in this book. I would like to conclude this chapter with two of my experiences.

A True Conversation with My Daughter

Once I participated in a workshop about communication that was held in a bank. There was a lot of defensive communication and we were apparently making little progress on the way to collaborative communication. However, months later, I was having lunch with one of the members of the group and he said, "As a result of that workshop, I had a true conversation, for the first time in years, with my 16-year-old daughter. Since then, we have real contact." If he hadn't spoken to me I wouldn't have considered that gathering to be all that effective. But it taught me to be careful with those sorts of conclusions. The seed has been sown, but you seldom know when it will germinate. In addition to creating a better father-daughter relationship, the assumption can also be made that both of them, in their work or social lives, will continue to use and encourage open communication, if not verbally then through their attitude.

"You Have Given Me Back My Husband"

I had another interesting experience with communication, but this time in an official institution. This institution had become bureaucratic and had lost its spirit, which had resulted in poor service, a negative public image, and a completely unsystematic administration, from which, after a reorganization, a deficit of millions came to light. This was the cause of an intensive process of change, and the work conference I participated in was used as a tool. One important part of this change process had to do with the head of administration, an elderly man who had lost his enthusiasm and any hope for improvement. He even stopped making any effort. However, after a number of work conferences that were in reality a spiritual community, he cheered up and turned into one of the driving forces behind the organization's transformation. At a party, his wife said to the director: "I am so grateful to you! You have given me back my husband. Before, when he came home from work, he collapsed on the sofa and he was of little use whatsoever. Now, he may be a little weary when he comes home, but afterward he is full of energy. Shall I tell you something else? I've fallen in love with him again!"

This demonstrates that a spiritual community in the workplace can be realized and is strongly desirable from the viewpoint of the individuals involved. It certainly isn't detrimental to the company and in my mind is absolutely necessary if the company is aiming for longer-term objectives—and not for the highest possible short-term profit—and for a valuable contribution to society as a whole.

Part 3:
Education

CHAPTER 8

The Soul

MOTTO: THE SPIRITUAL LEADER OBSERVES HIMSELF
WITHOUT JUDGMENT.

*"And out of this choiceless awareness perhaps the door will open
and you will know what that dimension is in which there is no
conflict and no time."*—J. Krishnamurti

WHY SELF-KNOWLEDGE?

Gnothi seauton. Know thyself.

These words were displayed above the entrance portal to the Oracle
of Delphi in ancient Greece. At that time, the Oracle of Delphi fulfilled
a function that has been taken over by therapists and organizational
advisors. I would like to see these people place more of an emphasis
on self-knowledge.

Why is self-knowledge so important?

In the first place, as the law of manifestation states, self-knowledge is absolutely necessary to create the reality we want and to take
responsibility for our lives. After all, we create that reality in our
minds, and we supply it with energy, consciously or subconsciously.
We must realize how we create our own reality and therefore what
lives in our subconscious. Thus, we must get to know ourselves.

Second, self-knowledge is essential for the preservation of creative tension, which I dealt with in chapter 2. The perception of reality is, after all, one of the poles of this tension. This means both the
reality outside ourselves and the reality within ourselves—our ideas,
thoughts, emotions, needs, perceptions, memories, etc. This inner reality must be accessible, allowing us to observe the relevant parts without any form of distortion. This in turn is required to form a solid
foundation for our creative process and for the utilization of the path
of least resistance (see chapter 2).

In addition, self-knowledge is essential for the ability to see and understand another person. The proverb "unknown, unloved" contains a lot of truth. We have the tendency to look upon the unfamiliar with suspicion and fear. While we do have an adventurous, curious side, the fear of the unknown remains, which may lead to alienation and resistance to what is new (this is also the root of discrimination and racism). What or whom we do not know is shut out. If we do not know ourselves, then we shut ourselves out. And if we do that with (parts of) ourselves, then we automatically do this (with parts of) the outside world. We project the unknown parts of ourselves onto others. But when we label other people we see our image of them instead of their true selves. This occurs prolifically: between parents and children, partners, colleagues, bosses, and staff. We see the other as we wish to, or assign positive or negative characteristics to them from the unknown part of ourselves. Much of the desperate search for appreciation, understanding, or respect (especially between parents and children) can be traced back to this. In order to truly know another, we must be prepared to know ourselves.

What's more, self-knowledge is a prerequisite for self-love. This is necessary for having a good feeling about yourself and, as will become apparent below, it is a prerequisite for personal strength and effectiveness. Loving yourself is required for loving another person, an important step on the way to "seeing" the other and toward awareness of unity. This is the core of the Bible's injunction to love thy neighbor as thyself.

Lastly, self-knowledge is a prerequisite for achieving awareness of unity. As Thomas said, "He who thinks he knows the All, but not himself, will remain in complete need." The way to the inside is the way to God, as we have already seen in chapter 5, and the way to God will lead to the awareness of the completeness of creation.

Perhaps what's most essential is that striving toward self-knowledge is a fundamental human need, together with the need for self-realization (Maslow). We all want answers to fundamental questions such as: Who am I? What do I want? Where am I going? We want to discover, develop, unveil, and unravel things. We crave discovery and adventure regarding the outside world just as we crave discovery and adventure regarding our inner world. The same goes for our fear of the unknown and our desire for safety and predictability. This is why resisting self-discovery is natural. Fear of getting to know oneself is then present in a conscious or subconscious form. The fear is real, even existential (it is even part of our existence), but is it unreasonable? It's therefore up to you whether you want to be stopped by that fear or not. If you pursue it, you must have the required will and discipline to continue. You can derive the will from the reasons above. The exercises in this chapter can assist you with the discipline.

It's almost impossible to see yourself and the world around you honestly and openly without striving to know yourself. There is no honesty without self-knowledge and no self-knowledge without honesty, and no spiritual leadership without honesty. It can also be said that without self-knowledge it is hardly possible to take responsibility. Therefore a spiritual (working) community is not possible without the three elements of attention, perception, and taking responsibility. The aim of this chapter is to provide tools for getting to know yourself.

Self and Soul

I have made no distinction between "self" and "soul." Is there a distinction? Is our soul not a part of ourselves? The deepest part, maybe? Or is our soul the part that remains after you have removed all the recognizable aspects from yourself?

In chapter 5 the soul was defined as the product of our life history. In ordinary terms the word "soul" is used for a deep part of ourselves, a sort of entity which exists free from our body, which, because it isn't attached to our body, may continue its existence after this life and was already in existence prior to this life. It may reincarnate, but then again maybe not. Even still, the word "self" is also often used in common language for a deep part of our personality, for example in the expressions "I wasn't myself," or "I'm searching for myself," or "I'm getting to know myself." But who is "me" who knows "myself"?

I will return to these questions at a later point in this chapter, but for the moment, I would like to use the following distinction. By "self" I mean the experience of what I described as the personality: our uniqueness, our individual character. This is made up of, among other things, our conditioning: what we have learned as well as our unique predispositions.

"Me" or "I" is the consciousness of this self. It is a part of what I referred to as "mind." It is the observer, the philosopher, the one who experiences things. When it functions it always brings with it a division in ourselves: the observer against the observed, the philosopher against the thought, and the one experiencing it against the thing being experienced. The dividing line can be randomly drawn, depending on where you focus your attention. If you think about it, "me" is not solely the consciousness of self, but also a part of it. Ultimately "me" and the "self" come together. The observer is the observed, the thinker becomes the thought. It's not so difficult to deal with this rationally, but it's difficult to experience this as a truth. (I'll explore exercises to do this later in this chapter.)

We experience our soul when we reach the core of our being (see also Thomas Moore). This means that we can only experience the soul when we're capable of letting go of the conditioned part of ourselves, when we can see and experience it for what it is, namely our conditioning. Growth begins, as I have repeatedly said, with letting go. We put things into perspective. We experience that we are not "really" our conditioned being, and we're liberated by this knowledge. We simultaneously experience that we are totally unique yet completely identical to others. We discover that contact—direct contact from soul to soul, being truly one, being a part of the world soul—is only possibly beyond the limits of our conditioning. This is also an aspect of awareness of unity.

An Exercise for the Self

The following is an exercise to directly experience what I mean here, taken from Danaan Parry. The exercise can be done with two people or with more people in the group. It goes as follows: you face someone and say: I'm different from you—but not really. The other person merely listens and allows these words to sink in.

This exercise gains considerable force when carried out in a (large) group. The members of the group face one another in two lines, and row A states the above line to Row B. Subsequently, each group member moves up a place (the person remaining on the end of the row takes his or her position in the other row, but this is also possible with two circles, an inner and an outer circle). The statement is repeated. When you get back to the starting point, the members switch roles: the listener becomes the speaker and vice versa. When everybody has been face to face with each other twice, the exercise is finished.

There are few exercises that I know of that can so rapidly and so directly provide a soul experience and a soul connection. It goes without saying that there must be a certain bond of trust present in order to make this work.

We are now able to drop the distinction between "me" and "self." In some situations, often under special circumstances, this soul experience can suddenly and immediately occur, for example in the group exercise I just mentioned, or in near death experiences, trances, experiences with nature, or during or after acute threats. This soul experience often comes after a gradual process whereby we have created space through the process of letting go. In general, we are able to—or dare to—permanently let go only when we know what it is that we can let go of. We must get to know and experience our "me" and our "self" prior to continuing on the path of letting go, which is why the way toward ourselves is also the way toward our soul. Self-knowledge makes use free if we know we can choose, put into perspective, and cease to identify ourselves with our conditioning (1).

Observing without Judgment

How do we achieve self-knowledge? By examining and observing ourselves, of course. This isn't easy. We always have a negative or a positive response—an affective reaction—toward our behavior or feelings. We like or do not like what we think, feel, find, and experience. We often disapprove or approve of this. We continually judge ourselves.

The problem with this is that through this affective response or self-judgment we interfere with the process of self-observation. We have the tendency to not want to see and not want to experience what we don't like and disapprove of. Just as "wishful thinking" or the opposite, being scared of something, results in the distortion or selective observation of the outside world, the affective response leads to selective observation of the inner world. In this way, we can of course never achieve self-knowledge.

There is also something else. If we judge ourselves, then we split ourselves in two: someone who judges and someone who is judged. We also do this with self-observation, but with judgment there is an additional factor because we introduce a hierarchy in the division. The judge is superior to the one being judged. The split then become a separation. There is a part of ourselves which has the arrogance or the pride to deliver a judgment on the other part. This results in a "top dog" and an "underdog." The underdog has the tendency to not feel good about himself. Even when he is being praised he's aware that it could all be different tomorrow and that there are always parts of him which are not okay. The top dog, on the other hand, feels superior, but not good, because, deep within he senses that arrogance, pride, and superiority do not form a basis for solid self-love. He is as such always afraid of being knocked off his throne. Pride comes before a fall, does it not?

In short: self-judgment distorts our self-observation and undermines our self-respect. It obstructs self-acceptance, a prerequisite for loving ourselves. And, finally, self-judgment always leads to judging others. With this we create a hierarchy with others and therefore avoid true contact, as we have seen in chapter 6. Self-judgment is therefore a considerable obstacle to awareness of oneness.

If judging others and ourselves has so many downsides, then why do we hold onto it? I think there are two reasons. The first is simple: we were taught about judging from the cradle. It has become a habit that we learned from our parents, by identifying with them and imitating them. However, there is a more fundamental reason, which is that life is a major detachment and separation process during which we learn to distinguish between inside and outside. At first our world is fully comprised of inside, i.e.: everything we experience is deemed as belonging to us. Later, the outside world becomes greater. Inside is familiar, safe, warm. Outside is unsure, unknown, full of adventure. We have feelings about this, and we transform these feelings into judgments. Those feelings are within us, but our judgments express that we do not want them, which has resulted in that, in the meantime, we have made something part of the outside which is situated within us. We have placed the separation in ourselves, as we have seen above.

Therefore, our fear of the unknown is closely linked to our process of judgment. This is why in the introduction of this book I stated that it takes courage to want to get to know yourself. Now I'd like to add that it takes courage to let go of your judgments. This is why it is also difficult to simply observe yourself. Self-observation always evokes resistance, which is why I will provide you with a number of exercises in the remainder of this chapter, things to do to discover more about ourselves and through which we can, to an extent, weaken the resistance and to get around our judgments.

These exercises can also assist with the development of discipline (see chapter 9), the discipline to regularly take a good look at yourself. In this chapter I provide a selection of exercises which I have found to be exceptionally effective and have withstood the ravages of time.

RESEARCH INTO OUR CONDITIONING

We commence our description of exercises with those that can assist us with getting our conditioning on the right track and, if necessary, letting go of it.

The Daily Question

The first exercise can assist us with getting our conditioning on the right track and, if required, to let go of it. The daily question provides insight into the structure of your process: how do I think, feel, observe, or communicate?

The exercise is quite simple: ask yourself the same question a number of times, for example three times, during the course of the day at set times. The question is: what am I occupied with? Then, take five minutes or so to analyze what is behind your actions, thoughts, focus, disposition, physical body, and whatever you are consciously aware of—or not. It's important to carry this out at predetermined times and to also actually take the time to do it. Setting an alarm is a useful method to remind you.

What's Hooking Me?

Getting hooked by something or someone means that we inadvertently and emotionally react to that something or that somebody. Oftentimes we do so the same way each time. For example, mother can always make us angry when she says "You don't really care about me," or our boss continually disheartens us by saying, "Very good, but..." We then react with our subconscious emotions—guilt, inferiority, sorrow, tenderness—without becoming fully aware of these emotions, but nevertheless our buttons are pushed. Where are those buttons that allow somebody to get you to react emotionally? To find out, ask yourself the following questions:

- What is off limits to others?
- How can someone always interest or excite me?
- Where am I always emotionally or physically vulnerable?
- Which subjects or situations continually make me angry?
- What always evokes my empathy or compassion?
- What do I disapprove of in other people?

- What do I approve of in other people?
- What do I lie about?
- What makes me outraged?
- When do I allow myself to be carried along in a discussion?
- When do I feel threatened?

Honest answers to these questions bring us to our vulnerabilities and also to the thought models we use to bring order to the world and for self-protection. But do they merely protect us, or do they also create an effect we don't really desire (any longer)? To answer this question, we must discover our thought models.

Thought Models

Our thought models color the world around us. What's more, they create the world around us because of the law of manifestation. We see what we think and we create what we think. If, for example, we think that people are untrustworthy, then we will observe signs of deceit and deception everywhere. We will also meet people who will deceive and mislead us. If, on the other hand, we think that people can be trusted, then we will attract trustworthy people and also be attracted by these people. There is, of course, a catch. It is about what we really, truly believe without misleading ourselves. If we want and therefore try and to a certain extent succeed to believe that all people are trustworthy, but deep down we don't believe it, then as a rule the deeper belief system is more effective.

It can be said in general that unconscious thought models have more effect than the conscious thought models. (That's why the theory of positive thinking has its limitations.) But how can we discover—and then let go of—our unconscious thought models? I've found two methods.

The first method is to take a look at where we find ourselves in life. Based upon the presumption that we create our own reality, our situation is the outcome of, among other things, our present thought models. If, for example, we've recently been deceived, then it's worth the effort to trace this back to our inner self. It is important that an attempt is made to remember our immediate reaction to the event. If we thought in a flash that the deception proves that people are untrustworthy, then that primary, immediate reaction is a good indication of our thought model. If we consider our current situation as the outcome of our own process of creation, we can consider this situation as feedback. Of course this method only works if we firmly subscribe to the theory formulated above, an issue I'll look at in the section "Core Beliefs."

At this point, stop reading for a moment and consider your own situation in this manner. Which images and thought models can you identify?

A second method for discovering one's thought models is to make a list of concepts which, if we think about it, played a significant role in our family life. After all, this is where we learned our worldview. Indeed, we may have adopted other concepts later on, but often the original concepts exist at a deeper layer. The newer concepts cover them, just like a new coat of paint, without the initial layer being removed. Furthermore, we must also remember to not only look for the concepts that were openly and verbally expressed by our parents, but also the ones they didn't discuss but which were expressed through their behavior. The behavior has in fact made more of an impact than words. If your parents advocated equality between the sexes, but your father was in charge of the family, then you are in the first place thrown into confusion and subsequently the example of the behavior most impacts your deepest convictions (see Laing about confusion in families). Ultimately, there are two types of concepts: concepts about how the world is, such as "people are only out for their own interests," and concepts about how the world should be, for example, "you have to take others into consideration." The first type of concept is of a factual nature, which may or may not be "true." The second type of concept is of a normative nature, and contains behavioral regulations.

To assist you in making the list of your own concepts, here is an overview of various areas of life, along with a number of examples of statements that are often made for each of these areas. (The layout is derived from David Gershon and Gail Straub's book *Empowerment*.)

Feelings

- Feelings are dangerous and must be controlled at all costs.
- Aggression is the most significant destructive force in the world. Aggression is bad.
- Aggression, in the form of the struggle for life and the survival of the fittest, is the most important way to advance in life.
- Men don't cry and shouldn't cry, especially in public.
- Men are very macho, but it's important that they get to know their gentle side and show it.
- Pain must be dealt with in silence.
- You may not inflict pain on another person.
- In a relationship, you cannot avoid inflicting pain on each other.

Relationships

- My partner will leave me if he/she discovers the real me.
- If you open up your heart in a relationship, you will end up being hurt.
- The monogamous relationship always results in entrapment, cheating, and attempts to control.
- The monogamous relationship is the divine way to spiritual development and freedom.
- One should lead a monogamous life.
- Rivalry and jealousy are necessary in all personal or business relationships.

- Relationships are wholesome if they are based on mutual respect and the preparedness to grow.
- Honesty in business produces the best results.
- In negotiations you must not lay all your cards on the table.

Sexuality

- Sexuality stands in the way of spiritual development.
- Sexuality is an important way to spiritual development.
- You cannot be in love for ever.
- Sex is dirty and one must not discuss it openly.
- If my partner isn't tender, then he doesn't love me.
- Men are only after one thing.

My Body

- You have influence over your body; it goes its own way.
- I have little energy, which is why I'm always tired.
- My body is the most important thing I have. That is why I pay a lot of attention to nutrition and exercise.
- I cannot lose weight.
- My body is dirty/the source of my pain/beautiful/a temple/unimportant/a source of pleasure.

Money

- You must keep money moving.
- If you were born poor then you will remain poor for the rest of your life.
- Wealth is not a good thing—it corrupts and makes people egotistical and gets in the way of spiritual development.
- Money doesn't make you happy.

- You cannot be truly happy without money.
- It is wonderful to have (a little) money.
- The devil shits in one big pot.

Work

- Work isn't pleasant. I work to earn money.
- One should work. Idleness is the parent of vice.
- Work is one of the most important sources of satisfaction and an opportunity for self-expression.
- In business, attack is the best form of defense. I cannot express my humanity in that world.
- Politics stink.
- If you are unemployed then it is your own fault.

Spirituality

- The world has a hierarchy: first comes the mother, then the father, then the pastor, then the bishop, then the pope, (or one's boss, then the CEO, then the queen), and on the top is a strong God.
- The world is a wonder.
- The world is a place of plenty; there is enough for everyone.
- The world is a place of scarcity; there isn't enough for everyone.
- It is God's will that I develop my talents and make them available to the world.
- My life is a mess. This is caused by my karma.
- If you have troubles/pain/illness then it's your own doing.
- God is love.
- God does not exist.

These are a few examples from the hundreds of thousands of potential concepts. I would like to note the following, though.

Up until now I have randomly used the terms "concepts" and "thought model." It is, however, practical to reserve "conception" for solitary thoughts and "thought model" for a coherent set of thoughts. Concepts are often linked to one another in various areas, which is why it is so difficult to alter them. If you alter one it's like removing a brick from a building: there is always the risk that the whole building will collapse, and then what? The great void? But that's threatening!

In addition, we can see from the above examples that the function of thought models is to arrange the (threatening) reality around us. We have been doing this since Adam gave the animals their names. This may be why the models, to a certain extent, are inflexible: we are afraid that if we give up our thought models then we are also giving up our safety.

I'd also like to note that no true distinction can be made between factual concepts and normative concepts. This also makes it difficult to change even factual concepts—there is often a standard or a value linked to it which is precious to us.

You may have noticed that you hold opposing thoughts. If this is the case, then you are lucky, because then you don't fall into the trap in which you desire to make your whole concept system uniform and so that you may have inner consistency. Holding opposing thoughts creates an initial prerequisite for the readiness to question your thought models, an almost necessary prerequisite for researching them at all. That is one of the reasons why spiritual teachers often contradict themselves. It's beneficial that students become aware of the function and the ultimate insignificance of their thought models.

Once again I advise you to stop reading here, and to identify your own concepts and thought models. It can also help to make your parents' concepts more explicit and to ask yourself in all honesty if you, deep down, still adhere to these concepts. You can also consider how your thought models influence your attitude (especially toward other people), your emotions, your behavior, your habits, your ideals, and your experiences. Another step is to consider which of those concepts, ideals, habits, emotions, experiences, and attitudes you wish to renounce. If you are truly determined and honest and wish to renounce certain elements, write them down on a piece of paper, tear it into small pieces, and throw it away or burn it—preferably in the company of one or more persons.

But be warned: only do these things if you feel you are ready to do so. Otherwise, the concepts will return and you will be disappointed and your self-respect will drop. In that case you are just like an alcoholic who says: "After today I won't touch another drop" or "I am trying to stop drinking." There is no "trying," there is no "after today"—there is only now.

The old conceptions and the habits will of course return, but if you are honest and determined then you will be capable of not paying any attention to them, which will result in them disappearing once more, just as a plant will wither if it is given no water.

Roles and Games (Transactional Analysis)

Yet another way to research our conditioning is to examine our interaction patterns such as those which take place between ourselves and others. Transactional analysis is an extremely applicable model for doing this. Transactional analysis itself is also a thought model—but a so-called "meta thought model," a thought model for the contemplation of thought models (and behavioral patterns). For more details, Berne and Harris deal with this subject more comprehensively.

We learn through imitating and identifying. This begins in childhood. We learn by imitating and identifying ourselves with our parents, older people, and also older children. This is clear from the games we play: father and mother, doctors and nurses, school. However, even if we don't play those games, then we imitate our parents and other older people and we identify with them. For parents it is often very amusing and sometimes difficult to recognize yourself in your child.

In this way, as a child, we introduce older people—our parents in particular—to our inner selves. This is particularly so regarding the parent of the same gender. We display their values, manner of thinking, behavioral habits, and much more. Furthermore, we also display the position of the parent: a position of power (from the child's point of view). This is referred to as the parent role or top-dog position.

But in addition to this, the child doesn't solely identify with the parent or older person; he or she is also a child in its uniqueness, playfulness, irresponsibility, lust for experimentation, and dependency. In the literature this is referred to as child role or underdog.

When we mature, these roles don't disappear, but continue to determine our thoughts and our behavior. However, a third role simultaneously develops: the role of the "adult." The adult is our own unique personality, the place where we are free and responsible and do not behave in accordance with the standard role patterns of parent and child.

An understanding of this model is of eminent importance for analyzing relationships between leaders and staff. Oftentimes, leaders take on the role of the parent. This calls for a (often unconscious) thought model consisting of: I am superior, I have power over others, I have the right and the duty to exercise this power, and I am responsible for the well-being of others. Such a thought pattern often results in an authoritative or patronizing attitude, sometimes veiled by friendly or kind behavior. Such parental behavior evokes childish behavior from the staff members, creating a parent-child relationship, which is known as a complementary relationship. The staff members then assume the following child-role thought pattern: I am not responsible, you (the leader) have to take care of me, and I will take on a passive role. This manner of thinking is known as victim/martyr thought. Neither parental thinking nor victim/martyr thinking results in satisfaction in life. As soon as we are aware of this type of pattern, we always have the opportunity to back out of it and to identify with and act in accordance with our adult side. The great benefit of this is that the relationship then develops into a relationship between free and responsible people, in which both partners can take the initiative and be creative. Equality typifies the relationship in this case, despite the possible existence of a formal hierarchy.

There are all sorts of variants of the parent-child relationship that play a major role in the personal and social realms. I refer you once more to Berne for a more comprehensive definition. It is important that these variants—referred to by Berne as "games"—be recognized, because they can have an extremely destructive effect and impede self-knowledge.

A common game is the dictator-victim-rescuer game, a game for three players (or two players with double roles) in which the players take on a continually alternating role of parent and child. A slightly extreme but common example is the alcoholic (or addict) game. The alcoholic plays the victim: he cannot help his addition—it is stronger than him, and, moreover, it stems from his unhappy childhood, or through the evils of society, or because of his constitution, or because of weakness of the flesh, or he is doomed, or whatever. His partner (or father, mother, child, or friend) initially plays the rescuer or helper and attempts to approach him with compassion, to listen to him, or to provide him with advice. If that doesn't help—and it won't, because the rescuer role is a parent role, which enhances the child role, the role of the victim—then the helper becomes either a victim or a dictator. In the first case, the helper, now victim, brings out the dictator role in the original victim (the alcoholic) who in turn becomes a dictator and goes on to terrorize his surroundings (note that the terrorist, also in war or freedom movements, is always to be considered as both victim and dictator). In the second case, the helper attempts to force the addict to give up the role of the victim (for example, by threatening them with desertion). No matter what the helper does, as long as he or she remains in one of the three roles, he will have a role-reinforcing effect on the alcoholic and thus contribute to the problem.

This may seem to be an extreme example, but upon closer inspection, processes such as these occur with regularity in so-called normal life. Consider, for example, a manager who tries in vain to encourage his unmotivated staff member to be more enthusiastic and make more effort, or the union negotiator who deliberately takes on the role of victim/dictator, or the teacher who cannot control his class. The question is always: Who is the actual victim, who is the dictator, and who is the rescuer? Closer inspection reveals that the roles are often interchangeable. However, the most important point is that interchanging roles never provides a solution, but maintains the destructive current system. It hampers self-insight. The only opportunity for resolution is for one person to let go of his or her role and with this let go of the problem. In this way, this individual enters into his or her own maturity and in doing so achieves freedom and responsibility. The individual must know that he or she is the one who has created this problem is therefore the one who can let it go. (This does not mean that the problem will disappear altogether, because after all the other person is responsible as well.)

About Roles and Games

I advise you to track down the parent and child behavior in your life, in particular in situations where there may be a "top-bottom" relationship (for example, boss-staff member, or parent-child). Do you often lapse into the dictator-victim-lifesaver game?

It is also interesting to perceive this game in situations in which you are not directly involved—for example, in politics. Which role can you identify with? Are you aware that if you can identify with one of the roles, that you are indirectly—with your focus and energy—responsible for continuing the situation? This is the reason why politicians and top managers have so much difficulty in stepping out of their roles.

These roles can also be seen in myths and fairy tales; we are evidently dealing with archetypes, which I'll explore in a later section.

Successes and Disappointments

The successes and disappointments we've experienced form a completely different angle for discovering more about our conditioning. This exercise is on the borderline between research into conditioning and soul-searching.

It's worth the effort to make a list of the successes in our lives, including the experiences we experienced as successes in the past. Begin with your childhood experiences and continue on to the present. Think of at least ten or 15 items, and write them down so that someone else can read and understand them. You can include anything from drawing a picture, performing in a concert or play, passing an exam, rescuing a stray cat, or earning an important position.

These items should make you feel positive and optimistic. After you list them, contemplate which characteristic or talent was responsible for each success (this is an aspect of soul research). It is often the case that the same characteristics will repeat. This provides insight into your talents that you can develop and offer to the world.

The following step is to consider why you have labeled those items as successes. This provides insight into which values you consider to be important and which you probably want to realize in your life and work. You can also make the distinction between acquired standards (code of conduct, conditioning) and the values that are located deeper in your soul (qualities or characteristics).

It is a completely different matter with the list of disappointments. This also has to be written so that another person can read and understand them. It often becomes apparent that the disappointments on the list have not yet been dealt with and have simply been hidden away. This is extremely dangerous with disappointments, because they will undermine both our hope and our faith, and as Paul said (I Corinthians 13), faith and hope are essential elements in our lives. Through time, they will also undermine our zest for living and even our life energy. This in turn can result in all sorts of unpleasant consequences, such as depression, reduced enthusiasm for work or relationships, or health problems.

It is important to examine how you have dealt with your disappointments. The only healthy manner is to feel them and express them in their entirety by sharing them with someone who listens with his heart. This can be embarrassing, because people tend to feel that they are exaggerating. However, not expressing oneself is much more dangerous. You can become irrationally desperate, and perhaps even cynical or skeptical. Cynicism is suppressed despair and skepticism is suppressed doubt, things that we do not need, not for ourselves or for the world. If ever it is essential to let go of your conditioned actions then it is when dealing with disappointment.

RESEARCH INTO OUR CORE (SOUL AND SPIRIT)
Core Beliefs

I believe that people become motivated through love or fear (often by both at the same time). We can feel love for ourselves, relatives and partners, work, and maybe even for enemies. We can fear losing our position, possessions, job, loved ones, prosperity, and, ultimately, life itself. If you think about it, fear is a perverted form of love (for yourself and your loved ones). If you are motivated through love, you create cooperation and harmony around you. If you are motivated through fear, then you create battle. In the first instance you have a win-win model, in the latter a win-lose model. I cannot imagine spiritual leadership in the battle model (even though there is a time and a place for everything occasionally—even for battle).

These models form the foundations of our thought models, which all the other models are linked up with. In order to investigate your situation I provide a system of two times two statements, which you can apply to determine your own position.

The system has two dimensions. The first is belief in self, which can be explained in two statements:

- I love myself
- I create my own reality

If you agree with these two statements to a high extent then it can also be said that you believe in yourself. You think positively about yourself, and you believe in principle that you are the master over your own life. We have previously seen this belief, in chapter 2. It is obvious that, according to the law of manifestation, these beliefs will not only result in an inner feeling of force, but also in a great personal effectiveness, influence, and charisma.

Loving yourself entails examining what it actually means to love another person. It is not so difficult to love someone you like or who is pleasant and does exactly what you expect of him. On the other hand, it's difficult to love someone if you disagree with his behavior or if he disgusts you. If you can see that the behavior of this person is merely skin-deep—no matter how much suffering it may cause on the face of things—and not in fact the person themselves, then you are well on the way toward loving him. This is exactly the same with yourself. It isn't difficult to love yourself if you think you are nice and do the right things. It becomes difficult to love yourself when you see things you do not like, such as envy, hate, or jealousy. Are you then capable of saying: you are all right, I love you as you are?

The second statement about your belief in yourself entails that you take on the responsibility for this reality. As we have seen in chapter 2, this does in no way mean that you have the process of creation under control. (This is why it is a misunderstanding to think that responsibility has anything to do with blame.) Unfortunately, this misunderstanding is widespread and gives cause to a gruesome and loveless attitude towards oneself and others, not unlike Calvinistic guilt and penance. However, it does mean that you say that everything in your reality is there because you, consciously or subconsciously, or at a point in time which you may no longer be able to recall, have "chosen" it.

While the first dimension has to do with belief in one's self, the second dimension of the system is trust in life. Once more this dimension can be interpreted with two statements:

- Life brings me with what I need
- I love change

It is easy to subscribe to the first statement when all is well, when we are prosperous, healthy, and happy, when we have friends and a loving family. But are we also capable of subscribing to this statement if we are confronted with illness, or even death? Or when we have financial problems or depression? Or when we have problems at work caused by the boss? In this context, the Bible book Job, which I dealt with in chapter 6, is a wonderful book. Only when we believe that life brings us what we need, without experiencing a sense guilt and penance, can we say that we subscribe to this statement in its entirety.

Do you love change? Personally, I only love change when it's pleasant. There are two types of change in life: changes related to reaching a new phase in life (see chakras in chapter 6) and unexpected changes. The first is a "natural" type of change. Things change when I leave my parental home, or when I live with someone, have children, or watch my children leave home. There are also natural transitional phases in my work and in my body. Life is a continual dying process, in the sense of taking leave of things and letting go of them. I sometimes have difficulty with this. However, I have also learned that each letting go creates the space for a new beginning—a possibility that something new will be born, yes, but also that I will be reborn. This also happened when I gave up my individual freedom to marry my wife. Space was created for something completely new and when my children were born I was reborn as a father. But to say that I welcomed every change in my life, that I love change—I am learning to do so.

I often have more difficulty with the second type of change— unexpected change. Not when change is pleasant, of course—if I win a prize in a lottery or fall in love, or am offered a great job—but if I become seriously ill or if someone close to me dies. I must say that, in retrospect, each and every one of these unexpected changes has been beneficial. I wouldn't wish to have missed out on any single experience in my life. On some level I'm able to say that I loved the changes in my past, but I'm not looking forward to the changes yet to come. I am busy learning to love change.

I suggest that you consider for yourself the extent to which you subscribe to the four previous statements. You can do this by allocating a percentage to each statement that indicates the extent to which you subscribe to it. One percent then means that you are completely in disagreement, and 100 percent means you're totally in agreement.

You will notice that the first set of statements seems to contradict the second set. But it only seems to be contradictory if we consider that the creation of our own reality is in fact a matter of co-creation. In chapters 2 and 3 I compared this process to a sailor who may be able to determine precisely where he wishes to reach land but is dependent on the wind and the current, which determine how and when he reaches land.

If you are capable of, to a large extent, subscribing to the above system of two times two statements, then you are a happy, strong, and effective person. If this isn't the case, then you have been leading yourself up the garden path. You are happy because on the one hand you can experience life as it truly is and on the other hand you have faith in your own mastery. You are effective and strong because you are truly attuned to the forces of life itself and waste little energy in attempting to go against the flow. In this case you also have an additional tool available for getting to know yourself. Your reality is, after all, based upon the statement that you create your own reality, a result of the "decisions" you have previously made, consciously or subconsciously. You can therefore use reality as feedback. Reality is a reflection of your inner world and by focusing attentively on your life situation (without judgment!), you can learn much about yourself.

The point of the question as to whether you agree to the above stated statements, is, of course, that you do not lead yourself up the garden path! It isn't about what you want to believe, but what you truly believe. Some people award 100 percent to one or more of the statements. I have seldom experienced that this was an expression of total belief, in harmony with our mind, heart, and soul. If this were the case, then we would be dealing with someone who, at the very least, has entered the first stage of total enlightenment (see further on in this chapter). I believe that this is a sign of a lack of self-knowledge, or sometimes even a lack of a consciously experienced life in which the statement concerned has not yet in fact been evaluated regarding its credibility.

But if you are truly honest with yourself, and you only partially subscribe to the above statements, how do you increase your percentage? Well, in principle, this adheres to the law of manifestation. You have identified your reality and in this way have found a foundation. You determine what you want and subsequently opt for one of the ways, which can be found in chapter 9, to supply this with energy. At the same time you will discover undermining thoughts, partially assisted by the methods previously defined, and you will provide them with no energy. Do not suppress them, but allow them to pass you by just as leaves in the breeze or the clouds across the sky.

With this we have in fact arrived at the method for changing all undesired beliefs and thought models you wish to alter. It is imperative that you no longer supply any energy to those thoughts you no longer want but are nevertheless still attached to. Therefore don't hide them or attempt to do away with them. That never works, as you in fact provide these thoughts with energy (think about the stopping smoking example in chapter 2). Accept their appearance calmly, do not deny them when they arise, and provide them with no energy. Through this action the thoughts will die a lingering death as a matter of course.

This in turn creates more space for new beliefs, which will form spontaneously, nourished from a deeper source within yourself. Allowing this to take place is often more effective and wiser than consciously creating new thoughts, which lose the link between heart and soul more rapidly and in turn will once more become outdated and dysfunctional. This is ultimately the fate of all thoughts. Life is eternal, but no single form or thought has eternal life. Do not cling onto any single thought or core belief. Holding on to any thought will ultimately hinder your growth process and with this will also threaten your inner peace as well as your effectiveness. The sole purpose of researching thought models is to learn how to let go.

The Fundamental Questions, The Growing Edge

I'd like to return to the questions that opened this chapter: Who am I? What do I want? Where am I heading? The answers to these questions provide insight into the direction of your life and indicate whether you are on the path to strength and happiness.

Since "Who am I?" is the mother of all questions and underlies this whole chapter and "What do I want?" relates to one's vision from chapter 2, I would like to focus on the question "Where am I heading?" This is the question regarding destiny. The answer to this question can be more readily found if it's split into three sub-questions:

- What must I do in this world during this life?
- What must I learn in this world during this life?
- What do I have to give in this world during this life?

Most people can, immediately or after a little contemplation, provide an intuitive answer to these questions, which can be refined further through contemplation. Everyone who truly wishes to know the answers shall find them (Matthew 7:7). "Where am I heading?" has an interesting hypothesis behind it, namely the existence of a predestined path, a destiny. In my personal experience this is true, but if you disagree, then I advise you to ask yourself these questions with the assumption that it is true. You can always decide afterwards whether you consider this to be the case and whether one's destiny is solely a projection of our own spirit or whether it has to do with a sort of life assignment.

These questions are particularly relevant for career planning and general life plans. Besides giving insight into one's talents or interests, these questions also provide, in my opinion, an essential guideline for assessing whether you are on the right track and where you actually should be heading.

To discover your destiny and direction in life, an effective exercise is to consider your "growing edge" (Gershon and Straub). This is the point to which you must reach or pass in your own growth process. It is something you must face up to, a situation in which you must proceed, or an action you must undertake in order to allow your growth process to proceed. You cannot get around it. If you attempt to avoid your growing edges then your whole growth process would stagnate. Growing edges can occur simultaneously in various areas of your life. They must always be considered as an expansion of your comfort zone, that part of your personality and your life where everything is safe and under control. You must be willing to leave your safe ground and take a step onto unknown ground, both within and outside yourself.

A few examples of growing edges are:

- Leaving a job before you have found a new one (to learn about integrity, courage, or liberating energy)
- Jumping from a high diving board, if that's daunting (to learn about dealing with fear)
- Learning to ski (to learn about the balance between letting go and having control)
- Learning to ride a horse (to learn a little about authority, faith, giving, and passion)
- Addressing a large group, if you have never done it and are not looking forward to it (to learn about daring to demonstrate yourself)
- Apologizing to your greatest rival (to learn about forgiveness)

In short, growing edges are always actions or situations that are challenging and exciting and also somewhat frightful and risky. There is no roundabout way that will achieve the same result. Your inner voice informs you that this is the route you must take to develop to your fullest potential. If you don't, you may experience sorrow, regret, or resentment at a later point in time, consciously or subconsciously.

In order to find out if you are dealing with a growing edge of your own, you must listen to your inner reaction:

- Excitement, delight
- Slight fear (if the fear overwhelms you or if it is completely suppressed, then you are probably too far away from your comfort zone)
- Intuition that you must do it—it cannot be avoided

I propose that you write down a number of growing edges for yourself before you read further.

Boundaries

Another aid for soul observation is to look into what you've hidden away within yourself, which boundaries have you defined within yourself. In general, we define three types of boundaries within ourselves (here I use Wilber's classification):

1. Between persona and shadow
2. Between psyche and body
3. Between ourselves and the outside world

Persona and Shadow

The classification is Carl Jung's, who thought of persona as being that part of our spirit (psyche) we know and accept. The shadow is the part we do not accept. Together, the shadow and the persona form the psyche—our thoughts and thinking habits, emotions, memories, concepts, values, and our role-concepts. These things are also located in our shadow, but those refer to the matters we would rather not know about ourselves. Specifically, the following elements are located in the shadow:

- Hidden desires that we have been taught are forbidden; for example, the desire to cause pain, unbridled egoism, tyranny, and homosexuality. It is irrelevant whether these desires are inborn or acquired.
- Feelings we would rather not face up to, perhaps because they are forbidden or are linked to painful experiences we'd rather forget. It could be hating a parent who (possibly due to his or her own powerlessness) has withheld something (such as love or respect) or has done something (such as committing abuse). Or it could also be the pain caused by previous rejections or desertions, or physical lust for someone who is off limits.
- Concepts we have been taught are indecent, but were taught to us while we were still in the cradle (sometimes

non-verbally through behavior). This could include racist or fascist ideas.

• Values which we actually do not want, such as a spirit of sacrifice or on the other hand sticking up for oneself.

• Elements from the collective unconscious (see chapter 4) that we don't accept or fear, for example, demonic symbols, or black magic, or visions. So-called archetypes are also included, concepts and images which symbolize a specific aspect of our humanity. These archetypes can include the dragon (all-devouring passion), the witch (our magical force), the sea (our immeasurable depth), and the triangle (being a part of the holy trinity or the holy family). In particular our "other" side can be found in the collective unconscious: the anima (the feminine) in the man and the animus (the masculine) in the woman (2).

If we do not investigate the shadow and instead put up a partition between the shadow and "ourselves" (the persona), then we effectively place part of ourselves out of working order. This results in a major loss of energy and life force. Moreover, the shadow does not allow itself to be put out of working order just like that. The shadow will indirectly reveal itself, and it does this in two ways: by affecting our actions, even if it isn't noticeable, or as a projection by attributing (negative) characteristics to other people which are actually located in ourselves.

Veiled aggression is an example of the first way the shadow reveals itself. There are numerous forms of this: irritability, bad temperedness, or the attempt to undermine others. Veiled aggression is particularly treacherous when it appears to be in the form of justification, as is the case when we ourselves are attacked, or in the case of so-called constructive criticism. But the tone and intention are the decisive elements. Are we purely focused on contact with another person, or is our shadow making an appearance? If it is the latter, then our actions will often produce side effects that do not agree with our conscious intention.

"It takes one to know one!" There is a lot of truth in this childhood taunt. We burden the other with what we disapprove of in ourselves, or what we may be lacking (maybe because we have suppressed it). This process is known as projection. It distorts our view of the world, as we have seen in our discussion about thought models. And it hinders true contact with another person, which, after all, requires that you see him for who he truly is. And, finally, this process makes it easy for us to avoid taking a look at ourselves. However, once we are aware of our projections, they form a unique tool for self-research.

Let's research our shadow and heal the fault in ourselves. We can do this directly, by asking ourselves which forbidden desires, emotions, concepts, values, standards, and elements from the (collective) unconscious we have hidden away and then openly and honestly examine the answer. We can also examine which projections we have put into the world. The following is a good exercise for this: Think of someone whom you admire greatly and assign five positive characteristics and five negative characteristics to that person. Do the same with someone who disgusts you. They may be people you know personally, but you can also evaluate public figures. Examine which of those characteristics also apply to yourself. Examine the extent to which your judgment of the other person is colored by characteristics you have or you lack. Exercises such as these are known as retracting projections and it helps us to re-integrate the shadow into our whole personality.

You will encounter a few more methods below that can help you get to know and integrate your shadow.

Psyche and Body

Do you have a body or are you your body? The majority of us say: I have a body. We talk about "my body," as if it were a possession or a thing, an appliance. We have therefore made a distinction between "me" and "my body." We subsequently transform that distinction into a boundary and before we are aware of it, we, in a manner of speaking, view our bodies in a hostile manner. "It" must simply do what we want it to do. Exercising doesn't alter that attitude if it is geared toward performance or only because we have to do it to maintain our body. It isn't surprising that we are capable of catching all sorts of illnesses. However, considering our body as being a part of ourselves has many useful benefits. First, because it is a part of ourselves. Is it not true that our face, our posture, the way we dress, and our fingerprints are highly personal expressions? And is it also not true that we protect our bodies from harm? Our physical integrity is very important and the reason why rape, incest, and physical torture for example are so terrible: they violate our integrity. We also experience our body as a personal, private area where only we can experience what is happening there.

Our body is us and this is why it is better that we consider it in this way, otherwise we will end up in a battle with honesty, which is the foundation of the leadership we are striving toward despite the accompanying inefficiency and discomfort. However, there are three more reasons why it is important that we consider our body as part of ourselves. The first is that we use the body to hide away part of our shadow. We store in our muscles the desires and emotions we would rather not have, and we in turn tense those muscles more persistently than is necessary. If we want to get to know the shadow then we have to get to know our body. Furthermore, we will never achieve awareness of unity if we do not integrate our body within ourselves, otherwise, how can we experience the connection with the world around us if we cannot even experience connection with a part of ourselves? And finally: if we continue to consider our body as a thing, according to the law of manifestation it will also start to behave like a thing. One of the properties of a thing is to become susceptible to malfunctioning. With a body these are known as illnesses. I may have an illness, but am I also an ill person?

The aim of it all is that we shift from thinking "I have my body" to "I am my body." There are various methods for accomplishing this, but the various physical methods that also develop consciousness are the most important, such as yoga, tai chi, martial arts, biofeedback, and bio-energetics. "I am my body" can also be advanced by providing it with more direct attention. That is possible through nutrition, physical exercise, or through guided fantasy.

The following is an example of a guided fantasy. This fantasy can be altered and expanded at your own discretion. Record the text and play it later or get someone else to read it out loud, otherwise you will have to continually refer to the text. If someone else is reading the text for you, you can also play gentle non-distracting background music, which helps to stimulate the right half of your brain and with that the power of imagination.

Make yourself comfortable and relaxed, but remain alert and close your eyes....Take a few deep breaths...become tranquil...focus all of your attention on the moment... imagine that you are becoming smaller, increasingly smaller...you are still becoming smaller...and ultimately you are no larger than the tip of your finger...and imagine that you have placed yourself in the palm of your hand just as you are sitting here ...and now enter your body via your mouth...you are in your mouth...have a look and see what it is like there ...what are the colors...what does it look like, what sort of atmosphere is there...pleasant or unpleasant...what is it like to be in your own mouth...take a walk around and take in the sights of your own mouth...now proceed deeper into your body, because we are going to undertake a journey through your own body...you are now traveling through your throat and through your esophagus into your intestines and you enter your stomach...have a look and see what it is like there…what are the colors…what does it look like, what sort of atmosphere is there…pleasant or unpleasant…what is it like to be in your own stomach…take a walk around and take in the sights of your own stomach…now we will continue the journey…go further and travel through your leg…now arrive in your foot…have a look and see what it is like there…what are the colors …what does it look like, what sort of atmosphere is there…pleasant or unpleasant…what is it like to be in your own foot…take a walk around and take in the sights in your own foot…begin the journey upwards…slowly rise upward and enter into your own lungs…have a look and see what it is like there…what are the colors…what does it look like, what sort of atmosphere is there…pleasant or unpleasant…what is it like to be in your own lungs…take a walk around and take in the sights in your own lungs …and now we are going to your heart…have a look and see what it is like there…what are the colors…what does it look like, what sort of atmosphere is there…pleasant or unpleasant…what is it like to be in your own heart…take a walk around and take in the sights of your own heart…now we are going further upwards and will arrive in your own head, in your brain…have a look and see what it is like there…what are the colors…what does it look like, what sort of atmosphere is there…pleasant or unpleasant…what is it like to be in your own brain…take a walk around and take in the sights of your own brain…we are on our way back to your mouth…and now you come back outside again and you are on your own hand…put yourself down…and become larger and larger, until you return to your normal size once more…you are once more sitting in your own chair…and slowly and when you are ready for it, open your eyes....

This fantasy can bring you more deeply in contact with your body. I have found that this method has helped people discover illnesses such as heart conditions, joint problems, and even tumors. If you aren't used to using your imagination, fantasies such as this are extremely difficult in the beginning, but if you keep at it you can do it. It is also useful to permit yourself to let yourself go a little.

Me and the Outside World

"The air is precious to the red man for all things share the same breath, the beast, the tree, the man, they all share the same breath."—Chief Seattle, 1854

A distinction can readily be made between oneself and the outside world, but where is the border? Around my persona, so that the shadow is my outer world? Around my psyche, so that my body is my outer world? Around my individual awareness, so that the collective unconscious is my outer world? At my skin, so that my wife, my children, and my house are my outer world? But if someone harms my children, he also harms me. If someone sleeps with my wife, then he has entered my domain. If an occupier or a dictator enters into my home, my country, or my world and takes possession, then he affects me. And the roles I play, are they part of me or part of the outer world? Where does the boundary lie? Where do I end and where does the outer world begin? This question is only of importance if we solely regard the boundary as being a partition and not as a place where the two parts can come into contact with one another, a place of connection. In practice we can think this, but it's extremely difficult to experience the connection. There are in principle two manners of achieving this: the reductionistic and the expansionistic manner.

The reductionistic manner is as follows. If we are attempting to answer the question "Who am I?" then we usually provide answers relating to the things we (think we) possess or the roles we play. For example: I am Erik; I used to be married and thus I am an ex-partner; I have three children, thus I am a father; I am a son; I am a man; I have a body, thus I am also a body; I have friends, thus I am also someone's friend; I am supportive to some people and a pain in the ass to others; I am an organizational psychologist and teacher; I live in a house on a canal; I swim; I compose, thus I am actually also a composer; I am a writer; I have memories and am therefore also my past; and so on.

But who am I? Now I am going to remove all of those "possessions" and roles one by one. If I no longer have any children, am I still who I am? Yes. If I should no longer be an organizational psychologist, am I still who I am? Yes. If I were to have an out-of-body experience, who would leave my body? It would be me, of course. Would I remain in existence if I no longer had a body? In fact I would. Thus I am not my body; I *have* a body. I remain in existence without it, also without my fatherhood, being a son, friendship, my house, my trade, my past, and my future, etc. If I were to describe myself it would be similar to a hole in a piece of wood (this analogy is derived from Daniel Cowan via Peter Russell): it is round, oh no—that is not the hole but its periphery; it is black, oh no—that is not the hole, that's the background; it is smooth, oh no—that makes a statement about the edge of the wood. You cannot describe the hole because you cannot describe nothing. It is empty, nothing. This is also the case with the self. It is a hole, it is nothing, therefore it also has no boundaries and is at the same time everything. This is known as awareness of unity.

The expansionistic manner is quite different. Just as we can expand ourselves from persona to shadow and persona—in other words psyche—and just as we can expand ourselves from persona to psyche, and from psyche to organism (psyche plus body), we can expand from our own organism to everything that lies outside this. This can take place in two ways: the possessive or imperialistic manner (that is what dictators do: everything belongs to them for the purpose of possessing and controlling), or the connecting manner, the search for and discovery of the affinity between yourself and everything around you. The latter is a process that occurs almost automatically if you have made the transition between persona to psyche and from psyche to organism. On the other hand, the imperialistic manner is the tendency we all have, as long as parts of our shadow remain which we have not yet recognized and accepted (compare "The King" and "The Businessman" in Antoine de Saint-Exupery's *The Little Prince*).

> A nice test to determine the degree of your imperialistic attitude is to ask yourself: How possessive and controlling am I? To what extent do I not try to control my wife, my children, and my staff? How strongly do I defend them against real or apparent threats from outside? How prepared am I to go to battle?

Meditation and Contemplation

We can also arrive at our core through meditation and contemplation. There are two forms of meditation: concentration meditation and insight meditation. The first is an uninterrupted focus of attention on a specific object, which could be a candle flame, a mantra (a word or expression—then we are dealing with transcendent meditation), your own breath, a paradoxical question or expression (a koan), or a thought. In the case of a thought we are dealing with contemplation. The outcome is ultimately what is known to the Buddhists as samadhi, a spiritual state of inner tranquility and peace.

Strictly speaking, concentration mediation is outside the scope of this chapter, as it is not in fact self-observation. The outcome is a certain composure, a less judgmental attitude, and being able to not let people get to you. Moreover, it is a good preparation for the second form of meditation, insight meditation, although it is possible to do this without these preparations. Love meditation is a unique form of concentration meditation, an ancient Buddhist meditation that can bring you in touch with your own capacity for loving. It is as follows:

> Sit down and relax, but remain in an upright position, with firm contact with the ground. You are to carry out each of

the subsequent steps for five minutes.

Step 1. In your mind, give yourself all the appreciation and positive thoughts you can think of and all of your loving attention. Do this continually for the entire five minutes, but you may repeat things as often as you wish.

Step 2. Now think of a loved one of your own gender. Transmit all appreciation and positive thoughts and loving attention to this person.

Step 3. Think of a neutral person. It can be someone you know personally, but it may also be a public figure you are familiar with through the media. Subsequently transmit all appreciation, positive thoughts, and loving attention to this person.

Step 4. Think of someone who you consider to be an enemy. This may also be someone you know personally, or someone you only know through the media. Transmit to him all your appreciation, positive thoughts, and loving attention.

Step 5. Expand this to all the people in the world. Begin with those who are physically closest to you and then gradually expand the range of your loving attention. And, finally, encircle the whole world.

With insight meditation, the course of consciousness is continually observed. There is consciousness of observing, and simultaneously consciousness of the flow of thoughts, feelings, sensations, etc. One should not become lost in this flow or be carried away by it; one is required to observe the flow without judgment or affect (conscientious reasons). (Judgment and emotions are part of the flow, not of the observation.) A method for not losing yourself in the flow is to label what comes to your mind. Insight meditation is not simple, but practice makes perfect. The outcome is not dissimilar to the self-reduction or expansion methods I already mentioned but in this is connected with an inner experience of tranquility and peace (the initial stage of enlightenment).

The result is another view of reality and therefore also of yourself. Both distance and unity are experienced. The awareness of unity is not merely intellectual, but is also experienced. The various schools vary regarding the duration and the effort required to achieve this stage, but it is highly probable that this simply depends on the individual and on the circumstances he or she has created.

Insight meditation is not easy to learn without the assistance of a teacher and without a group context. Therefore, if one wishes to choose this way, I recommend a course or a retreat. Furthermore, this form of meditation is not suitable for resolving all personal and relationship issues, as is often thought (see also Wilber). One of the previously stated methods is more likely to be suitable for this and if the personal issues are persistent, then professional guidance may be more suitable (for example, psychotherapy). In addition to this I refer you to the excellent literature on insight meditation, for example by Beck, Tulku, and Trungpa.

Although, strictly speaking, it is not within the scope of this chapter and this subject matter, I would like to touch on near death experiences. A rapidly increased process takes place during near death experiences, resulting in seeing and experiencing light and peace. The effects strongly resemble the effects of enlightenment. Those who have undergone this sometimes experience some difficulties because they and the people around them do not comprehend what's going on. This is also due to the fact that these experiences were not purposely experienced and were over so quickly. Time to deal with it is required. All of this is more intense if physical or mental rehabilitation is also required. However, once this has been dealt with, it results in a completely different view of reality. This often involves a new insight into the person's task or destiny in this life. This is an extremely rapid and effective method of achieving insight which for obvious reasons is not available to everyone.

Additional Tools to Attain Self-Knowledge

With this we have reached the end of the exercises for reaching our own core. I would like to conclude this chapter with a number of tools for getting to know our conditioning and reaching the essence of ourselves.

Dreams, (Guided) Fantasies, Hypnosis, and Reincarnation Therapy

Dreams and guided fantasies are another manner of observing yourself. An important principle when examining your dreams is to remember that you are everything that you dream. After all, everything in your dreams comes from yourself. Where else could it originate from? There are various theories regarding this. According to Jung, much of our dreams originates from the collective unconscious, in particular archetypes in symbolic form. Others say that external entities also influence our dreams, such as the deceased, (guardian) angels, beings from another reality, or God. Regardless, it all comes to us and through us, and taken from the point of view of awareness of unity, its origins are irrelevant. However, dreams should be taken seriously, as they form a source of information about ourselves, albeit sometimes in a veiled or symbolic form. This probably occurs because we couldn't cope with the information in a direct form. Dreams can provide answers to questions such as, Who am I? Where am I heading? What's my mission in this life? What should I do? And what is the solution to a problem I'm having? In short, dreams can answer the questions that matter. If we examine all the elements of our dreams we often become very much wiser.

Some people claim that they do not dream or cannot recall their dreams. That is nonsense, but if you choose it, want it, and focus your attention on it, then the dreams and memories will occur as a matter of course. It is also helpful to resolve to write down your dreams as soon as you have them or when you wake in the morning. This is also a very good idea for those who dream often—in this way we incite ourselves to focus more on our dreams.

Fantasies or guided fantasies (fantasies based on a text, an example of which was given in a previous section), can fulfill the same functions as dreaming, but have the disadvantage in being a controlled process. On the other hand, the material is often more accessible than dreams. It also occurs in fantasy that extraterrestrial beings address us or influence the content of the fantasy. This is more so for hypnotherapy, a sort of voyage of discovery under hypnosis, and reincarnation therapy, in which a journey is undertaken into other lives. (In general the reincarnation phenomenon is merely slightly comprehended and is not disputed, but one thing that's certain is that a well-guided reincarnation therapy session can provide a treasure trove of information, wherever it may come from.)

You can invent guided fantasies yourself. For example, you can go to a secret location, real or not real, where you feel completely safe and meet up with your guardian angel or your spiritual guide (from this world or another world) and unburden your heart or request advice. You can go to caves, up a mountain, or make a journey through time or space. The difference between a fantasy and a guided fantasy is that in the latter, you first devise the context, the structure, or the theme of the fantasy and only then do you experience the fantasy.

Study, Films, Novels, Plays

I have learned much about myself from books—from novels, but also textbooks or spiritual scriptures. If fact we have already seen examples of this, from chapter 1 to chapter 6, although the emphasis there was more on creating insight than self-knowledge. In order to truly acquire self-knowledge by reading books, it's mandatory that we do not merely get to know the intellectual context of the contents—we have to make a connection, it has to click. Novels, stage plays, and films we find truly touching often have a connection with something inside ourselves. You can watch films or plays and read novels with an attitude that's more or less geared toward self-discovery. You'll probably learn something about yourself.

The film *Chariots of Fire* taught me something about the various sorts of ambition within myself: to prove something and to provide something. *The Unbearable Lightness of Being* (both the book and film) moved me profoundly, probably because it brought me in contact with a number of my deepest desires, in particular the desire for an honest and pure life. Chekhov's *The Three Sisters* moved me, teaching me that I believe in beauty and love as something that exists outside myself and is more real that the world of form and time. *Who's Afraid of Virginia Woolf?* brought me into contact with games that I and others play and just how painful they are.

I encourage you to reflect on which books, films, and plays have moved you profoundly and what this says about you. I also encourage you to identify with all of the elements or characters in the narrative. If we read and go to the theater with this extra dimension, our lives will become richer and more profound.

Books, plays, and films have also helped me become aware of my vision and mission in this world. *The Tao of Pooh* by Benjamin Hoff and *Winnie-the-Pooh* by A.A. Milne brought me into contact with my desire for a Taoist life vision. *Illusions* and *Jonathan Livingston Seagull* by Richard Bach brought me into contact with my longing for faith in myself. *The Lord of the Rings* by Tolkien made me aware of the significance of living based on a mission, and how your mission chooses you. I will deal with this in more detail in chapter 9.

Which books, films, and plays inspire you, and how can you derive the contours of your vision from them? I hope that you write to me about this one day.

I was also enormously inspired by the Bible, Buddhism, and the *Tao Te Ching*. It was essential for me to bring the holy books into context with my inner experience before they began to reveal themselves to me. In my experience this is the case with the majority of people. This is why I advise you to approach the spiritual tradition with the questions What does it mean for me? and Which insights about myself discover?

Oracles

Oracles have been around for thousands of years. Around 500 years before our era, the Chinese were using the *Book of Change (I Ching)* and the Greeks were using the Oracle of Delphi. More ancient forms were used in Egypt by the Sumerians, and much earlier by the Native

American tribes and indigenous people. Ancient monuments such as Stonehenge still bear witness to the probable existence of oracles.

We've always had the desire to know what life has in store for us. But this isn't the purpose of oracles. No one can predict the future, apart from on a few incidental occasions. If we were able to predict the future, we would act on it and in doing so we would, in principle, make the future unpredictable. (For a fascinating example of this see for example part three of Frank Herbert's science fiction trilogy *Dune*). The purpose of oracles is to acquire self-knowledge and self-understanding, allowing us to, if desired, make better decisions. It was not for nothing that the statement at the beginning of this chapter was inscribed above the port of the Oracle of Delphi. One can seek advice by oracles with or without the intervention of an intermediary.

If the intermediary is an expert then there are irrefutable advantages in calling upon their skills, as oracles often speak in general or symbolic tongues. The expert can then act as an interpreter or an explaining agent. It is then of course essential that the expert is an authority in this field, well trained and honest. Some experts simultaneously act as mediums as they form a connection between two realities: on the one side the source of the information and on the other side the world of the questioner in the present. In this case their expertise and their honesty is all the more important.

There are many types of oracles. A few well-known oracles, which, after some study, can be practiced are Tarot cards and the *I Ching*. Numerology and astrology require more study.

I use the Transformation Game, which I mentioned in chapter 5, as a way to gain insight. In this game one walks the path of his or her own life. Besides attaining the answer to the question posed, one also gains a profound insight into their own life process and the process of life in this world in general. The Transformation Game can also provide insight into the following areas:

- What is intuition, as opposed to wishful thinking or reactions caused by experience, and how does one deal with it?
- What is free will? What happens if I use my free will in

a way that disagrees with the Way, the universal process of creation, or my own destiny?

• What is the process of blessing? We humans have apparently forgotten the art of blessing, but it can be picked up via this game.

• The insignificance of competition, except for in an exceptionally limited context.

• The significance and importance of giving, forgiving, and surrendering.

• The relationship between coincidence, causal, and trans-causal processes.

Above all the game is an opportunity to practice the process of manifestation, and in doing so players obtain a true insight into it. It also clearly reveals what you, at this point in your life, are actually manifesting.

As a rule, the game is played in small groups, but there is also an individual version and a version for organizations, which is suitable for larger groups and is called Frameworks for Change. The results are remarkable. The only disadvantage is that playing the game properly takes at least two days. Just as with numerology and astrology, I recommend that you first play it with a guide to really understand the essence of the game.

There are hundreds of other oracles. Many people spent a lot of energy wondering whether oracles can be believed, whether they are "true" or not. I don't consider this to be a particularly interesting question, though. The question for me is whether they can stimulate people toward insight; I think this is certainly the case. You must not expect that oracles will make specific predictions regarding the future or yourself, but that the predictions can encourage you to think about things, about who you are and where you are headed so that you don't have to resist what life has in store for you, but that you can go with the wind and the waves of life's current. As we have previously stated, "the wind and the waves always favor the best helmsman."

He Who Has Ears, Let Him Hear...

I believe that spiritual leadership is mainly about the development of people. I'm not just referring to professional development, but to personality development. I believe that everyone wishes to do this, but their motivation can often be extremely well-hidden.

Our enterprise, a medium-sized construction company, is in a continual process of change. One of the changes occurred during the introduction of a new activity, which was managed by an ambitious thirtysomething employee with a university degree. During this period, his mannerisms were inhibiting his personal development. He appeared to be haughty, hurried, easily irritated, and defensive. This blocked his development as a human being and employee, but it also disrupted the introduction of the new activity.

I spoke to him about his attitude on a number of occasions. I attempted to do this in an open and respectful manner, and I attempted to make a distinction between his behavior, which was an issue for us, and himself, because I didn't have any negative feelings about him as a person. I was also aware that I couldn't change him. However, this had little effect. He wasn't willing to see how he came across to his colleagues and he wasn't prepared to act on my suggestions.

I wasn't willing to leave it at this. The fact that his behavior didn't benefit the company and the work atmosphere also played a part, but still, I didn't like to see someone getting in the way of himself in this way. At one point I made the decision to not give him a raise. I was aware that he would interpret this as disapproval, but it was intended as a clear signal. He became exceptionally angry and didn't want to understand my reasoning.

Ultimately, he reluctantly decided to climb down a peg or two and attend a course that would help him understand his behavior and why he irritated people and help him change the situation. After following this intensive training course he returned to work as an inspired person. He talked to his colleagues and cleared up old irritations. He performed better and, moreover, he felt much better.

In the meantime he became a more balanced person who is employed as a director in another company, in which, I think, he feels very strongly about the development of people and the working community. He still thinks of the period I just described as an important one for his development.

I have a great deal of respect for people like him who have the courage to become aware of and radically change their behavior. Not everyone is prepared to—or capable of—doing so and I know from personal experience how difficult it is. Sometimes you wait so long to do it that you damage yourself and the people around you.

I am of course not certain, but I think my actions worked, as I know from personal experience that growing can be painful, but also that it provides a great deal. My initial motive was to stimulate his development. The fact that our company also has benefited from it, I consider as a natural consequence.

J. Th. Blok, director ERA Bouw Bv.

Good training programs can stimulate the group's development. I would like to once again mention the Transformation Game, in particular the Frameworks version, which is for individual development but also for team and organizational development. I will deal with the training aspect in more detail in chapter 10.

And Finally...

And so we have arrived at the end of our chapter about conditioning, soul, and spirit—about ourselves. As learning about ourselves is a prerequisite for spiritual leadership, I sincerely hope that this chapter has inspired you to "work on yourself," as it is known as in personal growth jargon, in a different manner, with joy (even though it sometimes hurts) and discipline. The old hands among you know that you mustn't expect immediate insights, breakthroughs, or revelations—although they aren't to be completely ruled out. As said by Jonker elsewhere in this book: "Working on your personal growth and development is an ongoing process for the duration of your life."

There is something else, though. The spiritual leader will always invite other people to observe themselves, perceive themselves, and take responsibility. As a rule, that invitation won't occur explicitly, but will be carried out through the leader's attitude and charisma. However non-forceful, this invitation will often inspire but also evoke resistance. In this case, the exercises in this chapter are often good tools for reaching the other person. They can also be carried out in groups and discussed together, amplifying their power.

This doesn't change the fact that we cannot force others to carry out self-research, although if we wish to create a spiritual working community self-research is necessary. If the others do not (yet) opt for observing themselves consciously then the group as a whole is not yet ripe for the spiritual community. Then there is nothing else left but our vision and example, although, we can sometimes break through a deadlock. See how Mr. Blok acted as a catalyst in the passage below.

CHAPTER 9

The Vision

MOTTO: THE SPIRITUAL LEADER ALLOWS
HIS VISION TO GUIDE HIM.

"Is there no vision of love to bind us together?"—John Denver

"We are all visionaries. Let it not be said of this Atlantic generation that we left visions and ideals to the past, nor purpose and determination to our adversaries. We have come too far; we have sacrificed too much to disdain the future now.—John F. Kennedy

"When people are united with their real power—the power to create what they want to create—they always choose what is highest in humanity."—Robert Fritz

EARLIER IN THIS BOOK I PRESENTED THE FOLLOWING definition of effectiveness: accomplishing what you want to achieve without the occurrence of—in the short term or in the long run—simultaneous undesired effects. It's obvious that effectiveness is a prerequisite for successful leadership, thus also for spiritual leadership. And as we saw in chapter 2, the only way a leader can accomplish what he wants to achieve without manipulating or pressuring people is by focusing on his vision. The harrowing lack of leadership that I mentioned in the prologue is primarily caused by a lack of vision. In this chapter we will illustrate how to develop your own vision, how to focus on this in a productive way, and how a common or shared vision can grow.

I define vision as the thing you want to achieve. You may already know exactly what you want to achieve and if so, you can skip the first part of this chapter. However, most of us have to focus on identifying exactly what it is we truly want to achieve, what we really wish for ourselves—not what we think we want or what we are obligated to want. In the following sections I invite you to investigate whether you are fully aware of your own—possible—vision.

WHAT I WISH OR DESIRE

It's wishing time. Just imagine that a good fairy comes along and provides you with the opportunity to fulfill your every wish. What are your wishes? Make a list of them.

Making an inventory of everything you wish for—or think you wish for—is the first step toward realizing a vision. Let your mind wander freely. You could want a beautiful house, an exciting job, five million in the bank, a journey around the world, good sex with your partner, quitting smoking (and with no difficulty!), a good physical condition, healthy self-esteem, developing your talents or a specific talent, the ability to play the violin, being able to speak in public, freedom, belief in God, eternal good health, immortality, world peace, or maybe just a good relationship with your neighbors.

Old wishes and desires, dreams from your childhood or adolescence, or dreams in general may re-emerge if they are still alive in you somewhere. You can play with fantasies that you gave up a long time ago because they weren't viable but are still attractive to you. It's wishing time. Do not worry about the feasibility of your wishes. We will deal with that later. You may wish for large and seemingly impossible things, but also for small matters that seem to be close by, whether they can easily be realized or not. Everything you wish for will have a place on the list.

It's helpful to repeat this process occasionally and to work at it for a couple of days or weeks when you begin this process. All the things that spring forth from your mind, old familiar things as well as completely new things, will surprise you. You will notice that this releases a lot of energy and is very exciting. If you aren't excited, two things may be at work. You may have already known your deepest wishes and desires and therefore this exercise doesn't bring any new desires to light. However, it may also be the case that you don't permit your deepest wishes and desires to emerge to your conscious mind. Perhaps as a child you were taught that wishing and longing is not allowed. "Children who ask don't get." Maybe your parents considered this life to be an earthly valley of tears, where you had to earn your daily bread by the sweat of your brow and to bear your children in pain, and where desire and enjoyment are signs of pride. And as we have seen in chapter 8, often these old ideas have more of an effect than we realize or desire. In addition, you may be afraid of being disappointed. You think that all of this is impossible anyway so it's better to ignore it. You do not long for the Promised Land, because you think you will never get there. In other words: you do not dare to face the maximum creative tension (see chapter 2). But let me tell you this: you don't know what's feasible in this or any other life, if that exists. As I already stated, if Martin Luther King and Gandhi had allowed themselves to be restrained by what they thought they could accomplish in this life, they wouldn't have had their dreams and therefore would not have had the enormous impact they had and still have today, long after their deaths. You don't need to be a Martin Luther King or a Gandhi, but it would be nice if you could fully be yourself. You wish what you wish, you desire what you desire, and you are what you wish and desire. Moreover, by forsaking your wishes before you have had the opportunity to convert them into a vision you deprive yourself of the energy to accomplish what you really wish to achieve. Thinking about what is or isn't feasible doesn't belong to the realm of vision, but to the realm of reality, and we saw in chapter 2 how important it is to distinguish between vision and reality. At the moment we are dealing with vision, but the relation between vision and reality will be discussed later.

You have now reached your first objective, taking stock of your wishes. You will feel pleasant, or gloomy, or tense, or whatever, but the energy of the game has disappeared. How are we to proceed from this point? How do we create a vision from this wish list?

Focusing Energy

Now we are going to make a few alterations to the list.

First, check to make sure that it contains only the items that you want and no items that you do not want. For example, it shouldn't say: I want to get rid of my migraine. This may be a wish of yours, but you'll allocate negative attention to something you do not want. According to the law of manifestation, this will actually create a migraine. Therefore you need to positively phrase these types of items. For example: I want to feel healthy and good. You can also change "no war" into "peace"; "no bad relations with the neighbors" into "a pleasant relationship with the neighbors (or all the people around me)", "quitting smoking" into "being true to myself" (or whatever you want to replace this with).

Then, check to see if the list contains items you already have such as, for example, good health. Maybe you wished for "good health until I die" even though you are healthy right now. Ask yourself if this wish stems from the hidden fear of losing your health. If this is the case, you shouldn't supply this wish with any energy, as you will also give energy to the fear, which will actually bring about health problems. Similar phrasings can be: "I wish that the relationship with my wife will remain good (or passionate)," or "I wish that all my relatives remain healthy," or "I wish that I will keep my job." These issues require a delicate touch. Of course these issues may concern things you really wish for, but if you have these things at the moment and they cover up a hidden fear of losing them, it's best to remove the wishes from the list. This requires a large degree of self-understanding, but after chapter 8 this should no longer pose a problem.

Then you must verify whether the list contains items that actually serve as a means to fulfill another wish. For example, perhaps your list contains 1,000,000 euro, but if I were to ask you what you would do with that money, you might say: "buy a beautiful house and decorate and furnish it" or "travel around the world" or both. In that case the money is not your true wish; the house and the trip are. You think that you need the money for these purposes, but, strictly speaking, you don't know this. You may win a prize in a lottery such as a house or a journey. Or you might get a job that requires that you travel around the world. But you wanted to take your wife along? Well, in that case you should have mentioned it. We must be accurate regarding our wishes and only wish for the ultimate result. Otherwise we will end up in the situation of the poor lumberjack from the fairy tale. You don't know this story? It goes as follows:

> One day a fairy came to the poor, hungry lumberjack and said: "You have been granted three wishes." So the lumberjack and his wife start an endless discussion about what they wanted to wish for. This went on and on and at one point the lumberjack's wife had had enough of it and said: "I'm hungry, I wish I had a sausage." There was a sausage on the table. One wish gone. The lumberjack was so infuriated by his wife's impulsive behavior that he yelled: "I wish this sausage was stuck to the end of your nose!" And so it was. You can guess the end. After long discussions and unsuccessful attempts to remove the sausage from the woman's nose, the only option left open to them was to use the third wish to remove the sausage from her nose. The moral of the story: be careful what you wish for, as your wishes may come true.

Remove all the items from your list that are a means to realize another wish. These are known as secondary wishes. Ultimately the only wishes remaining are those you want for yourself, the so-called primary wishes, even though the wish itself may have other pleasant side effects.

At this stage don't trouble yourself with which road you must follow to realize your wish or desire. Keep in mind that many roads lead to Rome, and there are many routes you can take to make your wish come true. But we are to aim at following the path of least resistance although we do not yet know which path this is. Don't bother with this yet; developing your vision requires your full attention. In order to be effective, focus your energy on one thing at a time.

The next step is verifying whether you really want to accomplish the items on the list. Ask yourself: if I could have that now, would I accept it? If the answer is yes, the item should remain on the list. But note that in order to answer this question, the item has to be so specific that you can identify the exact moment at which it has been accomplished. This is a guarantee against items that have been phrased in such vague terms that the relation with reality is completely lost. We said before that thinking big is recommended and to not worry about feasibility, but you must be able to compare your wishes to reality or you will not be able to build up creative tension and create any effect.

Now you must consider whether your list contains items that ask something specific from another person or persons. For example, "I wish that my wife were more assertive" or "I wish that my boss wasn't so bad tempered." These points are to be removed from the list or they must be rephrased in such a way that they are about yourself. It is perfectly okay to have wishes about other people, but they are of no use for the creation of a vision. Vision is about what you want to achieve in your life, such as respect for your wife or a good relationship with your boss, and not about how someone else should or could change.

Now comes the most important moment: reduce or extend your list until it contains approximately 10 to 12 items. Why this amount? Well, if there are fewer items, chances are that you left off a number of items. Keep in mind that there is no relationship between being content or happy and your desires. It isn't true that the more you want, the less content you are, or, conversely, the happier you are, the less you want. Check the examples at the beginning of this chapter again and see whether you suddenly think of things you forgot earlier.

To check whether you have forgotten wishes and desires pertaining to a certain realm, you could do the following exercise (derived from Gershon and Straub):

Write down the wishes, dreams, and desires you have in the following fields:

1. Your job
2. Your relationship(s)
3. Your physical environment (where you live, how you live, where you work, what your working environment looks like, and how each of these items relates to other items)
4. Your health
5. Your finances (income and wealth)
6. Special accomplishments and skills (special things you would still want to do in this life, such as traveling around the world or writing a best-selling novel, or certain gifts and skills you want to develop, such as learning to play the piano or understanding modern physics)
7. Miscellaneous (here you can put everything you haven't yet mentioned in relation to the previous fields, including issues concerning the world in general)

The next exercise (derived from Robert Fritz) will help you discover whether you are still overlooking some wishes. First, list all the items that are present in your life and whose presence you enjoy; for example, a beautiful house, a beautiful tree in front of your house, a good relationship with your spouse, or interesting work. Now list all the items also present in your life, but whose presence you do not enjoy; for example, a fight with the neighbors, getting stuck in traffic jams everyday, chronic backaches, increasing crime, and so on. List at least five items, but preferably more—as many as you can think of. Now make a third list in the form of the first list, but which is derived from the second one: a list with issues you would wish in your life, which, if they were present, would result in the items on the second list being resolved. For example: a harmonious relationship with the people around me (not: no more fights with the neighbors, because the point would not be included), living within walking distance from my work or living in a world where we could move unhampered and freely (not: no more traffic jams), feeling fit and healthy (not: no longer having backaches), or a peaceful society (not: no more crime).

You will probably be able to derive a number of vision issues from the third list.

If the list comprises more than 12 items, the time has come to concentrate and focus your energy. You are running the risk of dispersing your energy to such an extent that none of your wishes will receive sufficient attention. You must now determine which wishes are most important to you. These are known as fundamental wishes. These wishes are often related to faith in yourself, confidence in life, developing your talents, following and reaching your destiny, and caring and loving our world. This does not necessarily mean that the fundamental wishes must remain on your list—the wishes that demand the most attention and which create a great level of excitement will remain on your list. Often these are fundamental wishes, but it may also be primary wishes of a simple and/or material nature.

This is also a good moment to work out what is to be done with (seemingly) contradictory wishes and desires. If both of these are exciting and draw our attention, then they are to be left on the list for the time being. Life is somewhat greater than us and things that seem contradictory to us may be coherent in a manner that is completely unpredictable to us. This being said, the contradiction of wishes may nevertheless be a reason to re-check what we actually want. This may cause you to drop one of the contradictory wishes.

We now have a list with 10 to 12 items and they are to be phrased in such a way that every sentence starts out with "I want…" or "I intend…." For example: "I intend to earn an annual income of at least $70,000" or "I want to play the clarinet so well that I can easily play Mozart's clarinet concerto." Note that the phrases are as specific as possible, allowing you to identify the exact moment that they have been realized, even though you do not quite (or at all) believe in this. For some wishes it is evident that they can be phrased with a little less precision. For example: "I want to believe in myself" or "I want to love myself" or "I want to have developed my intelligence."

In general the wish must be phrased in terms of end results. Not "I want to develop my intelligence" but "I want to have developed my intelligence." However, there are a few exceptions. Sometimes phrasing in terms of results is not useful, as the development will proceed of its own accord. In the example mentioned previously this could mean that the first way of phrasing is preferable. It also possible that a process speaks more to the imagination than a static result, and then a process phrasing may be preferred as well. For example: "I want a world that is healing from its wounds" instead of "I want a sustainable society."

We now have developed the first version of our individual vision, our list of 10 to 12 items. Individual does not mean that it doesn't contain desires that have an impact that reaches further than our own personal lives, but it does mean that they are what we personally want. The vision is like a seed: it must now be sown, grown, and developed. Now most people think they have to convert the vision into action. However we are in no way ready for this yet. First we will investigate how solid and strong your vision is, how much you believe in it, and how resilient the seed is to the weeds of the undermining thoughts.

We'll Never Make This...

There are a few devils in your mind that will tell you why you definitely won't accomplish what you want. Say that your vision is that you want to feel fit and healthy, a point you included because you suffer from migraine. Here are a few of the devil's arguments:

• The predisposition for migraine is hereditary. It runs in the family. Mom suffers from it and so does Aunt Jo. It's in the genes; therefore nothing can be done about it.

• I tried so many things: allopathic drugs, homeopathy, psychotherapy, and alternative medicine. None of these things helped.

• Maybe I could get rid of it if I avoided all tension in my life. But that means that I would have to give up my job and I'm not prepared to do that.

Notice that these statements may contradict one another. If the first statement were true, then the third statement cannot be true, and vice versa. But each of these statements leads to the conclusion that the vision cannot be achieved. Now let's say that someone has the vision of developing self-confidence. The devils are:

• I've been hurt in my childhood to such an extent that it's no wonder that I have no self-esteem. It's no use crying over spilt milk.

• Psychotherapy might help, but I can't afford it. And in view of my friend Pete's experiences I have no faith in free psychological help.

Now try this for yourself with your own vision. Take one of the items from your list which is very close to your heart or the one you find the most exciting. Write down this item on a new piece of paper. Then formulate a number of statements that will make it clear to you that you are not going to accomplish what you want. Note these underneath the wish, but in such a way that you only use the left half of the paper. Leave a few lines free below each statement.

Formulate statements that contain a fact you believe in. You do not actually need to invent the statements; they're already present in your mind, sometimes consciously, sometimes subconsciously. These are undermining statements, real devils that require energy and attention and as such have a manifesting effect. Therefore, once you pay enough attention to them they become true—they turn into self-fulfilling prophecies.

However, devils aren't alone in your mind—there are also

angels. The angels deny the statements made by the devils using a different kind of statement, statements in which you also believe and which also contain facts. For example, the three statements from the first example can be refuted as follows:

• There are several contributing factors to almost every illness: hereditary disposition, lifestyle, and psychological state. I may have a predisposition for migraine but that doesn't mean I will actually have it.

• My friend Ken had hay fever; it is predominant among his relatives. But it suddenly disappeared after that serious depression he had, even when his disposition had improved for a long time. Therefore it is also possible to change physically. Maybe I have to undergo a crisis...

• Sometimes people say that the most powerful healing factor is faith in recovery. Maybe these therapies are ineffective, as deep down I do not believe in them.

• Of course I haven't tried everything. I may find the treatment or therapy that is suitable for me at any moment. Or maybe something new will be discovered...

• Recovery can also occur without therapy, as in the case with Ken.

• Why is tension actually necessary in my work? I could learn to not worry so much about everything, or else look for a more relaxed job. That may even be more pleasant...

• I sometimes think: this tension isn't caused by my work, it's in me. I take it along wherever I go, even if I did not work. But tension is certainly curable and that may cause my migraine to disappear as well.

The actual issue is not whether the arguments have an objective truth. The actual issue is that you believe in them, even if only in part. And you do; otherwise these statements wouldn't live inside you. Also note that the original arguments are not really refuted; in themselves they remain true, but the edge is taken off them. They lose their absolute validity. And indeed that is how it is in your mind: both groups of arguments are alive and even though they sometimes contradict each other, you keep attaching a certain credence to the devils as well as to the angels.

Try doing this with your own vision item. Put a few statements that refute the first ones alongside each of the statements you wrote down during the previous exercise. Gershon and Straub, from whom I took the exercise presented above, call this method "the turning around." The first statement in itself is not turned around. But your energy is turned around. The first group of statements undermines the vision; the second one supports the vision. That is why the second group is known as supporting statements.

Now we are going to draw up the balance sheet—literally.

You now have rows of statements on the left and right sides of your sheet of paper. Now ask yourself: which row do you supply with the greatest amount of energy or attention?

If you assume that the total amount of attention with respect to this vision item is 100 percent, how much of this attention will be allocated to the left hand side and how much to the right hand side? (Of course you can only assess this in a general and intuitive way.)

This can be a very revealing exercise. For many people, the number on the left side is larger. It will be clear that in such a case there isn't much chance of realizing the vision, even if you focus on it, because attention is constantly being undermined by the influence of the devils, the undermining thoughts. However, even if the number on the right side is larger, but you still allocate a significant percentage (30-40 percent) to the left side, then you're working on your vision with a considerable counterforce. This is like rowing against the current or driving a car with your foot on the brake.

The moment of truth has now dawned. Do you really want what you formulated in your vision? Even though the number on the left is greater than the one on the right, or maybe even smaller but still significant? If so, the time has now come to truly choose your vision. In the example above you do not simply state "I want to feel fit and healthy," or "I intend to feel fit and healthy" but you can state "I choose to feel fit and healthy." A noncommittal resolution has now become a primary or fundamental choice (analogous to primary and fundamental wishes).

I must advise you to do this only if you really want what you listed. For one, this choice will have consequences. It entails that you will have to do mental work and eventually you may have to take action to realize your vision. Should you be unsuccessful in doing so, you will lose faith in your own creative power and therefore in your own effectiveness. This will have a significantly weakening effect. In that case you would lose your self-respect too. This can be compared with apparently renouncing thoughts and feelings that you do not wish to have, which I discussed in chapter 8. I made the comparison with the alcoholic who says I will stop drinking tomorrow and continues to say so until he dies of a delirium or cirrhosis of the liver. In short, you will lose faith in yourself. (That is truly hell. Hence the expression: the road to hell is paved with good intentions.)

There is a second reason why you must only opt for your vision if you truly want it. If you do so, in time the vision will become reality. Well, that is wonderful, you say. Yes, if you have been truly accurate in your desires and have truly thought it through, it's wonderful. But this isn't always the case. For example, someone chose the vision that he wanted an intimate and passionate relationship with his partner. Although the relationship with his wife wasn't bad, it was distant. Two months later, his wife left him for someone else and took the children with her. And only after four or five years and a lot of misery was his vision realized with a new partner. Maybe this would have turned out differently if he had realized that in his vision he used the word "partner" and not his wife's name. If he had been aware of this, he might have chosen to work on his current relationship first in an effort to improve it.

You are free to choose whether or not to opt for your vision, but once you have chosen, your freedom of choice is limited. We already encountered this in our discussion of *Watership Down*, with Threarah and with General Woundwort and in a positive sense with Fiver and later with Bigwig and Hazel. This explains why so many people consider their lives as being predestined or forced: they walk well-defined paths as a consequence of fundamental choices they made long before. In many cases they unconsciously made these choices. If the vision you have chosen is in keeping with your (true) most profound wish this is beautiful but otherwise it may be quite frightening. Such a path can only be left if the underlying fundamental choice is revised and made anew. I have said it before: life is as a current with which it is better to flow. But if you don't like the direction of the current there is a way out—not by rowing against the current, which can only result in disaster and crises, but by changing the underlying structure. This happens in the same way one can only change the course of a river: by relocating its bed.

It is now time to repeat the above procedures for each of the items on your vision inventory. Afterwards for each item you either opt for your vision or you don't. In the latter case you remove the item from your list. (This also makes room for other items.)

You now have your purified vision inventory. Your vision is complete. The seed has endured its first attack and it has been planted. What now?

The first thing you must do is to alter the balance sheet for each item in your vision. You have to weed out undermining thoughts. How do you do that? Certainly not by suppressing the undermining thoughts, as this will make them stronger and cause them to manifest themselves. Nor will it happen through the autosuggestion of positive thinking—saying something like "I know I will succeed in this" or "I'm capable of realizing my vision." While you will provide your seed (the vision) with fertilizer, the weeds will also take advantage of it and you'll have a battle between your vision and the supporting thoughts on the one hand and the undermining devils on the other, a battle which is often fought underground, unconsciously. Even if you were to win this battle in the short term and realize the vision, then you will carry a defeated devil inside you who is planning revenge. As soon as a setback occurs revenge will be taken—the devil will say "I told you so" and you will lose faith and the setback will turn into an existential crisis.

So how should you go about eliminating undermining thoughts? We already tackled this problem in chapters 2 and 8. It is a matter of not supplying energy to or paying attention to the undermining thoughts. You do this by focusing your attention elsewhere as soon as these thoughts present themselves, for example to your angels (supporting thoughts). You will have to be consistent in this respect. In this way you work at strengthening your faith in the manifestation process which was dealt with in chapter 2.

So, we planted the seed and pulled out the weeds. What next? Can we finally proceed to action? No, we'll participate in non-action (chapter 3) and lend nature a helping hand. We will strengthen our seed further. We provide it with nutrition in the shape of affirmations and visualizations.

Affirmations and Visualizations

Affirmations are statements that show that you have already achieved the things you want. Visualizations are mental images or "films" illustrating the desired situation. Both of these techniques can supply your vision with more energy.

Affirmations

Affirmations must meet the following criteria:

1. They must be concrete and specific. The objective of the affirmations is to realize your vision. Therefore they have to create and focus energy like a laser. This is impossible if they are phrased vaguely and generally.

2. They must be phrased in a positive manner. Once again, the issue is what you want to accomplish, not what you want to avoid. Negative affirmations ("I no longer have migraines") direct the attention to the situation to be avoided. But this will enhance it.

3. They must excite you. If the affirmation doesn't excite you, there's no creative tension. This may either mean that the vision isn't

your real vision after all or that the affirmation has no direct relationship to your vision and is therefore not on the path of least resistance. In the first instance the affirmation can be a tool to verify the formulation of your vision. In the second instance it's possible that a dull affirmation points out the fact that you want to force and control the path to the realization of the vision instead of following the path of least resistance.

4. They must be phrased in the present tense as if the vision is already reality. In this way the affirmation supports the manifestation process, because this starts from the assumption that in fact the desired situation already exists, albeit at a different energy level. Phrasing it in the present tense helps increase faith in the manifestation process. Formulating it in this manner also creates momentum: i.e., that the process will increasingly gain momentum and generate energy and the energy will build on itself.

5. They must be about you. This is similar to what we discussed regarding the formation of your vision: you cannot make statements for other people. Other people create their own realities; you create yours. Therefore you should phrase the affirmation in the first person singular.

In addition, the affirmation can simply be a rephrasing of the vision or choice. For example:

- Vision: I want to feel fit and healthy
- Choice (in this case a fundamental choice): I choose to feel fit and healthy.
- Affirmation: I feel fit and healthy.

Strictly speaking, an affirmation is a lie. You know this, too, and don't fool yourself into thinking that you speak the truth. What you are doing is phrasing a future truth as if it has already been achieved. However, in case that you absolutely don't believe that the future truth will be accomplished in your life (which may be realistic or the consequence of strong undermining thoughts), it may be wise to formulate an affirmation which signifies a point along the road. For example:

- Vision: I want to be able to play Mozart's clarinet concerto without faltering.
- Choice (primary choice): I choose to be able to play Mozart's clarinet concert without faltering.
- Affirmation (secondary choice): I am having clarinet lessons each week with pleasure.

Another example:
- Vision: I want peace in the world.
- Choice (primary choice): I choose peace in the world.
- Affirmation (secondary choice): I have peaceful relations with everyone around me. When conflicts happen, I am solving them by adopting a loving attitude and communicating.

The danger of formulating a point along the way is that you are making a statement about the way instead of allowing the process to follow the path of least resistance. However, in the examples just mentioned, this danger is slight, as you are so certain of the path that the process will indeed follow that path. Your conviction is like the bed of a river and therefore it will determine the path of least resistance.

Sometimes an affirmation, which is a rephrasing of the vision, is so distant that you don't feel any connection to it anymore. In that case, contact with reality is broken and the creative tension is gone. You may long for world peace, choose it, feel energized by it, but in this case what really moves you may be your secondary choice. This evokes the creative tension. On the other hand, when you use a secondary choice as an affirmation you run the risk that there won't be enough creative tension. This could be the case in the example of playing Mozart's clarinet concerto. Maybe a better affirmation in this case could be: "I play Mozart's clarinet concerto without faltering and with pleasure, accompanied by a pianist" (a specific person may be mentioned here who is a good pianist, almost turning it into a visualization). However, it may be that you should determine which affirmation works best for you based on the above conditions.

The concept of the "growing edge," which I introduced in chapter 8, is a tool for the determination of the best affirmation. An affirmation that touches a growing edge can be highly challenging and stimulating. For example, I could imagine that the affirmation "I have peaceful relationships with everyone around me" is such an affirmation, particularly for somebody who often finds themselves in conflictual relationships. And for a migraine sufferer who continually allows himself to be influenced by tensions at work, an affirmation on the "growing edge" could be: "I work in a relaxed way and with pleasure."

Once more the time has come to put these ideas into practice by formulating one affirmation for each item on your list. Compare your statements with the five criteria above and rephrase them if necessary. You can only do this well after you complete the last exercise about undermining and supporting thoughts.

And finally, once you have formulated the affirmations, write them down and say them aloud, preferably in the presence of other people. Later, pay frequent attention to them by re-reading them from time to time and confirming them for yourself, for example in a meditation. This combines very well with the process of visualization.

Visualizations

Visualizations are inner images or "films" which show that you have achieved what you wanted to achieve, or at least that you are on your way. For example, if someone has a tumor, they could say:

- Choice: I choose to feel fit and healthy.
- Visualization: Five years after my treatment I will visit the outpatient's clinic for a check-up and be told that I am cured and that I don't have to come back again. I walk out-

side with a deep feeling of gratitude and buy a bunch of flowers and a cake.

• Optional visualization: I imagine a battle between my white blood cells and my cancerous cells, and my white blood cells are winning. I see fragments of the tumor cells being carried away in my blood. I can also perceive this as a battle in which the cavalry of the white blood cells gradually defeats the rank and file of the tumor cells. Another example:

• Choice: My choice is world peace.

• Visualization: In a century yet to come I see myself as a parent explaining to my son that there used to be wars. I see the disbelief in his eyes when I describe what they were like and I feel privileged to live in this time.

Both examples are rather profound; nevertheless, visualizations can be applied. Many of the things that hold true for affirmations also hold true for visualizations. Neither affirmations nor visualizations guarantee that you will actually accomplish your choice; they merely reinforce it. Whether you will realize your choice is also determined by your supporting and undermining thoughts, your faith in the process of manifestation, and your attunement with the visible and invisible forces in the world around you.

Visualizations can help to further investigate whether the choice involved really comes from your heart. You expect feelings of joy and fulfillment in the visualization but sometimes quite different feelings can be present as well: doubt, loneliness, fear, pain, or something else. This may indicate that the choice hasn't yet been made, but there can also be another cause. At any rate such feelings can indicate that you should examine whether the choice has completely crystallized. If so, this can only make you more determined.

Now I would advise you to take the time to create visualizations for each of your choice items. Each time you have completed one, make a drawing of it. With visualizations it's also important to share them with other people.

Now you have at least one affirmation and visualization for each choice issue. The time has come to pay attention to these affirmations and visualizations frequently—for example, by reading or stating them from time to time. Continue to do so for as long as you enjoy doing so. If you continually experience the same feelings of excitement and joy as the first time, even if they become somewhat less intense, you can continue. If, however, you sense that your energy is decreasing or that you get bored, the time has come to leave things be and allow nature to take its course. You do not want to over-fertilize your seed.

Letting Go

During all of this we should keep in mind what we saw in chapter 2 in relation to the process of manifestation: you cannot make grass grow faster by tugging at the blades. There is a time and a place for everything. Your vision will certainly become reality—but we don't know when. The only thing you can expect is a process that will in time result in the realization of the vision. The rate at which this will proceed depends on the aforementioned factors: the extent of your attunement, your inner balance between forces for and against the vision, and, finally, the universal process of creation itself. We cannot force anything. There is a time for conscious attention and there is a time for letting go. There is even a time for action, but not too soon. First we must complete the mental work and then we have to leave it to nature, to God if you wish. Only then it is time for action. But in which way? That's the question.

Action and Feedback

You have now chosen for your vision and supplied it with energy. Your vision differs from your current reality. This gives rise to a creative tension that wishes to release itself along the path of least resistance. It is now important that you support this force with your actions and do not get in the way of it.

Many people are strongly oriented toward action and once they have formulated their vision and chosen for it, they want to act, to do. But the book of Ecclesiastes teaches us that there is a time and a place for everything and the Taoist says: the Way never acts, yet nothing is left undone (*Tao Te Ching*, 11/48; see also chapters 3 and 6). The wind and the waves are always on the side of the best helmsman.

This means that you have to become sensitive to the forces which you personally evoked (your creative tension) and also to what's happening in the world around you. Life itself will provide you with directions on to how and when to act.

If you come across a hungry tiger in the jungle that seems about to attack you, you won't hesitate for a single moment—you act. You flee or shoot the animal. If your three-year-old son walks on a busy road, you act immediately. You grab him. Effective action stems from necessity. The same holds true for acting from your choice. As Perls said, "There is only one thing that should control, and that is the situation."

Let's assume you want to play a musical instrument. It's obvious that you will have to practice in order to do this. If you begin from your rational willpower, then you run the risk of evoking counter forces—practicing becomes a chore, a duty, and a burden on your time. Before you know it you no longer experience pleasure, which should be the driving force of your actions. This usually happens when you encounter setbacks—for example, if you make only a little progress. The issue is not so much willpower as willingness: the willingness to be open to opportunities and to submit to the forces you evoke yourself. Willpower is a force of the mind, while willingness is a force of the heart, the seat of all motivation. In this example, it's important to heed the signals you receive or the impulses which originate from your own heart. For example, let's say that at a party you talk to someone who, after a long and pleasant conversation, says all of a sudden: "Hey, do you by chance know somebody who wants to buy a clarinet? I have one that I want to get rid of." This can be the signal. Or let's say you pass a shop window that is filled with musical instruments and you see your instrument, and on an impulse you walk in and ask if you may hold the instrument for a moment. You buy the instrument. And so on. These situations are completely different than making a rational decision to buy an instrument, taking lessons, and dutifully practicing for an hour a day.

However, this doesn't mean that discipline has no place in life. But discipline is a secondary choice which should be more closely connected to the primary choice. It should be no more than becoming aware time and again of the primary choice and renewing the secondary choice each time. Therefore, discipline is a matter of want and not an obligation. As soon as discipline degenerates into an obligation a counterforce will arise. Where there is an obligation, there is also a no. Creativity, that is to say creating what you want, emerges at the intersection of spontaneity and discipline. Spontaneity cannot exist without pleasure and freedom of choice.

Life will provide you with directions as to whether you are acting at the correct time and place. If, for example, I have to make a number of phone calls for my job because I have to discuss issues or make appointments, or people have asked me to call them back (note all the "have to's" in the past sentences—are these obligations or necessities arising from choice?) and I am at my desk and start making my calls, I will receive feedback regarding whether I am acting in the correct manner. If I continually get the busy signals or answering machines or my phone is crackling and I try to persevere anyway, by the end of the morning I will end up being frustrated with the justifiable feeling that I have accomplished nothing. I tend to recognize this process after about half an hour and then I will proceed to do something else. However, I may be able to contact everyone immediately and do my business quickly and enjoy pleasurable interactions. The wind is in my favor and by the end of the morning I have accomplished a lot and feel satisfied.

Situations like these can also occur in other ways. If all the traffic lights are against me or I continually end up in traffic jams, then I may have to drive slower or do something else. If I am not being heard at meetings, or I leave each meeting feeling frustrated, my intentions might need some adjustment.

Fritz has created an exercise that may help in cases like these. It is a reflection exercise that is suitable for the end of the day, as a routine or if you don't have a good feeling about that day.

It proceeds in five steps:

1. Accurately describe the situation accurately that didn't turn out as you wanted.

2. What was your own action in that situation? What did you think, what did you (not) say, what did you (not) do?

3. Are you satisfied with your behavior? If so, proceed to the next point. If not, ask yourself if your behavior was in accordance with the choices you made?

4. If you still agree with your choices, affirm them. If not, change your choices.

5. Let it go and come back to the present.

Your behavior will become more in line with your choices if your choices are genuine. Sometimes our own behavior is feedback on what we truly do (not) want. Maybe we want to lose weight, but if we continue eating too much then this is never a primary choice (which doesn't mean that some people eat very little and are nevertheless overweight).

So does this mean that we never "have" to do something that we don't feel like doing? And does this not also mean that we won't accomplish anything if we always give up when there's a setback? Could it be the case that we cannot achieve our vision by firmly holding on to it? Or will we be like the would-be artist who is forever waiting for inspiration instead of working and in that way evoking inspiration, or at least increasing the chance of becoming inspired? The saying goes: "If at first you don't succeed, try, try again."

These are difficult questions. Our own feelings will provide the ultimate answer. If we feel good about what we do, even in adverse circumstances, we certainly must continue. It is more complicated in case of feeling discomfort if we do not act. This may indeed be the consequence of not being true to our chosen vision. But it can also be a consequence of our need to control, force, and manipulate the world around us as well as our own creative process. Then work and pressure may provide a kind of surrogate satisfaction, as with Bisy Backson (Rabbit) in *Winnie-the-Pooh* (see chapter 3). I call it surrogate satisfaction, as we never experience the profound contentment created when we realize our vision and make our contribution to the world. Surrogate satisfaction will never be enough—every new satisfaction evokes new pressure for action and then we become busier and busier, workaholics. In this case, as illustrated in chapter 3, we become dependent on the results. We must know ourselves very well in order to make the distinction between essential contentment and surrogate satisfaction, which links up once more with the thought models discussed in chapter 8. Do we become motivated through duty and obligation, or through the desire to develop our talents and offer them to the world? (Indicating a duty orientation versus giving orientation.) In the former case we do something because we have to do it, in the latter case because we really want to do it (secondary choice based on a primary or fundamental choice).

In the last resort maybe we should say that there's nothing wrong with acting, but there is something wrong with forced action. Forced action is based on arrogance, which stems from a lack of faith in life: we believe that nothing will be realized if we do not interfere with it. Natural action, on the other hand, stems naturally from our vision and is a joyful expression of ourselves, our creative power, and our love for creation. Again we refer to chapter 3 (*Tao Te Ching*, 46/2):

> Therefore the sage keeps to the deed that consists no action…
> It accomplishes its task yet lays no claim to merit.
> It is because it lays no claim to merit
> That its merit never deserts it.

A good intermediate step between steps one and two is to ask yourself what you want to achieve in the organization, to apply your own vision to the situation. The following questions may be particularly useful:

- Which situation do I want to see realized in (or with) this organization?
- Which talents do I want to develop in this organization?
- Which do I want to contribute?
- What do I want to get out of it?

You can also present these questions to your colleagues, provided that they interpret them in a personal way. The issue is what they really want and not what they have to want or should want. It isn't about arguments but about primary or secondary choices.

In working organizations a suitable additional step is to invite yourself and your co-workers individually to formulate their ideal working situation (whether it can be realized in this organization or not). In this respect you can pose the following questions to yourself and your co-workers and ask each individual to write down their answers:

In the ideal work situation:
- How do we deal with each other?
- Which values and qualities are central issues? (For example: care, profit, quality, skill, openness, love, the environment, personal development, efficiency, honesty, pleasure, or loyalty.) State three items that particularly appeal to you.
- Create a symbol or logo that represents you ideal work situation. For example, a special flower, an animal, the sun, a star, a tree, the sea, a circle, a network, a house, an abstract figure or whatever.

Toward a Collective Vision

In the introduction of this book I stated that there is a harrowing lack of leaders with vision. In the previous sections (and in chapter 2) we have illustrated how leaders can develop a vision. However, as leaders we should go at least one step further if we wish to be capable of creating the world that we want for us all. We should move on from an individual vision to a common vision, one vision of the whole. This is a dangerous subject, because we very much want to be independent people, not docile followers. Thus a collective vision is something quite different than an ideology or what is known in business as a mission statement. A collective vision is a vision of each separate individual in the whole that (in theory) is shared by each of the other individuals. Each individual freely opted for the vision, a continually ongoing process of choice that is continually activated, as we have seen in the preceding sections with regard to individual visions. Therefore it is not a rigid thought model (like for example an ideology) but a dynamic thought process. In practice, it's important to bear this difference in mind, as the effect of a collective vision is completely different from that of an ideology (mission statements are often more similar to ideologies than visions). A collective vision is based on a process of choice. So a vision refers to individual autonomy of the members of the community who take responsibility for their own behavior. A collective ideology, on the other hand, is based on an indoctrination process, which results in dependent group members, in followers. Modern ideology has illustrated the perils of this. A vision can result in enthusiasm and therefore in motivation from within. In contrast, an ideology results in fanaticism and therefore in a motivation which is supplied from the outside world.

Therefore, a collective vision is different from a collective objective, mission statement, or strategy. A vision is from the heart; the others are more logical (rational or irrational). A collective vision provides a good basis for open and efficient communication, as illustrated in chapter 7, and results in the actions of the various members of the community being brought in alignment. Without a collective vision this can only be achieved through instructing, indoctrinating, or convincing, the effects of which are considerably less motivating.

So how do we proceed from a collection of individual visions to one collective vision? This process consists of three steps:

1. The members of the whole (for example the staff of an organization) have to learn what a vision is and how develop their own visions.

2. The next step is that they develop a separate vision for the whole community. For example: what kind of organization do I want? What do I want this organization to accomplish? What do I want this organization to contribute to the world?

3. Begin a process of dialogue, as defined in chapter 7. This means creating a readiness to listen to each other's truths and having the courage to show your own truth. This is therefore completely different to discussing, convincing, negotiating, or communicating

We Make the World Lighter

This story is about a chemical plant that produces titanium dioxide, a raw material for everything that is white in this society: paper, white textiles, toothpaste, white paint, and so on. Due to environmental reasons, this factory was faced with the necessity to innovate its entire production process within a very short period of time. The general director had his doubts as to whether this could be successfully accomplished with the current management, particularly because of poor communication within the plant.

First, we investigated how the top and middle executives viewed the organization. The result was shocking: poor communication, a culture of shirking off responsibility instead of taking responsibility, and a lack of motivation and perspective. When the investigators presented the report, it wasn't accepted straight away. The executives involved suspected the investigators had presented the situation in a worse light than it actually was in reality. Subsequently, the investigators, who had simply noted what they had seen and heard, asked for a vote of confidence to be taken. Then the executives had to face the truth—their truth. It can be truly shocking when a truth comes to light! However, as a consequence, an on-the-spot decision was made to radically reform the company. The report was symbolically burned in a cremation-type ceremony on the beach—not because the report wasn't accepted, but because they were saying goodbye to the old reality (see also "letting go" in chapter 4 and in the following chapter).

Moreover, the decision was made to develop a new vision which was to have the following elements incorporated in it:

1. Which product and production process are we to choose?
2. Which values are central to this?
3. With what kind of organization do we want to accomplish this? How do we want to communicate in this organization?
4. What is the quality of the relationships with our environment (government, shareholders, clients, suppliers, unions, the neighborhood, and the general public) that we choose?

A study group was formed which collated the ideas from the group of executives. This resulted in an interim formulation of a vision, which was then submitted to everyone in the company. This was presented to some lower-ranking executives during the training meetings that were taking place within the framework of the transition to the new organization. It was presented to the remaining staff members during discussions that were led by these executives and were introduced by the general director.

Initially, the lower executives and the workers expressed significant skepticism regarding the purposefulness of this entire enterprise. But the director and the plant manager somehow managed to express that this was of paramount importance for them. They expressed their faith and their own personal visions without forcing the content of these visions onto the staff. It was moving to observe how the staff gradually began to adopt the opinion that they would be listened to this time.

And that is what happened. Each of the discussions was recorded in great detail. Not every remark was included into the vision but the ultimate result was still accepted as "our" vision. At a new year's meeting a mime artist inaugurated the vision in a festive manner. And during the following period the members of the organization, management as well as workers, frequently talked to each other regarding the realization of the vision.

Discussing the entire vision here would be too much. But I would like to expand on one element of the vision: the value that people would come first in this company. This didn't mean that everyone would get their own way, but that everyone would be heard, which on the other hand also means that everyone feels responsible for their actions, what they say, or the impressions they leave behind. This required a lengthy learning process, but the discussions about this were extremely worthwhile.

defensively. It's more like if you are in agreement with this item of mine, then I will agree to that one of yours. In this context, seeking compromise is completely wrong. There is a time and place for everything, and this is a time for dialogue. Whether or not you will be able to achieve a collective vision completely depends on the willingness to continue the dialogue with one another, even though there are misunderstandings, lack of consensus, contradictions, conflict, and it eats up time. This investment of time will yield ample benefit through the improvement of communication, harmony, and motivation. Exchanging the answers to the questions in the previously stated exercise is a fine way of beginning this dialogue process.

The following method, derived from Roger Benson, is fine for groups of up to 20 people. It requires two flip charts or two large whiteboards or blackboards. The person leading the discussion writes the following on one of these boards: "The Organization Now" and then says: "Just say anything." The members of the group begin to supply brief descriptions. Anyone who disagrees with the characteristic should shout "No!" If no one disagrees with the characteristic, it is to be written down on the board. Therefore only the items that everyone agrees with will be written on the board. There's no discussion and the exercise should proceed at a quick pace.

Once that has been done, the leader writes "The Desired Organization" on the other board. Then the same procedure starts. Eventually the group has a rough outline of reality and the building blocks for a collective vision (for this group). This has a highly motivating effect as the creative tension becomes perceptible and tangible.

If an organization wishes to arrive at a collective vision, all the members of this organization must discuss this vision in some way or another—or at least have the opportunity to do so. This isn't so simple in practice. It's even more difficult to not communicate in a defensive way or to end up in a discussion. Therefore organizations that want to achieve a collective vision often call upon the assistance of a facilitator.

Some people doubt whether achieving a collective vision in this sense is really feasible. It is possible, especially if we bear in mind that the development of a vision in itself is also a process of manifestation. We are in fact doing nothing more than making something visible that was already present on another energy level. Remember the quotation from John Denver at the beginning of this chapter. A collective vision is possible, but it requires courage, honesty, and effort. The benefits of a collective vision in terms of efficiency, pleasure in working (working with love), quality, and harmonious relationships with the outside world cannot be underrated. "The vision of love that binds us together."

The ultimate result should be based on the input of everyone who has contributed to it. This is not to say that it is a democratic result. Democracy belongs to the realm of discussion. What we are dealing with now has much more to do with the development of a working community as discussed in chapter 7.

Marjorie Parker comprehensively defined an example of developing a collective vision in a Swedish company. For those who wish to see how this process evolves in practice, I refer you to her book. Also Richard Semler's book *Semco-stijl* portrays how you can involve everyone in the company in the development of that company (and therefore its vision). For those who have no opportunity to study these books, I will present a short description of one of our own projects in the Netherlands.

Toward a Global Vision

Just as we must develop a collective vision within organizations, we are faced with the challenge of developing a global vision. We must make it visible, manifest it. And here too, we can become aware of the fact that this vision actually already exists—but it hasn't yet become manifested in the sense that it is consciously shared by a large majority of global citizens, even though generally speaking each of us wants the same things.

Furthermore, we know that there's a great deal more to say about this global vision that has not yet manifested. At the end of chapter 4 I stated the following two elements:

1. A world in which the Goddess has regained her rightful position

2. A world in which we have learned to love and to live with the awareness that we are at one with each other, with the Earth, and with the cosmos

The development of a global vision is to be perceived as a paradigm shift. In principle, manifesting a common global vision is no different than developing a vision in an organization. In this case, the central issue is also exchange, dialogue. However, the form of dialogue differs. Without a doubt computer networks and other technical connections such as interactive TV will play a great part in this. However it is apparent that we are connected at a mental level, often without being aware of this, long before these gadgets were invented. For example, there are many examples of simultaneous inventions being made in different locations across the globe (for example, the art of printing books), and ideas often simultaneously occur at different locations. There is a parapsychologic connection between people which in this day and age can only become stronger (consider also Peter Russell's global brain concept in chapter 5, and Sheldrake's morphogenetic field theory). Among global citizens, the global vision is, admittedly, less well organized and sometimes also less visible than a dialogue within an organization, but nevertheless it goes on all the time. As spiritual leaders we can enhance this dialogue by:

- Explicitly presenting our "piece of the planetary puzzle"
- Working at our own vision for the world and conveying this vision
- Being open to the explicit and implicit dialogue that occurs around us

Growing, Blossoming, and Bearing Fruit

In chapter 2 we saw that we are creators and that we are part of the total process of creation. Just as it is the calling of an apple tree to grow, blossom, and produce apples, it is the calling of each and every living creature to grow, blossom, and bear fruit. The problem with us is that we no longer seem to be in touch with what our fruits are. We think we are an apple tree or want to be one, but in actual fact we may be a gooseberry bush. "But as the river doesn't wish to be a mountain, so, too, I am content with me" (*Essene Book of Days*).

Therefore the issue is to discover which unique talents we have and to enable them to blossom, in turn allowing us to present to the world our fruit. This will result in feeling contented and fulfilled—if we do not succeed in that, we can at most achieve only temporary satisfaction. And it is also true that only then do we contribute to the harmony and wholeness of creation.

Discovering our vision—and as a part of that, discovering the talents we want to develop—is our starting point in this process. The process of creation which will subsequently be set in motion is only partially under control. It proceeds in stages:

- Discovering the vision (the occurrence of the seed)
- Making the choice (planting the seed)
- Investigating and allowing undermining thoughts to perish (removing the weeds)
- Discovering and strengthening supportive thoughts, affirmations, and visualizations (reinforcement, nutrition, and care)

- Non-acting and acting (growing and blossoming)
- Achieving a result (bearing fruit)

We have been made aware of the requirement for a careful balance between activating and enhancing on the one hand and waiting and surrendering on the other. Again this is the balance between yin and yang. We, especially men, tend to lean too much to the yang side, to want to do too much. But we can't push the river, and "within me lives the be-er and the do-er, the meditating monastic and the builder of temples . . . It is my monk that keeps me centered, as my builder builds castles of love" (*Essene Book of Days*).

There was an interesting quote from Robert Fritz at the beginning of this chapter: "When people are united with their real power—the power to create what they want to create—they always choose what is highest in humanity." What is the "real power" in people? "The power to create what they want to create." You will find that power in yourself at the moment when you get into touch with your fundamental wishes and desires. That is your piece of the planetary puzzle. That is the piece that moves you.

You are also moved by your compassion. That is based on your pain which enables you to suffer along with other people in the world. If you had no perception of suffering, you couldn't empathize with the pain and grief of your fellow human beings. You wouldn't even know what it was. But you do know; therefore, the pain is also present in you (1).

In your heart the pain and the vision combine into passion. This passion is your driving force and makes you powerful. It's an incredibly powerful flow—the flow of the man or woman who is exuding power and love, the leader. However, you cannot become a leader by suppressing this force—by suppressing yourself—with all your might. Why people try to do this is one of the greatest puzzles. But you aren't doing this, are you? You want to build on reality, the future you want for yourself and your children? Just like John Kennedy, you think that we came too far in this world and sacrificed too much to disdain the future now.

CHAPTER 10

The School

MOTTO: THE SPIRITUAL LEADER IS AWARE THAT LIFE IS A
LEARNING PROCESS AND ACTS IN ACCORDANCE WITH THIS
IN HIS DAILY ACTIONS.

*"The world is your exercise book, the pages on which you do
your sums."*
—Richard Bach, *Illusions*

A FREQUENT QUESTION IS: CAN LEADERSHIP BE TAUGHT?
It is often said that leadership is a talent you are born with or not.
While all kinds of management skills can be learned, good leaders are
born and not created.

I disagree with this statement and very much believe that it's
possible to shape or form a leader. This also applies to spiritual leaders. However, in order to fulfill this goal I will first define what learning actually entails. I will then look at what in my opinion are the
optimal learning prerequisites for developing spiritual leadership.

LEARNING

Learning progresses in a number of phases. At the beginning of our
lives the first phase isn't always necessary. However, once we have
actually learned things and become stuck in our ways—are conditioned—the first phase is absolutely essential. The phases are:

1. Letting go. First we must create space for new things. We cannot pour wine into a glass filled with water. This is also the case with
ourselves. We must first empty ourselves, and to do so we must first
let go of what we have learned up until that point. This may be concepts, ways of thinking, behavioral patterns, or habits. The intention
is not to totally abandon all we have learned, but that at the very least

we distance ourselves from it. We must be capable of putting our existing behavioral habits into perspective and realize that there may be other options.

This might seem relatively simple, but experience often shows just how attached we are to the ways we have thought and acted up until now. We presume that this is truly the best manner. This isn't so surprising, as our existing working methods and thought models have brought us to where we are now, and at the very least we have a reasonably good feeling about that. Sometimes we are unaware of the extent of our attachment to our patterns. Becoming aware of this is the first step in the letting-go process.

2. The second phase is attuning and receiving. Just as a radio has to be tuned into the correct wavelength to receive the program being transmitted, we must also be on the correct wavelength. We must attune ourselves to what is being projected toward us from outside and inside—insights, skills, and indications. We must also truly want to and be capable of acknowledging and accepting what is projected to us; to incorporate or let in.

3. The following step is integration. Everything we have taken in must become a part of our organism: body, mind, soul, and spirit. This is also the phase where it can be helpful to practice and experiment, also the phase in which an attempt can be made to find the equilibrium between a new routine and at the same time remain open to change (otherwise we will become stuck in our ways once more). This is also the phase I identified as "mindfulness" in chapter 6 because we must handle this new aspect with attention.

4. This last phase is the generation of a willingness to learn, the realization that life is a continuous learning process that we must be continually open to. Should this willingness be lacking then we would once again create attachment and with that unnecessary crises in our lives. We would undoubtedly learn form this, but it makes the learning process unnecessarily arduous. It goes without saying that this phase can in fact always be active. It is therefore no longer a phase: it continues infinitely.

These learning phases always occur, no matter what it is you wish to learn, whether it's a manual trade or broader knowledge and understanding. For example, if you wish to become a psychologist and to continue to develop yourself as one, then you will first have to place aside your opinions of people and their behavior. You initially have to create space, and subsequently make yourself open to observe, listen, and hear what another has to say about the matter; you may subsequently have to accept ideas or views which differ greatly from your own concepts and understanding. This isn't easy, as your familiar manners of thinking may very well be thrown into total confusion and you must also fit your new insights into your ways of thinking and then allow your behavior to be determined through them.

And this is in fact always the case, whether you want to learn drama, become a carpenter, or exercise spiritual leadership. You will always have to go through these phases: letting go, attuning, allowing, and integrating. Even with a technical skill, for example woodwork, learning is always first letting go (your notions as to how it should be done) and then making yourself open (to your teacher, for example). Knowing that nothing is certain forever and living in accordance with this knowledge is the fourth phase: learning as a habit, a learning attitude.

It is clear that this is much more than a technical process: obtaining understanding, acquiring a skill. The whole personality is always involved if you wish to learn as comprehensively as possible. Only then does learning lead to craftsmanship, to true professional skill. And when we see this it evokes an emotional reaction: admiration, perception of beauty, respect. We are in fact always moved by true craftsmanship, as I have previously stated.

If learning can takes place at this level, then spiritual leadership can of course also be learned. Then we can personalize our spiritual insights, through which we will achieve experience of unity. Only than can we truly learn to communicate openly, whereby we can also coach. Then we can learn to develop our vision and convey it to others, which will stimulate and inspire others instead of manipulating them. We can also learn to advance the development of a group vision. We can learn how to manifest this without wanting to change the other person. Ultimately, we can learn to face ourselves in an open and honest manner.

Things are very much the same at a group level. Groups must also go through these learning phases. The prerequisite is of course that the majority of the group is open to learning. However, there is something else. It's absolutely essential to have open communication within the group. This requires sensitivity to group processes and the readiness to communicate about this on a meta-communication level.

Enough about the learning process itself. What are the conditions under which the learning process, and specifically the development of spiritual leadership, will progress to an optimum? First let me describe my ideal learning situation.

I HAVE A DREAM...

I imagine a building, an old castle-like manor house with a large gate. It is situated on the grounds of a country estate where all kinds of buildings lie tucked away behind the foliage. I see people walking through the gate and the grounds: young people, older people, men and women from a variety of ethnic backgrounds, some dressed formally but others casually. The sun is shining and there are people sitting on benches reading books and newspapers.

A business school has been established here. However, it isn't an ordinary business school, it is the International School for Personal Leadership, a school with the aim of training middle and top level leaders. These aren't managers with a good head for figures, who are good at planning, administering, and supervising, but leaders who can train, inspire, communicate, and unite.

The school is located on a campus, readily accessible by public transport. The majority of the students reside there. The fee for the one-year course is substantial, but many banks and corporations are prepared to assist with a low-interest loan. The school is intended for those who consider meaningful lives more important than career and position, and for those who consider personal fulfillment through work to be more important than money and power, position, or status. In short, these people find that their personal development is more important than climbing the social ladder and are consequently seeking to supplement the higher education they've already completed. Thus we are dealing with a post-graduate course for those who are eligible to learn something about leadership and make a significant contribution to society.

A Typical Day on Campus

The day begins at 7:00 with mediation in a room which has been specifically designed for this purpose. This class is attended by a small number of students and teachers. At 7:30 there is tai chi for a small group of people and because the weather is nice; this takes place on the sports field (otherwise it takes place indoors in the sports hall). Other people can be seen entering the restaurant for breakfast.

The actual educational program begins after breakfast. The morning is split into two sessions: 9:00-10:30 and 11:00-12:30. These classes teach the theoretical subjects which are also taught at business schools—economics, computer science, system dynamics, etc.—but also subjects which are not standard business school fare, such as philosophy, spiritual movements, languages, (para)psychology, anthropology, knowledge of brain functions, theoretical physics, environmental issues, and much more. All subjects are taught in a practical and non-dogmatic manner. The teachers let go of the idea of a value-free science and alternative sources of information are freely drawn upon. The values which the school wishes to realize form a guideline for the choice of subject matter.

After lunchtime, there is an hour set aside for relaxation or individual study. From 3:00 to 5:00 there are workshops and presentations on drama, music, sports and physical exercise, communication, conflict management, group dynamics, literature, writing groups, painting, aikido, and martial arts. Naturally, all of these workshops do not occur simultaneously. A specific workshop will as a rule last for eight sessions spread over four to eight weeks.

It is then time for dinner. The evening is set aside for study, hobbies, and for the study group which meets at least once a week with the purpose of integrating all of these various learning processes. The progress of each individual is also evaluated and the learning objectives are determined for the coming week. There is also time set aside for self-discovery and feedback. Films are also shown, for entertainment and also to tie in with the curriculum.

Visions and Values

A course such as this can only be successful when all aspects are attuned to one another based on a vision. This vision must entail what you wish to teach the students, but also how to go about it. The learning process itself must be an illustration of the subject matter. You must practice what you preach. The subject matter for a course such as this must be subordinate to the objective—namely, developing spiritual leadership. This means that certain sections will receive more emphasis than others that would be taught in a regular business school program. It also justifies the inclusion of non-traditional subjects in the curriculum. This book is an example of this. I am convinced that if the subject matter, learning environment, and the teaching methods are all totally attuned to each other then better results can be achieved. This is mainly because the process of letting go and attuning, as defined above, takes place more effectively in this type of environment. There is significantly less conscious and subconscious resistance to the process of change, the learning process. Teaching methods have been developed in management and communication training and adult education which are far more effective than those currently used in universities and business schools. A one-year study period must provide students with a solid foundation, so that they can further their own development and discover how they can manifest themselves as a spiritual leader. This is certainly the case if, for example, the daily program is supplemented with intensive three-day workshops and work experience, from working on a shop floor to taking on a managerial role. The subjects for the workshops could include empowerment, the Transformation Game, intercultural communication, and conflict negotiation.

It is important that one be aware that a course such as this can never be free of values. The values stem from the vision and as such form a counterpart of the objective. They function as criteria for the continual evaluation of the subject matter and procedure. The values of unity, openness, honesty, courage, responsibility, and creativity would be in keeping with a school for spiritual leadership. And, finally, an extremely important value that must be realized with an educational course such as this is the value of the spiritual community. Otherwise nothing will come of spiritual leadership.

International

The school of my dreams is an international one. This means that both students and lecturers are recruited from across the globe, with English being the official language. Why is this so important?

First, spiritual leadership is leadership that embraces the world as a whole. Every local action will have an impact on the greater whole. This is both at the spiritual and material levels. Consumer behavior, energy consumption, and the way we dispose of waste all have worldwide implications. In the same way, everyone and everything is affected by the psychic and spiritual energy we transmit. If we wiggle our toe, for example, this could cause a storm elsewhere, as everything is linked to everything. The outcome of fostering resentment or hate will be very different than if we were loving or forgiving. Hence it is of paramount importance that we are aware of the underlying intention of our actions. The spiritual leader knows all of this. However, to become fully aware of the extent of this it's beneficial to have contact with people from many races and cultures.

Another reason is that there are many great teachers in this world who could contribute and they speak many different languages. It would of course be impossible to engage each and every one of these excellent teachers. However, there are some methods and insights that are so crucial that we may wish to go to their source, and in many cases this is a teacher. If the school were internationally orientated this would ease the process of reaching the source.

The third reason as to why the school should be international is that an international school could contribute to a better understanding in the world and as such could make a contribution to world peace. Ideally, I'd like to realize a network of such schools across the globe, each with its own style and influence, but which are connected in spirit regarding their objective and their vision. They would form a network, both physically (by means of electronic communication) and spiritually, whereby all aspects would support and enhance each other. This network may even become one of the lobes of the new world brain, which was dealt with in chapter 5.

One final reason as to why the school should be international is that our local perspective is in fact too limited and parochial. I see this everywhere, not only in the Netherlands. Those who do not become familiar with what is taking place elsewhere in the world become limited, sometimes even narrow minded, in their manner of thinking. An international orientation makes us modest, broadens our horizons and increases our compassion and creativity.

DEVELOPING SPIRITUAL LEADERSHIP
ON A DAILY BASIS

What does my dream of a leadership school offer to a manager or executive who has been actively employed in business for a considerable time? It's perfectly normal for a football team to spend the majority of their time on training. If the team wishes to perform well, the time spent on the training field must be many times greater than the time spent playing the match. This is no guarantee for success, but it is the minimum requirement for a good result.

Nevertheless, the general view within organizations is that we must be capable of doing things straightaway. This is of course not the case. Business also requires practice. And the most effective training would mean a training period of several days, in particular in combination with in-service training.

Experience also shows that successful managers, more than anyone else, find themselves stuck in their fixed ideas and patterns, which is why the letting-go phase takes up a lot of time and energy. Moreover, a very good outcome could be achieved in shorter or longer training (for example in a summer retreat). How can we best describe such a retreat? Well, if a lasting result were to be achieved and the participants were to take irreversible steps on the path to spiritual leadership, then the course should have the duration of two, preferably three weeks. The schedule for the day would have to be the same as that for the regular course, but with more time for meditation and contemplation. The morning session would be less theoretical, though. A typical day might be:

7:00	Meditative physical exercise
7:30	Meditation
8:00	Breakfast
9:00	Individual discussions
9:30	Morning session: theory and exercises: getting to know yourself
1:00	Lunch
3:00	Afternoon session, or sports, relaxation, or informal discussions
5:00	Contemplation, mediation
6:00	Dinner
7:30	Evening session: training, arts, music
9:30	Free time
11:00	Meditative close to the day (optional)

If large groups were to participate in such a retreat they could alternately work in large groups and smaller sub-groups.

I explicitly use the word retreat to describe this training to reflect the relaxing and spiritual elements. Becoming aware of yourself and your link to the greater whole are pivotal. I am of the opinion that this is particularly necessary for mature managers with more of a fixed routine, because letting go and attuning oneself is a more difficult process for them. People have the tendency to go in search of practical solutions and formulas, but this won't make them spiritual leaders. Rather, awareness of unity and vision must be developed or enhanced and one must learn to face up to oneself. The time must be taken to stop and allow one's soul to catch up and to re-establish contact with the Great Spirit. This is difficult when we're pressed for time and oriented toward results. This is about being nourished, not about returning home with as much knowledge as possible.

Meeting other students is an important aspect of the retreat. Establishing contacts across the generations can contribute to a unified awareness and the reflection of the underlying values of spiritual leadership. Intercultural relationships could also be another important aspect.

And while subject matter may vary greatly, it must always be primarily geared toward personal and spiritual development, not the acquisition of specific knowledge and skills. The knowledge and skills taught are aimed at understanding, developing, and enhancing an attitude that supports spiritual leadership, a service-oriented attitude.

A program such as this is only effective when the participants have attuned themselves to the fact that contemplation and self-observation are more important than theoretical knowledge and cutting-edge management techniques. Managers that send people to such a course will also have to be convinced of this.

If everyone in a managerial position—and that is in fact everyone within an organization of responsible people—were to participate in such a retreat course on a regular basis, the process of spiritual leadership would be greatly advanced. Spiritual leadership naturally cannot be taught in a single course or retreat; it's a life-long learning process, but one that can be accelerated and enhanced (see also Jonker's contribution elsewhere in this book).

This doesn't change the fact that young students who are able to undertake a one-year course have a considerable advantage. Their learning process will begin at a point reached by mature managers and directors only after years of learning experiences (not always pleasant) in daily practice and workshops.

I have defined the ideal learning situation. But what must be done if the ideal doesn't exist? Then it is of paramount importance that these conditions be created within your organization. This in itself is also important because you'll fulfill the requirements for a learning organization and also for the development of spiritual leadership.

LEARNING PREREQUISITES

It's also important that the current program of courses, retreats, instructional courses, and summer schools be "screened" for the learning prerequisites portrayed above. Those programs are the ones best suited for teaching spiritual leadership. To help you evaluate them, I'll outline the most important learning prerequisites.

The conditions under which optimal learning can take place can be derived from the dream I've outlined. It can provide an example for the conditions which good leadership training must comply with and the conditions under which optimal learning can take place in daily practice.

Internal Learning Prerequisites: The Motivation to Learn

I think of internal learning prerequisites as being the conditions that exist within the student. There is in fact only one internal learning condition: the motivation to learn. However, a distinction must be made between extrinsic and intrinsic motivation.

With intrinsic motivation the motivation to learn is located in the subject itself. For example, you may wish to study psychology or carpentry because this interests or even fascinates you, or because you feel that your talents lie there. Extrinsic motivation, on the other hand, is the desire to learn in order to reach a goal that's not related to the subject matter. For example, you may want to learn psychology or carpentry because you wish to acquire prestige, power, or money. Intrinsic motivation is always a stronger and more reliable motivation than extrinsic motivation, as with extrinsic motivation the question always remains as to whether there is a more rapid method of reaching the goal. It may also be the case with extrinsic motivation that the subject matter or the learning process itself is experienced as boring. This is unfortunately the case in the greater part of the current educational system.

Be that as it may, spiritual leadership can only be learned based upon intrinsic motivation, as spiritual leadership can only be exercised based upon intrinsic motivation. You exercise it because you like it or because it is on your path, or because your vision incites you to do so. You don't do it to achieve a specific aim through it. Moreover, intrinsic motivation urges you to learn to develop your talents and share them with the world; it doesn't make you attempt to learn something for which you have no aptitude.

The intrinsic motivation for spiritual leadership means that you must be fascinated by people. You must be fascinated by the cosmic miracle that you are and which you see all around you. This means that you have an investigative spirit: you want to know who you are and what gets you going and also how this connects to other people. You must also be fascinated by development, the conditions under which we develop and the direction in which we develop. You must also be fascinated by communication, how we arrive at connection and unity or, conversely, at conflict and battle. You must be fascinated by creativity, how we create, individually and collectively. You ask yourself, What is creation and what's the relationship between creation, growth, love, and life itself? Is life creation? And, finally, you must be fascinated by the greater whole—the cosmos, the world, where we come from, where we're going, and what it means to be a part of the greater whole.

Our natural love for ourselves and each other may be the most significant source of intrinsic motivation. This is clearly shown in chapter 1, where love is the factor for Hazel and his troops. In this context, the story about the leader and his daughter is also a clear illustration of this. Love exists in each and every one of us. But if this love is to be made available as a motivation for spiritual leadership, then this love must be unleashed. Unfortunately, love is often shut behind a barrier of old pain, disappointments, wounds, rage, resentment, and hate. Should this love be made free then spiritual leadership would follow as a matter of course.

External Learning Prerequisites: Material Conditions, Vision, Quality, and Competence

The external conditions for learning are the conditions to which the learning environment must comply to create an optimal learning process. I'll describe a few, including situations outside of a corporation, such as a school, training institute, or a conference center. I will then deal with the extrinsic conditions within an organization or corporation.

Material Conditions

There must be room for study. The material conditions must ensure that not all energy is required for survival. This is why the students in my dream are capable of financing their study. It's also beneficial if the school is located in supportive surroundings. Good classrooms, good equipment, nature and beauty, recreational areas, and sports facilities all contribute to creating a safe and inspiring environment in which it's possible to make the effort and to take the risks that are necessary for learning.

Vision

As I previously stated, there must be a collective vision of the learning situation. The elements necessary for a collective organizational vision also apply here. To summarize once more, there must be answers to the following questions:

1. What is the essence of what we wish to learn?
2. What are its central values?
3. How do we realize this product and these values? Which learning organization do we want and how do we deal with each other?
4. What is our relationship to our surroundings?

A collective vision in a school or a training program is initially developed by the staff exactly as defined in the previous chapter. In long-term situations or schools, the collective vision must expand until it is the vision of the students as well as the teachers. Therefore, this vision must be continually redeveloped when a new group of students begin their education. This continuous process is one of the most important factors of the learning process and is not only educational for the students, but also for the staff.

If we apply this to spiritual leadership, then it can be said that my personal vision of the first question has in fact already been expressed in the introduction of this book and I will return to this in the epilogue. As far as I am concerned the second question is answered in the earlier passage "My Dream, Vision, and Values." However, I would like to deal with the third question more comprehensively here.

You cannot teach spiritual leadership if you yourself do not apply it in practice. You have to "walk your talk," practice what you preach, or at least strive toward doing so. This means that lecturers must be spiritual leaders themselves and must form a spiritual community. They are in touch with their own spiritual growth process and practice open communication.

They are also intrinsically motivated to practice their form of spiritual leadership, which in this case means that the students' development is their most significant motive (obviously without lapsing into pressuring the students). Just as the collective vision has to be continually developed, the spiritual learning community must also be redeveloped until it can be said that the learning situation is a collective undertaking. Following this line of thought, you'll arrive at the answer to question three.

Regarding the fourth question: the surroundings of the learning situation must be established initially. This of course depends on the course or program. In my fantasy school, the surroundings comprise parents, society (in particular the organizations), investors, politics, neighbors and neighboring businesses, and other schools with similar objectives. "Practice what you preach" also applies to the relationships with the surroundings. Therefore, you must strive toward cooperation, openness, unification, and a collective vision. Battle and competition are only in keeping with spiritual leadership when essential values are threatened by an external factor. There may very well be a time for fighting (and a time for peace), as stated in Ecclesiastes, but it's always important to remain aware of the three elements of spiritual leadership (which is in this case extremely difficult!) and to imagine where this will lead.

I would like to add this about the environment and ecology of the society in which the school functions. Spiritual leadership means awareness of unity and this means a connection with nature. While the purpose of nature is to nourish us, it must not be exploited. Therefore, a school for spiritual leadership must act in an ecologically responsible manner with its surroundings. This concerns matters such as energy and mineral use, waste management, nutrition, perception of nature, and many more things. This must be incorporated into the collective vision.

Competence and Quality

The competence and the quality of the teachers within a school or a training program is an important learning prerequisite. We are all aware of the importance of a good teacher, from our own time at school and from our children's experiences. The results achieved with a specific subject are often determined by the quality of the teacher, not the student's aptitude.

In my mind, quality depends on two matters: the teacher must love his profession or the subject he teaches, and the teacher must be capable of both open communication and clear communication. Love cannot be learned (although it is possible to liberate love), but, in principle at least, communication skills can be learned. While I've already discussed open communication in chapter 7, I'd like to discuss clarity here. Everyone who feels love for a subject or for the process of teaching can in principle learn to communicate clearly, although this comes more naturally to some people than others. Knowledge of presentation skills and didactics can be applied as well.

One of the most significant faults in the teaching practice (standard education and adult education and management training) is that teachers don't have an adequate feedback system that allows them to hear how effective they are or why they are ineffective. Or, if there is a system, in many cases there are no consequences. If a teacher isn't performing well, he or she must be given the opportunity to improve, and if this doesn't work then they must do something else. If this principle were to be applied consistently, then the quality of education would advance in leaps and bounds. The fact that quality and competence aren't taken seriously, or becomes subordinate to other interests, is responsible for the poor quality of our educational system and a great amount of suffering, both on an individual and a social level.

I dare to propose that the social issues we confront and struggle with and deal with so un-creatively are at least 25 percent due to the inadequate education system.

External Learning Prerequisites Within the Organization: Time, Culture, and Systemic Thinking

Learning must be permanent and thus must occur in service. Even though these types of schools and courses are available, to achieve a lasting result learning must be an integral part of daily practice. This is the condition for the fourth learning phase with which I started this chapter.

This requires time and money, at least initially. I refer to what I previously stated regarding the relationship between training and achievement: time for practice must be incorporated into the structure of the organization. Regarding money, it's my firm belief that the budget for training purposes must amount to somewhere between two and five percent of the personnel costs.

A second important learning prerequisite in the organization is its culture. The importance of learning must be central. But this isn't enough. There must also be a readiness to undergo soul-searching, to discuss personal and collective thought models, to learn about manifestation, to communicate openly, to give and receive feedback, to support each other's learning process. These prerequisites are almost parallel to the characteristics of the spiritual community in chapter 7, which are both the ideal condition for and the result of the learning organization.

Systemic thinking is a third important prerequisite (see also Senge). This is learning to perceive reality as a system of feedback. It entails being sensitive and learning to gain an understanding of the strengthening, (de)stabilizing, and delaying processes in reality. Here we must consider snowball effects and vicious circles (positive and negative strengthening processes), achieving equilibrium (for example, between supply and demand in an ideal market), and the fact that some of the effects of your actions only occur at an extremely reduced rate (such as global warming).

Systemic thinking is an aid for holistic thinking: seeing yourself, the organization, and the world around you as a related system or an organism. This is the first step toward unity of consciousness.

An effect of systemic thinking is that we welcome the future in an open manner. We are aware that many types of futures are possible and, contrary to our assumptions, that the future isn't a projection of the present. As a rule more than one possible scenario can be imagined. This helps us keep an open mind and live with uncertainty. This manner of thinking also advances our awareness of the forces around us and our sense of the co-creative process. It simultaneously makes us free and sensitive, just like the sailor on the lake. Our hope and faith can be given a more realistic basis with the aid of systemic thinking.

With this last point we once more find ourselves at the beginning of this book: the spiritual leader follows what his hand and his heart direct him to do. He doesn't live based on plans and strategy, but in the present. With this I want to conclude this chapter and make up the balance sheet. I'll do this in the epilogue.

EPILOGUE

I WOULD LIKE TO BEGIN THIS EPILOGUE BY LISTING ALL OF the mottos at the beginning of each chapter, collectively the ten commandments, or rather, as the Jewish say, the ten words, or characteristics, which form a guideline for the spiritual leader.

THE 10 CHARACTERISTICS OF SPIRITUAL LEADERSHIP

1. The spiritual leader follows what his heart and his hand direct him to do.

The spiritual leader doesn't live his life according to a schedule. Of course he will have to draw up a plan and make appointments from time to time, but his plan and agenda are not sacred. He allows himself to be led by what the situation requires of him, within the scope of a broadly necessary aim. He is also aware of what the situation requires of him and what is better left to others. In short, he has an understanding of his specific talents and role. He is as a sailor on a (larger) sailing ship—and the wind and the waves are always in favor of the best helmsman.

2. The spiritual leader is a manifestation leader.

He knows the law of manifestation and how to apply it. He is therefore capable of creating the situations he desires—without forcing and pressuring his fellow man. He is aware of the direction of the universal process of creation and works together with it, not against it. He is therefore outstandingly effective. The wind and the waves . . .

3. The spiritual leader looks after his affairs without acting and yet nothing remains undone.

The spiritual leader is aware that there is a time and a place for everything. This doesn't mean that he never does anything, as there is a time for action and a time for waiting. It does mean that he is truly convinced that nothing is capable of existing if it is not in keeping with the universal process of creation, the Way. Therefore his most important task is to establish and sustain contact with that process and to stimulate others to also experience this.

4. The spiritual leader lets himself be led by the Goddess within himself and in nature.

The spiritual leader is aware of and acts upon the feminine energy within himself and around him. He is aware of how this energy was forced into the background, and that forces are active now which are attempting to restore the balance between masculine and feminine energy. He wishes to strengthen these forces. However, he must first strengthen the feminine side within himself. He does this by being open and receptive, by listening, (literally, but also with his inner ear), by making himself open to the "gentle forces" (including the "gentle" emotions) and to connect with nature. He is more eco- than ego-oriented.

5. The spiritual leader allows himself to be guided by the Great Spirit.

The spiritual leader knows that there is something greater than himself. There is a greater consciousness, a greater spirit, a greater unity of which we are all part of if not physically then certainly spiritually. We ourselves are the very place where this unity manifests itself. He is also aware that it isn't always easy to experience this unity. However, he knows that it is necessary if life is to be meaningful. This spirit is also the source of compassion and love and care for one another. It is the basis of an attitude of service to a unity greater than just yourself. Conversely, this spirit can be found while experiencing these processes, for example, while caring for your family and staff members.

6. The spiritual leader allows himself to be inspired through one or more religious traditions.

This point links up with the previous point. This doesn't mean that the spiritual leader has to be a follower or practicing member of a specific church or religion. It does mean that he is open to the profusion of wisdom handed down through the centuries, such as the wisdom contained in the great world religions. He allows himself and his daily actions and non-actions to be inspired through one or more of the great religions.

7. The spiritual leader allows himself to be nourished by the spiritual community with the aid of open communication.

A leader is not a leader without other people. However, to be a true spiritual leader others must not be dependent on him; they must be autonomous and free. This requires a spiritual community, which the spiritual leader can partially assist in creating by truly listening and speaking openly. This requires courage and honesty.

8. The spiritual leader observes himself without judgment.

The spiritual leader knows that self-knowledge is the source of all wisdom. He also knows that self-observation is the way to this knowledge. And, finally, he knows that self-observation without judgment is the most difficult thing in existence. Nevertheless, this is what he strives toward. Not so much to attain wisdom, but because he is aware that only by taking this route will he be in a position to provide the world with his unique gift. Feedback concerning oneself is obtained through self-observation without judgment, and this is the only thing that will enable you to develop into a more complete person.

9. The spiritual leader allows his vision to guide him.

The spiritual leader is aware that vision is not the same as an objective. Vision comes from the heart and is therefore passionate. He will therefore work on his vision to clarify it, which will subsequently have an impact on others. Moreover, he will further the development of a common vision within a community and he knows how to do this.

10. The spiritual leader knows that life is a learning process and acts in accordance with this in his daily actions.

This guideline is in fact a sort of summation of all the previous guidelines. The spiritual leader knows that nothing in life is coincidental. What exists is there because he has put it there, or because it is what he needs. He therefore assumes 100 percent responsibility and his mindset is geared toward learning and developing himself and others.

If we take a comprehensive view of all of these points then it becomes clear that leading is in fact being led. In each and every point there is the principle of following or surrendering to something or someone else. This entails that the spiritual leader must be receptive. There are no options open to the spiritual leader other than living with feminine energy. This is why spiritual leadership is exceptionally challenging for men, or for women who, due to the influence of our culture, have taken on male behavior (unfortunately is often the case with female managers who have become managers as a result of this behavior).

There is something else. The underlying thought behind all of these principles is that leading is not so much an activity as a manner of being. It is not based on actively proceeding outwards, but on turning to the inner self. It is my belief and experience that if someone does this in one of the ways defined in this book, he will automatically become charismatic, which will result in his ability to exercise a powerful influence on his surroundings. However, this influence is gentle and allows the other person to be valued for who he is.

As leading is more a manner of being than an activity, it is therefore not so easy to provide a recipe for it. This explains the general skepticism about management, leadership, and organization books and courses which profess to provide a ready-to-use technique which will solve all of your problems. On the other hand, managers continue to request such techniques. It would be very easy indeed to pick up a practical technique that would be a cure-all for all of our complaints and the company's complaints. However, if there were such a cure-all, then it would have been discovered a long time ago. This would result in management becoming simple, but also boring and non-challenging.

It is much more difficult to learn leadership by means of self-development. It also costs a lot more time and effort. Accordingly, self-research requires courage and the preparedness to take personal risks. It is in fact an undertaking with yourself. This is the main reason why managers, politicians, and executives, against their better judgment, continue to request techniques, while at the same time are sick and tired of them.

The Sacred Wound and the Higher Purpose

> We want to strive towards the highest,
> Dig to the deepest,
> And to enfold the world with friendship.
> —"The Law of the Migratory Birds"

Do you know the ancient Celtic legend of Cuchulain? It goes as follows:

Cuchulain was a great warrior—greater than the world had ever known. He protected his clan against all evil influences and against rival clans. He had received the blessing of the Goddess. Through time all of the other clans came to realize that Cuchulain was unconquerable and therefore Cuchulain's clan was no longer prey to attacks. Peace reigned.

However, Cuchulain needed challenges and victories to nourish his pride. Therefore, he continually provoked other warriors, who sooner or later felt that their honor was under threat and accepted the challenges—and of course lost. In this manner Cuchulain left behind a trail of humiliated and beaten warriors and in doing so caused more suffering than pleasure.

After some time the Cuchulain clan elders had had it and after lengthy consideration they decided to request that the Goddess revoke Cuchulain's special protection. And so it happened. Cuchulain was wounded in the next fight. The wound he received wasn't fatal. Instead, it had the characteristic that it would never heal.

This resulted in unbearable suffering, so much so that Cuchulain could no longer endure it and he retreated into a cave. After years of isolation and repentance and through an abyss of utter desperation, he finally submitted and renounced his pride. He was only able to do this when he had actually looked into the wound and was able to see his own destructive side in the depth of the wound. He also saw his own beauty. With deep dismay he turned to the Goddess and prayed for mercy. "Not my will, but thy will shalt be done, but if it be your will to release me from this ordeal, so shall thy help me." And so was it. The physical wound healed. However, the memory of the ability to suffer and feel compassion remained. The bitterness was transformed into compassion.

Cuchulain returned to his clan and was welcomed with open arms. He spent the rest of his days at the service of his fellow man. He was transformed from a warrior to a "warrior of the heart," from a warrior into a spiritual leader.

The legend of Cuchulain, and in particular the concept of the wound that would not heal, can be seen in many different forms in world literature and tradition. For example, there's the Greek myth of Prometheus, who stole fire from heaven and had to pay the penance of "eternal" suffering until Hercules released him. There's also, in the Legend of the Holy Grail, the wounding of the Fisher King, which was brought to an end by Perceval. Evidently, the way to spiritual leadership for many of us is through an ordeal. This could be the awakening of Kundalini energy from the yoga tradition or the dark night of the soul, which we know from both the Christian and the Buddhist traditions. We must give up what we are truly attached to, whether it's our pride, our power, our focus on results, our attachment, our planning, our control—and maybe, ultimately, our fear.

The process forces us to face our deepest wounds, the "wound that never heals." This is also a sacred wound, as it's linked to our mission, what we are here to provide on this Earth. You could also say that only after facing up to our deepest wound are we capable of developing our talents to their fullest and offering our gift to the world. Only then does our life become complete, completely fulfilled and yet free from our ego-oriented thoughts and needs.

This process is in fact the same as the learning process defined in the previous chapter. However we are now examining it at its most fundamental level. It is also the same as choosing between God and Mammon.

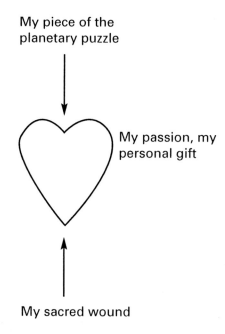

My piece of the planetary puzzle

My passion, my personal gift

My sacred wound

By looking into our sacred wound we can discover our piece of the planetary vision and the planetary puzzle.

The sacred wound will never heal, but if we have the courage to look at it for long enough—or even better, look into it—then the wound will transform. What's incredible is that by doing so we can come into contact with our vision (What do I want?) and our destiny (What must I do?). I also believe that we humans also have one vision and destiny: our planetary vision and our planetary mission (compare with Teilhard de Chardin's noosphere discussed in chapter 4). By looking into our sacred wound—which can be an exceptionally painful process because we convert the physical pain into emotional pain, and the emotional pain into mental pain and then greater understanding—we discover our piece of the planetary vision and the planetary puzzle, the questions as to where we as a whole wish to go.

If we have reached this point then we can integrate our vision with our wound. This takes place in the heart. Passion and the personal gift we have to give the world are located there. The process is represented in this figure derived from Danaan Parry and Jerilyn

Brusseau.

I would like to bring this book to a close by sharing with you a little about my own wounds and gift. It also sheds light on my deepest motivation for writing this book. I also hope that this description will compel you to go in search of your own sacred wound and piece of the planetary puzzle so that you can come into contact with your own specific form of spiritual leadership.

My Piece of the Planetary Puzzle

I am a Capricorn. The painter Johfra placed the goat at the top of a mountain, completely alone at the top of the world, but, like a true goat, with its feet placed firmly on the rocks. Like the goat, being alone and feeling lonely, coupled with a firm connection to physical reality are the foundations of my sacred wound.

Due to wartime circumstances (I am half Jewish and was born in 1940), I spent the first five years of my life in an atmosphere of fear and isolation. Since we didn't have a stable home life, I wasn't able to develop permanent relationships with friends. Later on in life I felt extremely alone within my family, and with my keen insight into reality and my belief that I was way beyond my age, I observed the void in my family relationships and ultimately withdrew into a world of books and fantasy. As a result of this I acted precociously and older than my age, which also resulted in my becoming isolated at school. Ultimately, I became an outcast in my class. I often felt totally alone, not truly part of any family or community. There was no one I with whom I could discuss my feelings. I hid this unbearable situation in a corner of my spirit and covered it up with courage, arrogance, and the desire to control fellow human beings. This is the core of my wound. I don't want to be melodramatic about it, as I believe that this isn't extraordinary. I believe that the majority of people have similar stories to tell about their own lives if they were only brave enough to recall them and face up to them. (See Miller, for example.)

When I, at the closing stages of a long process of consciousness-raising, had relived and experienced these feelings, my vision came to me of its own accord. I passionately desire a world of unity, a world in which we can all be aware of unity with each other and the Earth itself. A world in which we know that we are not alone. A powerful world, a world without fear.

What can my contribution be? The answer to this question also arose automatically. My contribution can be to be completely present and allow contact to be established. I can provide my talents—keen insight, compassion, and sympathy—in that contact. I developed my insight in a sense because of my wound and the pain I felt; as a result, I can now use it to contribute to my happiness and others' happiness. I also became more sympathetic and compassionate because of feeling hurt. Through my compassion with the small, lonely, arrogant boy that I used to be, my ability to feel compassion and sympathy for fellow human beings has been enhanced.

These two talents—keen insight and compassion—contain both my motivation and my form of spiritual leadership, which up until now I have utilized in my work as a therapist, consultant, trainer, and author. I am curious about your form of spiritual leadership. I hope that you may go on to make new discoveries with the assistance of this book.

NOTES

Prologue
1. I have based this book primarily on Taoism, the Judeo-Christian tradition, and Buddhism, but not because Islam, Hinduism, and other religions could not provide a significant contribution to our spiritual understanding and to the foundations of spiritual leadership. It is because I have never studied or practiced these religions and can therefore not say very much about them. I hope that this book inspires experts to do this. Also due to a lack of knowledge, I pay little attention to shamanic traditions, even though my dealings with the female principle and the soul in chapters 4, 5, and 8 have definitely been influenced by these traditions.

2. In this manner we refer to the Holy Ten Commandments. See: Whitlau, Tenachon 12.

Chapter 4
1. Much in this paragraph is based on the book *Brain Sex* by Anne Moir and David Jessel. For the sake of brevity I have left out other significant aspects of the brain research. See for example Pribam (the brain functions like a hologram) and Vroon (the brain functions simultaneously at reptile-mammal level and at "typical" human level).

Chapter 5
1. In accordance with the older Judeo-Christian tradition, God, to me, seems more Becoming than Being. In the new Bible translation God reveals himself as "I am who I am." However the old translation states: "I will be who I will be." This appears to be more in line with the original Hebrew tenor. God accordingly reveals himself as a dynamic happening, as a development. I am of the opinion that the later churches have lost sight of this viewpoint in a way.

2. For information: In the US: Innerlinks, P.O. Box 10502, Asheville, NC 28806; E-mail: angel@innerlinks.com. In England: Findhorn Foundation, The Park, Game Office, Forres IV 36 OTZ, Scotland; E-mail: minglis@findhorn.org. In the Netherlands: Erik van Praag, SPL bv, Oudeschans 3c, 1011 KP Amsterdam; E-mail: spl@antenna.nl.

Chapter 6
1. If you write the word "live" backwards it becomes "evil." I attach no special significance to this coincidence, but it's amusing.

2. I found it stimulating to compare these principles with my definition of spiritual leadership. I believe there's a clear link. Is there also one for you?

3. In the Bible, it is assumed that the sabbatical year and jubilee year is collective and simultaneous. Although this would reap significant benefits, my argument is based upon the fact that each person counts for himself. Consider also the anthroposophy traditions, which define the individual life as a successive series of seven-year phases, each with its own significance.

4. For the experts: this order is based on the Mahayana Buddhism. The objective

of this branch of Buddhism is not exclusively about reaching enlightenment, but also about being caring toward fellow human beings.

5. Buddhism believes in reincarnation and states that this cycle takes place through many lives. The path to enlightenment is also through many lives. Until we escape this cycle, we are reborn. Only when the ultimate insight has been achieved (see also step eight of the eightfold path) are we free to pursue our life as a free spirit unattached to earthly existence. See also chapter 2 under Karma.

6. For the more philosophical reader, a link can be seen here with Sartre's existentialism. With Sartre "nothing" is the polarity of "being"; that what we experience is eventually a deed of choice. The difference is that Sartre perceives "nothing" as something, which may very well be an inextricable part of life and fascinates us (simultaneous attraction and repulsion), but which at the same time is also the source of meaninglessness. The Buddhists however perceive this as being the way toward perfect enlightenment. See also J.P. van Praag.

7. The years between 21 and 28 years are also known as a period of development of this chakra. This was perhaps the case in former times, but now we conquer our position in society later, probably because of social developments.

8. See the example titled "If You Do Not Have Enough Time, Go and Sit Down for a While" and also my book *Room for Happiness* for more information about the meaning of crisis (from the Latin for turning point). For that matter, it wouldn't be such a bad idea to introduce collective transitional rituals into the organization, for example, for those who reach a specific age in a specific year, or for those who have been with the organization for a specific period of time. This can be seen as a part of the spiritual working community (see next chapter).

Chapter 7
1. The group in the organization, as has been explained, is to be viewed as the "extended family." As such the group forms the "soul" of the organization, whereby the community can be seen as the spirit of the organization (see chapter 5). The history is reflected in the group; the sustainability in the community.

2. It is sometimes said, especially in New Age circles, that "in my mind the conflict between the sexes doesn't exist. Men and women are the same to me. We are all humans and the purpose is that we all get to know ourselves as humans." But I think this viewpoint omits some of our reality. We were not put on this Earth as men and women for no reason—the task is probably to learn from it and learn about it and to extract joy from it.

Chapter 8
1. For those with a professional interest, conditioning, personality, self, and me are mainly psychological concepts, while soul and spirit are more spiritual concepts.

2. One of the fascinating aspects of the collective unconscious is that it surpasses cultural differences. Specific symbols can be seen in every culture, such as fairy tales and the myths of that culture.

3. For information concerning Frameworks: In USA: Innerlinks, P.O. Box 10502, Asheville, NC, 28806, Email: angel@innerlinks.com. In Great Britain: Findhorn Foundation, The Park, Game Office, Forres IV 36 OTZ, Scotland, Email: minglis@findhorn.org. In the Netherlands: Erik van Praag, SPL bv, Oudeschans 3c, 1011 KP Amsterdam, Email: spl@antenna.nl.

Chapter 9
1. As long as Perceval did not experience his own pain in the Legend of the Holy Grail, he was unable to pose the question to the Fisher King that will heal both the land and the king. See chapter 4. This is why the "hero" in fairy tales, and also Perceval, must endure all sorts of adventures before he is able to help.

BIBLIOGRAPHY

Achterhuis, Hans; *Het rijk van de schaarste*, Ambo, Utrecht, 1988

Albee, Edward; *Who's afraid of Virginia Woolf*, 1962

Adams, Richard; *Watership Down*, Avon, New York, 1976

Bach, Richard; *Jonathan Livingston Seagull*, Avon, New York, 1976

Bach, Richard; *Illusions, the adventures of reluctant messiah*, Dell, New York, 1977

Beck, Charlotte Joko; *Everyday Zen*, HarperCollins, San Francisco, 1989

Berne, Eric; *Games people play*, Grove, New York, 1967

Beukel, A. van den; *De dingen hebben hun geheim*, Ten Have, Baarn, 1990

Bhagavad Gita, Bhaktivedanta Book Trust, Amsterdam

Blue, Lionel; *Bright Blue: The wise and witty confessions of a unique rabbi*, BB, London, 1985

Bordeaux Szeleky, E.; *The Essene gospel of peace*, 1978

Chang, Johan; *The tao of love and sex*, Wildwood, London, 1977

A Course in Miracles; Routledge & Kegan Paul, London, 1975, 1985

Fentener van Vlissingen, P.; *Ondernemers zijn Ezels*, Balans, 1995

Fritz, Robert; *The path of least resistance*, Fawcett Columbine, New York, 1984,1989

Gershon, David and Gail Straub; *Empowerment, the art of creating your life as you want it*, Dell, New York, 1989.

Gibran, Kahlil; *The prophet*, Heinemann, London, 1926

Gleick, J.; *Chaos*, Contact, Amsterdam, 1991

Godwin, Malcolm: *The holy grail*, Viking Penguin, New York, 1994

Gore, Al; *Earth in balance: ecology and the human spirit*, Houghton Mifflin, Boston, 1992

Harris, T.; *I'm OK — you're OK*, Avon, New York, 1969

Hartog, Jan de; *Hollands Glorie*, De Prom, Baarn, 1988

Hartog, Jan de; *De kapitein*, Elsevier, Amsterdam, 1974

Hawking, Stephen; *A brief history of time*, Bantam, Toronto, 1988

Hay, Louise; *You can heal your life*, Hay, Santa Monica, California, 1984

Hoff, Benjamin; *The tao of Pooh*, Dutton, New York, 1982

Houtkooper, Joop M., *Observational theory, a research programme for paranormal phenomena*, Swets en Zeitlinger, Lisse, 1983

Johnson, Robert A.; *He, understanding masculine psychology*, Harper and Row, New York, 1974

Jung, Carl Gustav; *The Archetypes and the Collective Unconscious*, Vol. 9 of *The Collected Works of C.G. Jung*, edited and translated by G. Adler and R.F. Hull. Princeton University Press, Princeton, New Jersey, 1970

Kelder, Peter; *Fountain of youth*, Harbor, Washington, 1985

Krishnamurti, J; *Freedom from the known*, Gollancz, London, 1969

Kushner, Harold S.; *When all you've ever wanted is not enough*, Summit Books, New York, 1986

Laing, R.; *The politics of the family (and other essays)*, Pelican Books, London, 1969

Lao Tse; *Tao te ching: the classic book of integrity and the way*, Bantam, New York, 1990

Lansdowne, Z.F.: *De chakra's*, Schors, Amsterdam, 1988

Linden, Nico ter; *Schoffelen in de wijngaard*, Gooi en Sticht, Hilversum, 1982

Lovelock, James; *Gaia, a new look at life on earth*, Oxford University Press, Oxford, 1979

Maslow, A.; *Motivation and personality*, Harper, New York, 1954

Meester Eckhard; *Waar God naamloos is*, Mirananda, Den Haag, 1994

Miller, Alice; *In den beginne was er opvoeding*, Wereldvenster, Houten, 1983

Jessel, David and Anne Moir; *Brain sex, the real difference between men and women*, Dell, New York, 1989

Moore, Thomas; *Soul mates: honoring the mysteries of love and relationships*, HarperCollins, New York, 1994

Moss Kanter, Rosabeth; *When giants learn to dance*, Simon & Schuster, New York, 1989

Murphy, Joseph; *The power of your subconscious mind*, Bantam Books, New York, 1982

Nayak, P.R. and J.M. Ketteringham; *Breakthroughs*, Rawson, New York, 1986

Pagels, Elaine; *The Gnostic gospels*, Random, New York, 1979

Parker, Marjorie; *Creating shared vision*, Norwegian Center for Leadership Development, Oslo, 1990

Parry, Danaan; *The Essene book of days*, Sunstone, New York (yearly edition)

Pirsig, Robert M.; *Lila*, Bantam, New York, 1992

Potok, Chaim; *The chosen*, Penguin, New York, 1966

Praag, Erik van; *Room for happiness*, America House, Baltimore, 2001

Pribram, K.; *Languages of the brain*, Wadsworth, Monterey, California, 1977

Rajneesh Chandra Mohan (Osho); *The way of the white cloud*, Rajneesh Foundation Publication, Poona, India, 1972

Raphael; *The starseed transmissions*, Carey, Mountain View, Missouri, 1983

Rietdijk, C.W.; *Experimenten met God*, BRT, Brussels, 1989

Roberts, Jane; *Seth speaks*, Bantam, New York, 1974

Russell, Peter; *The global brain: speculations on the evolutionary leap to planetary consciousness*, Tarcher, Los Angeles, 1983

Schutz, W.G.; *FIRO, a three-dimensional model of interpersonal behavior*, Palo Alto, 1958

Semler, Ricardo; *Turning the tables*, Times, New York, 1993

Senge, Peter M.; *The fifth discipline*, Doubleday, New York, 1990

Sheldrake, Rupert; *A new science of life: the hypothesis of formative causation*, Blond and Briggs, London, 1981

Slavenburg, J.; *De verloren erfenis, inzicht in de ontwikkeling van het christendom*, Ankh-Hermes, Deventer, 1993

Snelling, John; *Elementen van boeddhisme*, Strengholt, Naarden, 1993

Spangler, David; *The law of manifestation*, Findhorn, 1975

Stikker, Allerd; *Tao, Teilhard en Westers denken*, Bres, Amsterdam, 1986

Teilhard de Chardin, Pierre; *Het verschijnsel mens*, p. 64, 119, 152, 329. Het Spectrum, Utrecht, 1958

Thich Nhat Hanh; *A guide to walking meditation*, Fellowship, Nyack, NY, 1985

Tolkien, J.R.R.; *The lord of the rings*, Allen & Unwin, London, 1956

Tollmann, Edith and Alexander; *De zondvloed, van mythe tot historische werkelijkheid*, Tirion, Baarn, 1993

Trungpa, Chögyam; *Mediation in action*, Stuart & Watkins, London, 1969

Tulku, Tarthang; *Gesture of balance*, Dharma Publ. Emeryville, California, 1977

The Home Planet, Addison-Wesley, Reading, Massachusetts, 1988

The Urantia Book, Urantia Foundation, Chicago, 1955

Vroon, P.; *Tranen van de krokodil*, Ambo, Baarn, 1989

Whyte, David; *The heart aroused*, Bantam Doubleday Dell, New York, 1994

Wilber, Ken; *No boundary*, Shambala, Boulder, 1981

Wilber, Ken, Jack Engler and Daniel P. Brown; *Transformations of consciousness*, Shambala, Boston and London, 1986

Whitlau, Eli; *Tenachon, afl. 17*, Libresso, Deventer, 1987

Zimmer, Heinrich; *Philosophies of India*, Princeton University Press, Princeton, New Jersey, 1969

Zimmer Bradley, Marian; *The mists of Avalon*, Dell-Balantine, New York, 1982

INDEX

Printed in the United Kingdom
by Lightning Source UK Ltd.
102991UKS00002B/13